Looking in Windows

To Ron:
Happy reading!
George Mills

Looking

in Windows

Surprising Stories
of Old Des Moines
by GEORGE MILLS

Iowa State University Press / Ames

George Mills, longtime *Des Moines Register* staff writer and reporter for WHO-TV (Des Moines), is also author of *Rogues and Heroes from Iowa's Amazing Past* and *The Little Man with the Long Shadow*, both published by Iowa State University Press.

Articles and illustrations that appeared originally in *The Des Moines Register* are reprinted here with the permission of *The Des Moines Register*. Unless otherwise noted, all illustrations courtesy George Mills.

First edition, 1991

Library of Congress Cataloging in Publication Data

Mills, George
    Looking in windows: surprising stories of old Des Moines / by George Mills. — 1st. ed.
        p.   cm.
    Includes index.
    ISBN 0–8138–1573–8.—ISBN 0–8138–1574–6 (pbk.)
    1. Des Moines (Iowa)—History—Anecdotes. I. Title.
    F629.D4M55 1991
    977.7'58—dc20   90-45892

Contents

Sin City

Des Moines was known as "sin city" for generations.
It always had been much more than that, to be sure:
the state capital, a center for merchandising and medicine, a city of
strong pioneers and great editors, of big religious revivals, of major
political battles, of strong theater, art, education and literature, of the
state fair.

Nevertheless, the "sin" label stuck and served to lure some
Iowans to town, seeking gusto and relaxation, and added an element of
spice to the city's history.

It has been my privilege to observe the Des Moines scene as a
political reporter and free lance writer for fifty-six years. My avocation
in the same period was delving into Iowa history, with a particular focus
on Des Moines. The combination of activities has inevitably led to a
head full of fast-moving historical tales.

The purpose of this book is to bring together a selection of those
stories, told with an emphasis on action and hopefully, readability. In
the selection are a number of previously untold narratives and
long-hidden facts, secret information of the type any veteran reporter
long has known but has been constrained from using for one reason or
another. Or perhaps he discovered in later research.

Not often does a writer come on to situations so richly diverse in
personalities and events as are to be found in Des Moines' past: from
Ronald Reagan to Ruthie the barmaid for example. Or from Indian
warriors to abolitionist John Brown to the Hiroshima bomber pilot to
bootlegger Louie Siegel; from crooks in the courthouse to "burn down
The Register"; from great presidents to that big disappointment Prince
Rupert.

How could a writer miss with such a cast of characters and such
adventures to work with?

But the question arises: is the slambang, hurry-into-print newsman out of place in the august field of history? Not at all, in my opinion. News and history are allied fields. Both deal with communicating matters of importance and interest to humanity, but with this obvious difference: the reporter gathers and disseminates his products right now; the historian takes the longer view and has the luxury of time to uncover previously undisclosed but pertinent material that often is entirely new or clarifies and explains in greater detail a situation of long ago. News actually is relatively short and fast, history longer and more deeply presented.

Each profession may benefit by the example of the other to some extent, the reporter from the painstaking standards of the historian, the historian from the ability of reporters to spot quickly the drama of an important story and to present the personalities and/or issues in a lively and interesting way.

Also, you might ask: doesn't a political writer usually operate in the rather narrow field of candidates and elections? What is such a writer doing in the broad historical scope of human interest? The fact is that broad scope is very much in the political spectrum any more. Ever since the New Deal of Franklin Roosevelt greatly expanded the role of government in the realm of human affairs in the 1930s, politicians have had to deal much more closely with every phase of life. That development has correspondingly widened the range of political reporting.

It can be said that this book was more than thirty-five years in the making. Some of the stories first appeared in a series *The Register* carried in the 1950s under the title "In Old Des Moines," others since in the news sections and on the page opposite the editorial page in the newspaper. As previously mentioned, a number of the stories are appearing herein for the first time. The time range of the book is from 1735 to the early 1960s.

The Population of Des Moines

1846	127	1915	105,652
1850	502	1920	126,468
1855	2,278	1925	141,441
1860	3,965	1930	142,359
1865	5,722	1940	159,819
1870	12,035	1950	177,965
1875	15,782	1960	208,982
1880	22,696	1970	201,404
1885	32,469	1980	191,003
1890	50,093		
1895	56,359		
1900	62,139		
1905	75,626		
1910	86,368		

Source: Federal and state census reports. Note: No figures are available for years ending in "5" after 1925 because the state census ended with that year.

Out on the Frontier

Indians Win One

The Indians took it on the chin from the white man nearly all the time in early Iowa. But not in a battle they fought mainly against the French at or near the present location of Des Moines in 1735, more than two and a half centuries ago. The French were the ones who slunk away, cold and hungry, along with some Indian allies.

The present Iowa was part of a vast area of North America that belonged to France. Most of the Indians in the northern Mississippi valley and Great Lakes region were on good terms with the French. The tribes helped France fight wars against England and Holland. French trading posts did a big fur business with the Indians.

The Fox tribe was an exception. The Foxes stayed aloof along the Wisconsin River in Wisconsin. Not only that, they had the nerve to stage roving attacks on Indian allies of the French and thereby seriously interfered with the fur trade. That came to an end when the Foxes suffered a major defeat and had to flee across the Mississippi River into the land of the Ioways.

The Sacs had been neighbors of the Foxes and were not so unfriendly to the French. But a French officer was killed in 1733 in a Sac village. The Sacs realized they were in big trouble. They retreated across the Mississippi and joined the Foxes.

The French were not about to let the officer's death go unavenged. Back in Quebec, the French capital of North America, the government organized a small military force to teach the recalcitrant Indians a lesson, and to separate the Sacs from the Foxes. The expedition promised adventure to the French settlers, and sixty-four volunteered to go. They were joined by 200 friendly Iroquois, Potawatami, and Huron Indians. Captain Nicholas Joseph DeNoyelles commanded the force. He was known as a tough fighter.

The little army started from Montreal late in 1734 and moved out of Detroit on January 1, 1735, with a Fox village on the Wapsipinicon River in Iowa as the objective. It took until March 12 in the snow and cold to reach the village, which was found abandoned. A captured Indian said the Foxes had gone to the Des Moines River in what is now central Iowa. Chilled and already short of food, the French with their Indian friends tramped over the empty wilderness to the banks of the Des Moines. Arriving April 19, they found the river full of floating ice and Sacs and Foxes in greater numbers than expected. Advance information indicated the invaders would encounter only four lodges of Indians. Instead there were fifty-five lodges on the west side of the river, with an estimated 250 warriors.

The DeNoyelles force crossed the river and opened battle, pushing the less well-armed foes back into the woods. The Sacs and Foxes counter-attacked. The fighting raged for several hours with one French officer killed and probably other Indians on both sides killed as well. The Foxes crept forward as night fell and tried to scalp wounded Iroquois.

The French commander saw he wasn't getting anywhere and ordered a retreat. He divided his men into two groups, one to continue fighting and the other to build a shelter for the wounded and to guard against harassing raids.

The Iroquois didn't like the outlook. They called a council of war, which was attended by DeNoyelles and some Sacs from the other side. DeNoyelles told the Sacs that all would be forgiven if they would desert the Foxes and return to Wisconsin and trade with the French. The Sacs rejected the offer. They said they didn't want to take their women and children on such a hard journey. More likely, the Sacs may have realized the French were up against it and in no position to bargain.

DeNoyelles laid siege to the Sac and Fox village. The impasse continued for four days. The French food shortage grew critical. All they and their allies had to eat in that period were twelve dogs and a horse. Some ate their moccasins.

DeNoyelles knew he was beaten. He retreated eastward after concluding a meaningless agreement with the Sacs that they would end their alliance with the Foxes. The Sacs did no such thing. Indeed, the heat of battle had fused the two tribes into a permanent close relationship. The exact spot where the French-Indian battle took place in central Iowa isn't known. One respected historian said it was "not far from the present capital of Iowa."

Plenty of Indian blood flowed again in the area a century afterwards. In 1841 a band of Sioux attacked 24 Delawares hunting in the Raccoon River valley west of the Des Moines River and killed all but one. The lone Delaware survivor brought the news to a Sac and Fox band camped near the site of the present state capitol.

An old chief named Pash-e-pa-ho, also known as the "Stabber," swung into action. He rounded up 500 braves who pursued and caught the Sioux after a chase of more than 100 miles. "With a fierce battlecry," the pursuers charged the Sioux camp. A vicious battle resulted in an overwhelming defeat for the Sioux. The Sioux lost a reported 300 braves. Pash-e-pa-ho's force reportedly lost only seven.

Pash-e-pa-ho, the stabber

No Go! No Go!

The anguished Indians cried: "No go! No go!"
They didn't want to leave the Iowa territory. But there was no way to avoid it. By treaty they were supposed to have gone two months before.

Soldiers unceremoniously routed two hundred Sacs and Foxes out of hiding places in what is now Boone County. The troops took the unhappy Indians south to Fort Des Moines, an army post at the junction of the Des Moines and Raccoon rivers in what is now Des Moines.

Like it or not, the Indians were soon on their way to new places to live in Kansas. The time was late in 1845, a year before Iowa became a state.

Under a treaty negotiated in 1842, the Indians sold 12 million acres of land in the center of Iowa to the United States government. The price was forty thousand dollars, to be paid each year. The government

The Indian land cessions of 1842
(State Historical Society of Iowa)

also agreed to pay off $258,000 in Indian debts owed to white traders. The land involved constituted about one-third the present area of the state. It was the single biggest real estate transaction in terms of area in the history of Iowa.

The treaty permitted the Indians to remain in Iowa for three more years, or until October 11, 1845. That deadline was well past when the band was evicted from the Boone area hiding place.

The 1842 deal barred white settlers, often called squatters, from moving in during the final three years of Indian occupancy. That proved difficult to enforce. The government thereupon built Fort Des Moines for two purposes: to prevent whites from moving in and to keep rival Indian tribes from fighting each other—principally to keep the northern Sioux from attacking the Sacs and Foxes. (Man for man, the Sac and Fox warriors could hold their own and then some, but the Sioux had more manpower.)

The fort soldiers did drive some squatters away. But the relentless westward tide of settlers was too much. The pioneers were not to be denied.

It must be said that the Indians willingly agreed to sell their vast domain. Hard times had settled in on the Sacs and Foxes in the early

1840s. For one thing, food was scarce for them, but unfortunately whisky wasn't.

Large quantities of firewater sold contrary to law by greedy traders debilitated the tribes. A government agent said Indians of all ages and ranks and of both sexes presented "a continual scene of the most revolting intoxication."

The traders also lured the Sacs and Foxes into further debts by selling them such outlandish items as fancy ties and vests as well as beads and bright calico cloth. The Indians had a strong sense of honor and they didn't want to welsh on those obligations.

Government agents decided that at least some of the items foisted on the Indians were far out of line. The agents scaled down the traders' claims $54,000, from $312,000 to the $258,000 that the government paid.

Constant bickering among the chiefs also weakened the tribal organization in that period. In 1840 Chief Hardfish declared that Keokuk, Wapello, Appanoose, and Poweshiek had cheated in distributing earlier federal annuities to the Indian families. That crisis was solved in 1841 by the government making the payments directly to heads of families rather than through the leadership.

As to troublemaking traders, one of the worst was an outlaw named Jonas Carsner. He did considerable damage in the Fort Des Moines neighborhood. He sold bad whisky to the Indians and then stole their horses while they were in a drunken stupor.

Captain James Allen, commander at Fort Des Moines, determined to punish Carsner. Allen dispatched a unit that caught Carsner and brought him in for trial. The evidence against the outlaw was too scanty for conviction, however. The angry Allen turned Carsner over to the Indians. They tied him to a tree and gave him a "most unmerciful whipping."

The punishment didn't change Carsner. He stole another horse from an Indian and was given another beating. He promised to go straight but that same night stole two horses belonging to a trader named Fish.

The Indians sympathized with Fish and lent him a horse. Fish pursued Carsner and unluckily caught him. Carsner knocked Fish out of the saddle and made off with that horse as well. It was a case of the bad guy winning all around.

Fort Des Moines came into being May 9, 1843, when the first contingent of troops under Allen arrived from Ottumwa via the Des Moines River aboard the steamer *Ione*. The soldiers were "dragoons," or cavalry, fifty-two in number. A company of forty-six infantrymen followed, bringing the total fort strength to nearly one hundred.

The dragoons carried swords so unwieldy the scabbards dragged along the ground as they walked. That was no real handicap since they did most of their fighting on horseback. It was said each dragoon was capable of handling five Indians by himself in combat. That kind of confrontation never happened. The soldiers did have to discipline Indians once in a while but the white settlers were the main problem.

Fort Des Moines really wasn't much of a fort. No stockade was built to protect the troops in the event of a major attack because none was expected and none took place. The fort consisted of twenty-five or thirty one-story double cabins built of rough logs and stretched in an "L" along the confluence of the rivers. The whole layout was north of the present Des Moines baseball park. The fort flagpole was said to have been near the present intersection of Second and Market streets.

The army didn't waste much money improving the fort. There was no point in it. Everybody knew the operation would be over in three years.

While no squatters as such were permitted to settle in numbers near the fort, Allen did allow some whites to take up residence close by. Trader Robert Kinzie set up his quarters near the present Third Street and Court Avenue. On the east side of the Des Moines River, brothers Washington George and George Washington Ewing also were given trade permits and allowed to claim some land. So was John Scott who contracted to provide supplies for the garrison. West of the river Ben Bryant, John Sturdevant, and Alex Turner grew vegetables for the military.

Allen allowed Peter Newcomer, who may have been the first civilian settler, to file a land claim in return for building a bridge over Four Mile Creek along the route of a military road east of the fort. Thomas Mitchell, founder of Mitchellville, was granted the same privilege in return for building a bridge over Camp Creek.

Allen might have been accused of a conflict of interest today. He and one Moses Barlow went into partnership in a sawmill ten miles south of the fort, to produce lumber not only for the fort but to sell to future settlers as well.

Also, there was no mill in the region to grind grain. The closest was at Bonaparte in southeast Iowa, 150 miles away. Allen got one John Parmalee to buy out Barlow and to establish a grain mill near the sawmill. Once the gristmill got going, Allen sold out his total interest to Parmalee. There might have been a congressional investigation today.

Meanwhile, anticipation had been building up for a forthcoming historic and dramatic event. The time approached when the Indian waiting period was to expire and the land thrown open to legal settlement by whites. It was an opportunity for each pioneer to lay claim to 320 acres of the richest land in the world.

Fort Des Moines, 1844

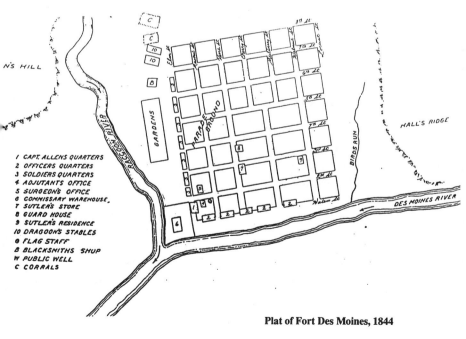

N'S HILL

GARDENS

PARADE GROUND

HALL'S RIDGE

BIRDS RUN

DES MOINES RIVER

RACCOON RIVER

1 CAPT. ALLENS QUARTERS
2 OFFICERS QUARTERS
3 SOLDIERS QUARTERS
4 ADJUTANTS OFFICE
5 SURGEON'S OFFICE
6 COMMISSARY WAREHOUSE,
7 SUTLER'S STORE
8 GUARD HOUSE
9 SUTLER'S RESIDENCE
10 DRAGOON'S STABLES
0 FLAG STAFF
B BLACKSMITHS SHOP
W PUBLIC WELL
C CORRALS

Plat of Fort Des Moines, 1844

Settlers made deals with each other as to who should claim what. Some measured acreages and drove stakes ahead of time even though such early action had no validity.

A shot was fired in east Des Moines at midnight October 11, 1845, signalling the end of the Indian era and the opening of the whole region to white control.

Precisely at 12 o'clock, wrote historian H. H. Turrill, "the loud report of a musket fell upon hundreds of eager ears. Answering reports rang sharply on the night air in quick succession from every hilltop and every valley, until the signal was conveyed for miles around, and all understood that civilization had commenced her reign in central Iowa."

Using colorful language, Turrill went on: "The moon was slowly sinking in the west, and its beams offered a feeble and uncertain light for the measuring of claims for which so many were engaged.

"Ere long the landscape was shrouded in darkness, save the wild and fitful glaring of torches carried by claims makers. Before the night had entirely worn away, the rough surveys were finished and the Indian lands had found new tenants. Throughout the country thousands of acres were laid off in claims before dawn.

"Settlers rushed in by the hundreds and the region, lately so tranquil and silent, felt the impulse of change and became vocal with the sounds of industry and enterprise."

A few bands of Indians remained for months afterwards. The soldiers found another 110 tribesmen in wretched condition thirty miles up the Des Moines River in March of 1846. The Indians were fed and started on their way west out of the state.

On March 10, 1846, the last of the troops abandoned Fort Des Moines. The era of the first Fort Des Moines in central Iowa was over.

Polk County, named for the current President James Polk, was created January 17, 1846, by an act of the Iowa Territorial Legislature then meeting in Iowa City. That same day the federal government gave the new county 160 acres which became the site of the village of Fort Des Moines.

Somebody cut down the fort flagpole soon after the troops left. The log cabins were gradually demolished as well over the following years. All there is today to recall the distant heritage of the fort is a restored cabin near Elm and First streets and not far from the Des Moines River bank.

The first Fort Des Moines newspaper, the *Iowa Star*, was printed July 26, 1849, in one of the log cabins vacated by the troops.

The land given to Polk County went on the market immediately. The highest priced lot, at the corner of First and Vine streets, sold for $105. A lot 132 feet square where the Kirkwood Hotel is located went for $35.

A French Name

The city of Des Moines got its French-sounding name from the Des Moines River, but what is the origin of the name? Several answers to that question have been advanced for a century or more.

The army post located at the confluence of the Des Moines and Raccoon rivers was named Fort Des Moines when built in 1843. The word "Fort" was dropped in 1857 when Des Moines became the capital of Iowa.

One theory ascribes the name to the thousands of Indian burial and religious mounds found in the river valley. (One mound was on the site of the Polk County courthouse and another on the southeast corner of Fourth and Walnut Streets in Des Moines.)

It was said that French traders back in the 1700s consorted with Indian women in substantial numbers in interior Iowa. The result was a hardy race of half-breeds in the upper river valley above Des Moines. They reportedly called the stream the "River of Mounds," and thus ultimately "River Des Moines."

Early French map showing Des Moines River

Another theory suggests that the river got its name from a band of Trappist monks [*de la Trappe*] located on the banks of the Mississippi River in Illinois, opposite the mouth of the Des Moines. Hence the "River of the Monks."

Still another idea put forward was that the name originally was the *Des Moyen* river, in the middle between the Mississippi and Missouri rivers.

The best explanation, however, dates all the way back to Father Marquette, the French Jesuit priest who explored the Mississippi in 1673 with his counterpart Louis Joliet. Their party was the first to set foot on Iowa soil.

Father Marquette recorded in his journal that on July 25, 1673, his group found a large Indian village he charted as *Moingowena* not far from the mouth of a river flowing into the Mississippi.

A 1720 globe in Dijon, France, and other French maps of the times designate the stream as *Rivière de Moingowena*. The Indian name is an Algonquin word that was difficult for the early traders to pronounce and they are said to have shortened it to *des mons*.

When President Thomas Jefferson bought the huge Louisiana Purchase west of the Mississippi in 1803, the document mentioned a "River Moingona" or "River de Moin."

There was nothing standard about the spelling of the name in the early years of Iowa history. An 1854 map of the area spells it all in one word "Fort DesMoines," with no intervening space. An early prominent hotel at First and Walnut streets, the site of a Polk County office building, carried the name "Demoine House."

Demoine House

But for the reaction of official Washington, the town might have emerged with the name "Fort Raccoon." At the time, Captain James Allen suggested it be named "Fort Raccoon." Nothing doing, Washington said, and the Fort Des Moines name, with an earlier spelling, was adopted.

Stolen Land

I t may be that Des Moines is the county seat of Polk County only because of territory "stolen" from Warren County, its neighbor to the south. Without that additional land, the Polk courthouse might have gone elsewhere.

The transfer of 144 square miles of northern Warren to Polk County in the late 1840s was one of the slickest real estate deals ever pulled in Iowa. Warren pioneers regarded it as thievery.

A hot battle raged in 1846 over where the Polk courthouse should be located. Fort Des Moines wanted it in the worst way. The fort was the largest town in the county, with a population of 127, and twenty-three families in all.

One rival for the county seat was Brooklyn where practically nobody lived. Brooklyn was laid out by Dr. T. K. Brooks in what is now the Dean Avenue and East Fourteenth area of Des Moines' east side. Dr. Brooks was Fort Des Moines' first postmaster but one of his principal goals in life after he retired seems to have been to keep the town from becoming the county seat.

Polk City was another county seat candidate. So was Dudley, a now-vanished tiny town down the Des Moines River not far from the present Carlisle.

Battles among towns over county seats were common in early Iowa. One authority says such conflicts "were the source of enmities and feuds that lasted for generations."

In early 1846 both Fort Des Moines and Brooklyn sent lobbyists to Iowa City where the Iowa legislature was meeting. The lawmakers appointed three commissioners to visit Polk and decide where to locate the courthouse. The Brooklyn lobby did all it could to run down Fort Des Moines.

"The Fort is too far south in the county," the legislators were told. "The county seat should be more in the center of the county. The people would be better served that way."

The statement in general was true. Fort Des Moines was, and Des Moines is, in the south part of the county.

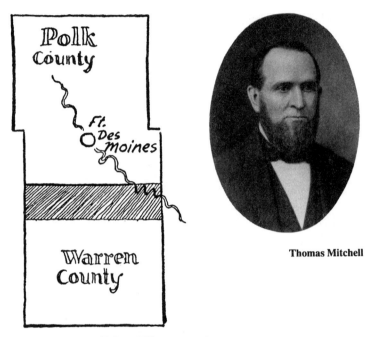

Thomas Mitchell

The contested area, Polk and Warren counties

The Brooklyn lobby came home, confident that Fort Des Moines wouldn't win. Brooklyn, of course, also was too far south. But that was all right. The important thing was to keep the Fort from winning.

Fort Des Moines lobbyists didn't come home right away. Two of its members were Thomas Mitchell, founder of Mitchellville, and Dr. Pierce Fagan. They concocted a scheme.

Before the Brooklynites woke up, the Fort group pushed through the legislature a bill annexing to Polk County the equivalent of the full tier of northernmost townships from still-unorganized Warren County. That expansion gave the Fort a more central position in Polk.

A few weeks later the location commission arrived and proceeded to decide the contest.

"They were eight days investigating the claims of the various towns," says one report. "When they finally decided in favor of Fort Des Moines, the people of the place gave themselves over to unrestrained manifestations of joy. Cannons were fired, bonfires burned and there was ample board spread at Colonel Tom Baker, and the best of music, consisting of two fiddles."

Commissioner Giles M. Pinneg of Scott County received sixty-two dollars for his work in locating the Polk county seat. Commissioner M. Z. Williams of Mahaska County got twenty-eight dollars. There's no record of what Commissioner Thomas Hughes of Johnson County received.

Meanwhile, Warren County was organized in 1849. Warren became impatient. It wanted the territory returned. Polk was loath to give it up.

For one thing, Dr. A. Y. Hull objected. He was Polk County's state senator in the legislature. He lived on the north bank of the Des Moines River in Camp Township in the southeast corner of the county.

If all the land taken by Polk were returned, Dr. Hull would find himself living in Warren County. He feared he couldn't be elected in that county.

Warren had a state representative named P. Gad Bryan. Gad fought for return of the land. He failed in the 1850 legislature. In 1852 a petition was signed by a majority of the voters in Warren asking the legislature to restore the land.

The 1853 legislative assembly did just that, except for a piece of the north side of the river in Camp Township. Dr. Hull had won his battle to keep his homestead in Polk County. To this day the boundary between the counties in that area is not a straight line but follows the river. And, of course, Des Moines is on the southern edge of Polk County and nowhere near the center.

Warren was luckier than some other Iowa counties, notably Humboldt. It has only twelve townships instead of the usual sixteen.

Humboldt County was created in 1851. The county was eliminated in 1855 and the territory divided between its north-south neighbors, Kossuth and Webster counties. The Humboldt people wanted a county of their own, however, and the county was re-created in 1857. In the re-creation, the southern tier of Humboldt townships remained in Webster County. The only explanation given was "some unexplained manipulation."

Traffic Jam

A motorist today is likely to blow his top if he is stuck for half an hour in a traffic jam. Imagine how unhappy he'd be if he were caught in a jam for two or three days.

There were such long tie-ups in the village of Fort Des Moines in the spring of 1850. Dreams of great riches were the cause.

Gold had been discovered in California! Men dropped everything all over the nation and headed west. Waiting vehicles lined up from the Des Moines River all the way east to Four Mile Creek. The vehicles were not automobiles but wagons pulled by horses and oxen. Cars were far in the future.

Impatient drivers tried to buy their way to better positions in the line. All cooked meals over fires as they waited. Some whiled away the time playing cards and drinking whisky. What they were waiting for was a ride over the river on Aleck Scott's flatboat ferry. The ferry operated a little south of what is now Grand Avenue.

There were no bridges across the river. If you wanted to cross you either waded or rode the ferry. The water was too deep for wading at that

Westward-bound traffic was huge. The ferry carried 1,049 teams of horses and wagons and 2,813 people in six weeks that spring. In one April week 252 wagons and 675 persons were ferried to the west side. Pulling the wagons were 215 oxen and 717 horses. Most of those travelers were from Wisconsin and Illinois, with some from Jackson County and other eastern Iowa areas. The number of emigrants on this and other roads was tremendous.

Human beings were just as interested in attaining great wealth quickly in the mid-nineteenth century as they are now. A Des Moines editor wrote: "From a gentleman just returned from the Bluffs [Council Bluffs], we learned there are encamped around that place near 2,000 teams. [He] met 300 or 400 on the way between there and here."

The traffic was wonderful business for ferryman Scott. He was the same Scott who donated part of the hill on which the statehouse stands. He is the Willson Alexander Scott who is buried in the southeast part of the statehouse grounds. His is the only grave on the grounds.

Scott charged thirty-seven-and-a-half cents to take a driver with animals and wagon across the river, twelve-and-a-half cents for a horseman and his steed, and five cents for a foot passenger. The gold fever infected Polk County pioneers too. Said one report: "The excitement grew daily as the people heard marvelous reports from the Pacific coast. The one great subject around the fireplaces and in the log cabins that winter was the gold of California."

One such "marvelous" report came in a letter to the *Fort Des Moines Gazette* from Jacob Thrailkill in California. He told of making a fabulous $30 a day, not from gold but by selling lumber he had sawed. He did dabble in gold as well: "Each day we worked we did not make less than $16 to $24 per day, and one day we made $55 and yesterday we made $112 apiece. I have now laid up between $1,000 and $1,200."

That was big money in those days. No wonder Iowans were tempted to head to the gold fields.

Another California report said, however: "Let everyone remain

Des Moines' biggest traffic jam (Frank Miller/George Mills)

at home who is at home, for out of 100, 99 are sick or broken in spirit, or lose their all by gambling."

The *Des Moines Journal* of 1851 carried a poem which said in part:

> How many tearful partings
> And how many lives untold
> Have been laid upon the altar of
> This raging thirst for gold.

There's a feeling of excitement in this Polk County report of the huge migration: "It seemed that bedlam itself had been let loose. A continuous line of wagons stretched away to the west as far as the eye could reach. If a wagon was detained by reason of being broken down, or by reason of a sick horse or ox, it was dropped out of line and the gap was closed immediately.

"If a poor mortal should sicken and die, the corpse was hurriedly buried by the wayside, without coffin or burial service.

"When night came on, the line of wagons was turned inside and their proprietors would go into camp. Very often the sound of revelry would begin around the campfires thickly set on every hand, and whisky, cards and curses would follow in their course."

Another report said the "gold hunters from Polk County crowded eagerly into the gaps of the wagon trains, bidding farewell to their nearest and dearest friends, and many of them never to be seen again on this earth. . . . Very few gained anything and the great majority lost everything. . . ."

It was said the only real gainers were those who "remained on their farms and sold their produce to the gold-crazed emigrants."

Dealing with gold rushers wasn't all profit, however. They were believed to have brought disease with them. "Those poor, deluded votaries of Mammon," one report said, "scattered the dreadful scourge of smallpox everywhere they came in contact with the settlers."

Littering the trails with trash occurred even in those times: "Glass bottles, after being emptied of their nefarious contents down the throats of men, were dashed against the wagon wheels . . . game cards and broken and empty bottles were strewn all along the line of travel."

Each wagon did carry a supply of liquor for medical purposes. Dysentery was the most common sickness. A newspaper story advised: "By all means include nutmeg and a keg of good brandy. Thicken the brandy with sugar and nutmeg. A good dose will cure [dysentery]."

What the rushers appeared to need and enjoy most of all was coffee. The *Gazette* urged rushers to take along a coffee pot "large and of good quality" because there was "more coffee used than anything else."

The trip by wagon over the plains and mountains must have been unbelievably harsh. One experienced traveler recommended that rushers go by ship to Panama, cross the isthmus and proceed by ship up the coast to California. He wrote that travelers who used that route "were in condition to go to work immediately." Which evidently wasn't true of those who traveled overland.

In 1858 a sudden batch of a different kind of gold reports thrilled the nation. Gold discovered in Iowa near Osceola! Three or more places in Madison County! In Adair County! Lucas! Warren! Near Panora! In Des Moines!

The Des Moines report said gold had been found in the Des Moines River in the downtown area. Said a newspaper story: "In a short time hundreds of people had gathered at the interesting spot. Pans and spades were placed in immediate use to eke out the precious metal.

"It was soon found convincingly true that gold is embedded in the heart of our city. We saw specimens that were unmistakably gold. It is generally believed that when the river recedes to the ordinary summer stage, rich deposits of the precious metal will be disclosed by the mining." The excitement infected even the most easy-going citizens. A Des Moines editor wrote:

"Inveterate loafers who have never been known to pass an industrial hour at any honest employment, have taken their pans, shouldered their spades and [have] gone out to try their fortune in pursuit of gold."

Meanwhile, traffic into Iowa greatly increased, lured by gold reports printed in New York and other eastern papers. Steamboats arrived in Des Moines from Keokuk on the Des Moines River "bringing . . . gold seekers from all parts of the country."

But the boom collapsed as fast as it had come into being. There was and is gold in Iowa but in such slight amounts that the cost of recovering it exceeds its value. Traces are found in rocks brought into the region by glaciers eons ago. Nobody has ever been known to mine gold profitably in the state.

Incidentally, not nearly all the westward migrants in the 1850s were motivated by lust for gold. Many only wanted to establish homes. Tens of thousands came to Iowa for that purpose and stayed.

A great number of others went on through, such as the Mormons on their way to Utah to establish their own religion and way of life. Such a band passed through Des Moines in 1856, pulling handcarts containing all their possessions. Said a report: "In the broiling sun these poor creatures, the majority of whom are women, moving slowly along in Indian file, dragging behind them in little carts the necessaries of the journey, sometimes two women dragging the carts, at other times a man and a woman together.

"The company was from Europe and mostly consisted of English people, who left their comfortable homes, their early associations and all the attachments which render the English people such unwilling emigrants. Here, with a journey of more than 1,000 miles before them, of which 200 would be through a perfect desert, without shade or water, these . . . people are trudging forward."

Going back to the Des Moines River ferry: But for a swimming ox, there might never have been a Kingman Boulevard in Des Moines.

Albert Smith Kingman worked on the river ferry in 1850 as a young man. The ferry was crowded one day and Kingman was knocked into the water. He couldn't swim. Luckily there was an ox swimming

Albert Kingman

near him. Kingman grabbed the animal's tail and was pulled ashore. He later bought nearly 100 acres of land between what is now University Avenue and Center Street and 28th and 31st streets. He donated an eighty-foot strip to the city for what is now part of the boulevard.

Water, Water Everywhere

Please God, stop this awful rain." Many a devout pioneer in the Des Moines and Raccoon river valleys must have whispered such a prayer when he went to bed in the spring and summer of 1851.

Rain! For more than six weeks rain fell almost constantly, mercilessly. The rains began the middle of May and didn't let up until July. Early settlers said the rain period exceeded the forty days and forty nights of biblical times.

The storms were frightening. One pioneer said in his memoirs: "The rain would be pouring down in torrents, with intense lightning and crashing thunder. Sometimes I would be kept awake nearly all night by the blinding lightning, even when so distant that the thunder was scarcely heard. I don't think that before or since, in any equal amount of time, I ever witnessed such fearful electrical disturbances."

Nobody knows for sure how much rain fell in the Des Moines area in 1851. There was no official weather bureau station to take readings. One early history claims the rainfall that year reached 74.49 inches. A fantastic amount and by far the greatest annual volume of moisture in the area's history. Normal for Des Moines is about 31 inches a year.

Either the weather of central Iowa was unusually wet in the middle of the last century or the weather gages of the pioneers were too optimistic. Those unofficial records reported: 1850, 49.06 inches; 1851, 74.49 inches; 1852, 59.49 inches; 1853, 45.76 inches.

But the pioneers did record dryness the next two years in a row: 1854, 23.35 inches; and 1855, 23.38 inches.

The enormous 74.49 inches in 1851 could have happened. One record says there was 36.75 inches of rain at Muscatine, Iowa, in June, July, and August of that year. There were twenty-one rainy days in June at Muscatine and the rainfall for the month totaled 14.75 inches. July was cold and wet with 8 inches. August was cold and rainy with 14 inches, the Muscatine report says. Whether or not the early figures are accurate, it is undeniable that raging floods choked central Iowa pioneer life in 1851.

There was a little town of Dudley on the Des Moines River then, two miles east of Carlisle and southeast of Des Moines. Jerry Church had founded the town. He had high hopes that Dudley would become the state capital of Iowa. He also wanted Iowa State College (now University) and the Polk County Courthouse located there.

The flood of 1851 washed Dudley off the map for good. Jerry seems to have taken his bad luck rather light-heartedly. One report says: "With wild waters surrounding his store, the waves carrying off everything that was movable, Uncle Jerry climbed the roof of that last building that defied the current and fiddled over the destruction of his city, as Nero did when Rome was burning."

Uncle Jerry Church fiddles while flood waters rage.
(Frank Miller/George Mills)

LaFayette, another little town below Dudley, also was washed away. One historian wrote of Dudley: "The water covered the town plat deep enough to float a large steamer."

The town of Fort Des Moines had a population of less than 600. Even so, the damage was tremendous. Says one report: "The Des

Moines River was a rushing torrent three miles wide in many places. Houses were carried off, sheep and swine swept downstream. Rails and fences ditto. It seemed that the spirit of ruin had taken possession of the bottom lands which lay in beauty a few weeks before." Another report said it was "almost impossible to estimate the losses. Roads (trails) were impassable, bridges swept away, mails stopped, travel by land to any distance utterly vetoed." Still another report quotes early settlers as saying the current from the Raccoon River swept across the lower portion of Court Avenue, Walnut and other streets. "East Des Moines was overflowed entirely, and the swollen waters covered all the bottoms and swept around the hill upon which the capitol now stands."

Nearly all the mills in the county had to be shut down. Flour and meal were difficult to obtain for weeks. The settlers had to use pounded corn for food, which was called "samp."

The west side of Fort Des Moines didn't appear to have been damaged much, although business was paralyzed. Water partly covered the street at Third and Court. Young men who boarded at the old Marvin House at Third and Walnut used a raft to get back and forth across the street. Walnut Creek west of Des Moines was passable only to swimming horses and oxen.

Boats sailed all over East Des Moines. Dr. Thomas Brooks even succeeded in floating considerable building material to a house site a mile east of the present statehouse. A strong current flowed on East Fourth Street.

With all the high water, only one life was lost in Fort Des Moines. Huge trees were torn loose from banks upstream and came rolling down the river. Settlers made quite a little money catching these trees and turning them into saw logs. A young blacksmith was out in a boat with two other men intercepting the trees. The boat overturned and the blacksmith drowned.

The damage, of course, was not confined to the Des Moines area: "Ottumwa, Eddyville and other towns along the [Des Moines] river were in the same overflowed and injured condition."

Some unusual losses were reported. For example, a Des Moines river boat had gotten as far as Croton, Iowa, in Lee County with a cargo of 500 pairs of wooden shoes. The shoes were destined for the Dutch town of Pella, Iowa. There was a dam at Croton and the boat could not proceed upstream. The shoes had to be unloaded. They were stored in a Croton blacksmith shop near the river. Then came the flood of 1851 and "the thousand wooden shoes were washed down the river."

Floods devastated the Des Moines River valley again in 1892 and 1903. The latter year was particularly bad.

"Probably the greatest disaster in the experience of those now living is upon us," said the May 31, 1903 *Register*. "Thousands are

The flood of 1892

suffering for the want of food and clothing. There is not time for ceremony and the demand is for immediate personal service.

"Let all who can constitute themselves committees on the alleviation of some pain today. Food and clothing can be left at any drug store in the city, where committees will properly dispose of them."

The water was so high in 1903 that Deputy Sheriff George Kelly caught "three fine little fish" in the Polk County courthouse basement.

Floods of 1947 and 1954 plagued Des Moines and other Des Moines River cities. The flood of 1954 was the highest in history for Des Moines. Damaging floods haven't been believed possible since the Saylorville dam and reservoir were built upstream. But what if 1851 happens again?

Liquor Champion

The liquor-drinking champion among early Des Moines newsmen had to be Dr. W. H. Farner. He was editor in the late 1850s of *The Iowa Citizen,* predecessor of *The Des Moines Register.*

This is what his assistant wrote of Farner, undoubtedly exaggerated somewhat but with some truth nevertheless: "He was a prodigious consumer of whisky. He drank early in the morning and he drank often; he drank after breakfast and drank frequently; he drank before dinner and he drank untiringly; he drank after dinner and he drank persistently; he drank before tea and he drank inveterately; he drank after tea and he drank tremendously; continuing to drink on in that way when in congenial company until every other man was under the table; and yet this little fellow, so fragile and bloodless in appearance, so destitute of muscular development, so wan, cadaverous and ghostlike, was never known to be unsteady in his gait nor maudlin in his conversation. . . . He was the most remarkably sober drunkard with whom I was ever acquainted."

Dr. Farner left Des Moines as the Civil War came on. He was last heard of in 1861 serving as surgeon of a Confederate army regiment in New Mexico.

A Capital Move

The safe of the Iowa state treasurer got stuck in the mud. The safe full of cash stood marooned for four days and nights in the muck and snow near Four Mile Creek northeast of Des Moines. Twenty oxen pulled the big strongbox free and brought it to Des Moines on a bobsled.

The problem occurred while the entire Iowa state government was being moved from Iowa City to Des Moines. The government opened for business November 10, 1857, in a capitol located on the site of the Civil War monument south of the present statehouse.

There were no railroads as yet and the moving, with horses and oxen pulling the vehicles, took about a week. For four days Iowa literally had a "capitol on wheels," as one authority said. State offices closed in Iowa City November 6 and opened in Des Moines November 10.

One major task was moving the safes of the state treasurer, state auditor, secretary of state, and superintendent of public instruction. Dr. Jesse Bowen of Iowa City was awarded the contract and delivered the safes.

Colonel Hooker

The heavy treasurer's safe was hardest to handle. One report said its arrival in Des Moines was "hailed with great delight, not only by the citizens of Des Moines but also by the state officers and their deputies, for in it was the gold and silver to pay them their last month's salary."

The present Iowa constitution was adopted in 1857 and it designated Des Moines as the permanent capital of the state. The shift from Iowa City was made because a majority in the state believed Iowa needed a more centrally located capital. Des Moines at the fork of the Raccoon and Des Moines rivers was chosen. Des Moines was a town of under four thousand.

The moving job was so difficult a task that the teamsters of the time turned it down. Des Moines was eager for the capitol, however, and recruited owners with horses, oxen and vehicles, plus other volunteers, and got the job done.

Colonel E. F. Hooker was the boss of the Great Western stagecoach line that was a principal link of Des Moines with the outside world. Hooker grandly offered to transport the top state officials from Iowa City free. The offer was quickly accepted. Fresh horses every ten to fifteen miles speeded the journey.

Governor James Grimes and the other elective state officials got to Des Moines in a hurry, comparatively. They traveled by the fast stage from Iowa City and the journey took only a day and a half. (The trip by auto today takes little more than two hours.)

Deputy state officials, however, needed nearly three days. They left Iowa City in a hack (a coach of sorts). The first night out they stopped at Brooklyn. A snowstorm came up the second day. They stopped that night at a Mr. Piper's in Jasper County twenty-five miles east of Des Moines.

The snow was twelve to sixteen inches deep the next morning. The hack driver refused to go on. The deputies hired a farmer and his lumber wagon and he took them the rest of the way.

John M. Davis, deputy secretary of state was especially glad to reach Des Moines. He had the responsibility of delivering to the 1858 legislature the results of the state general election.

Davis packed the records in his own trunk along with his clothing. He reportedly sat on the trunk the last twenty-five miles of the trip to make certain the records would not be stolen. Actually he may have sat on the trunk only for convenience. He was riding on the lumber wagon and he had to sit somewhere.

The new capitol in Des Moines didn't cost the state anything, at first at least. An east Des Moines group pledged thirty-five thousand dollars and built a three-story brick statehouse 100 feet long and 56 feet wide. The group went broke in the depression of 1857, however, and the state ultimately footed the cost. The building served as the capitol until the 1884–1886 period when state offices were opened in the present golden-domed statehouse.

Flight to Freedom

The load of cornstalks in the wagon moving through downtown Des Moines looked innocent enough. If you had peered under the stalks, however, you would have found four weary and frightened human beings.

The driver was a stern-looking old man with bushy hair and a flowing beard. His mud-spattered wagon and dusty clothes told of long travel on trails over the prairies.

It was barely dawn on a cold winter day. The rutted streets were all but deserted. The wagon crossed the Des Moines River and continued slowly east on the old stage route then known as Keokuk Road (now East Grand Avenue). The vehicle stopped at Isaac Brandt's home on the northeast corner of Keokuk and East Twelfth streets.

Brandt was in his yard. He said "hello." The driver responded by grasping his right ear between thumb and finger. That was the underground recognition signal. Brandt asked how many. The driver held up four fingers. Brandt, a merchant, invited the driver to stop. The driver said he had to be on his way but would stop the next time. Brandt looked under the stalks and saw the shivering passengers.

The hidden human beings were all blacks. They were escaped slaves from southern states. The year was 1859. The driver was the famed John Brown, fanatical foe of slavery. Brandt's home was a "station" on the underground railroad. That "railroad" was a series of individuals and organizations that helped escaped slaves to reach

Flight to freedom (Frank Miller/George Mills)

freedom and safety in the north in pre–Civil War days.

Brown is best known in American history for his merciless battles against slavery in Kansas and for his unsuccessful attempt to start an insurrection of slaves at Harper's Ferry in Virginia. He was hanged in Virginia. Later Northerners in the Civil War were to sing: "John Brown's body lies a-mouldering in the grave, but his soul goes marching on."

Brown had at least one other firm friend in Des Moines. He was John Teesdale, editor of what is now *The Register*. Brown stopped to see Teesdale in Des Moines while en route east to launch the Harper's Ferry attack. The editor urged Brown not to do anything rash but to go back to his farm in northern New York for good.

John Teesdale

The old fighter told Teesdale, as he had told editor Horace Greeley of the *New York Tribune:* "No, the battle is raging and I must fight. My mission is direct from God Almighty."

Before Brown was executed, Teesdale advised in an editorial that the sentence not be carried out. "His death can add nothing to the security of slave property," the editor said. "The spectacle of that old snowy-haired man, driven to madness by the violence of his pro-slavery enemies . . . standing on the gallows, will deepen and widen the tide of public feeling that is now settling against [slavery]."

Des Moines had no railroads, no improved highways, no lasting bridges across either the Des Moines or Raccoon rivers. (Those which were built were likely to either break down or be swept away by floods.) Travelers had to ride ferries to get over the Des Moines. Teesdale paid Brown's ferry fee at least once.

Brandt's home stood just east and across the street from the old State Historical Building until the mid-twentieth century. It was a funeral home at the time it was razed.

Helping fugitive slaves to escape was high adventure in Iowa in the 1850s. Says one authority: "The country was full of secret agents and slave hunters, so that the utmost caution was necessary to get the 'passengers' through. . . . They [the blacks] were packed in sacks, boxes, barrels, coffins, under loads of straw or cornstalks, men in women's clothes, women in men's clothes."

It may be that underground railroads have been overdramatized in history. Nobody knows how many slaves were helped to freedom. (Some were taken all the way to Canada.) The number who succeeded in reaching the north, however, was not large in comparison with the then-black population of the south.

There were many stations in Iowa, at least five in the central part of the state. Brown had come that morning from Jimmy Jordan's house in what is now West Des Moines. Jordan was a state senator. The next station after Brandt's was the Reverend Demas Robinson's place on Four Mile Creek in east Polk County.

Brown and his passengers continued past Robinson's that day on to Uncle Tom Mitchellville's inn near what is now Mitchellville. The next day they journeyed to Grinnell for a stopover, and then to Cedar County which was the eastern terminal of the western division of the railroad.

So far as it is known, the four fugitives reached freedom. There is no record of escaped slaves ever having been caught in this state and returned south. Officers did try at least twice to gain possession of fugitives but were balked.

Brown once went through Des Moines with eleven blacks. He had entered the state from Nebraska City, Nebraska. The number of fugitives had grown to twelve by the time eastern Iowa was reached. One of the women had a baby en route.

It appears that two black women were held as slaves in what is now Des Moines in the 1840s. One Joseph Smart bought the women in Missouri and brought them to old Fort Des Moines. He "held them for some time" at the Fort and then sold them in Missouri.

Smart probably could have been forced to set the women free. The Iowa courts held as early as 1839 that a master who brought a slave into the Iowa territory lost all ownership and control over the individual.

Blacks drifted into Iowa all during the 1850s and 1860s. There were between 400 to 600 in Des Moines in the late 1860s. Marcellus M. Crocker, Des Moines' famous Civil War general, reported favorably in 1864 on the black regiments in the Union army. He said they fought "as well as any troops." In that year the "first African regiment from Iowa" reported the deaths of twelve Des Moines men in action at Helena, Arkansas.

A "little race question" arose in as long ago as 1899 when the noted Booker T. Washington, a former slave, addressed a crowd of several thousand in Des Moines. A report said: "There was a little race question because everybody on the stage went down in the main part of the auditorium because they wanted to (better) hear him. Mr. Washington nevertheless felt he had been treated with disrespect. He felt that the prominents on the stage left it before his speech just because he was a black man."

A Hanging Councilman

A Des Moines city councilman hanged two men by the neck until they were dead. This drastic action in January 1860 shocked central Iowa. The victims were horse thieves.

Stealing a horse was about the worst crime you could commit in pioneer days. A horse was a principal means of transportation. It was true there was some boating on the rivers. But people mostly traveled by animal power, horseback, horse and wagon, horse and buggy, and maybe oxen and wagon. And they walked.

The Reverend Thompson Bird, pioneer Presbyterian minister and Des Moines' first mayor, walked all the way from Des Moines to Cedar Rapids to attend a church conference. And then walked home.

Councilman Lemuel Small took great pride in a team of two horses that he kept in his stable at home. He represented the old Fifth Ward and lived at Thompson's Bend, on the south side of the Des

Moines River, across the water from the present Union Park.

When Small got up on a cold winter morning in 1860, the horses were gone. The enraged councilman grabbed his gun and mounted another horse. He enlisted the help of Constable Al Simmons and started after the thief or thieves. The trail was easily discernible through the snow and led eastward from Des Moines.

Small and Simmons stopped at the village of Rising Sun and got a blacksmith, whose name isn't known, to go along. All three were members of a vigilantes committee formed to wreak vengeance on perpetrators who escaped punishment in legal proceedings. Many miles to the northeast, in Tama County, Small and his companions spotted two men camping in the woods. The vigilantes rode up quietly and covered the pair with guns. They were the Bunker brothers, widely known for taking other people's horses.

Small determined to make them confess. Leaving Simmons to guard one brother, the councilman and blacksmith took the other brother to a tree. "We're going to hang you unless you want to tell us what you've done with all the horses you've stolen in the last few years," Small said. "We want to know the names of the members of the gang. If you don't tell us inside of two minutes, up you go!"

"If you don't tell us inside of two minutes, up you go."
(Frank Miller/George Mills)

The suspect refused to talk. They seized him, slipped a rope around his neck and hauled him kicking and struggling into the air. "Confess, damn you, and we'll let you down!" yelled Small.

At this point the other Bunker wormed out of Simmons' grasp and ran away. The vigilantes had to make an immediate choice. If they stopped to lower the first brother, the second might escape. They didn't want that. So they tied the end of the rope around the tree trunk and ran after and caught the fleeing brother. When they got back, the first Bunker was dead.

Small and his companions realized they were in a serious predicament. They had killed a man. What to do? If they stopped now, the surviving brother was sure to tell what had happened. "We might as well make a good job of it," Small said unhappily. They thereupon hanged the second Bunker and returned home.

Somebody learned of the deeds and who was responsible. Tama County authorities filed murder charges against Small and Simmons.

Several days later Tama officers appeared in Polk County. They stormed into the houses of Small and Simmons in early morning, woke them at gunpoint and threw them into a wagon. The officers ate breakfast at an eastside hotel and started out of town. Isaac Brandt was just opening his eastside grocery when the wagon passed. He saw the handcuffs on Simmons. Within half an hour Brandt rounded up thirty vigilantes and went after the wagon. They caught up with the officers and their prisoners near Rising Sun. The vigilantes brushed aside the angry lawmen and freed Small and Simmons. The officers returned to Des Moines and started legal proceedings to take Small and Simmons into custody again.

One Des Moines judge refused to honor the request. An immediate appeal was taken to a higher court. The record isn't clear as to what higher court it was. The case was argued all day. In the end the judge decided to deliver the two men to the Tama authorities.

"Lemuel Small and Al Simmons, you are ordered to stand up!" the court crier shouted. The Sheriff looked around for the prisoners. They had disappeared.

The escape was another sensation. The officers were fighting mad. They searched around the county, to no avail. Months and years passed. The case began to be forgotten in the blood and suffering of the 1861–1865 Civil War.

In 1865 Small came back to Des Moines for a few days in disguise. He disappeared again but not for long. When he returned a second time, he was arrested and taken to Tama County where he stood trial. He was found guilty of murder in the first degree. He appealed to the Iowa Supreme Court which ordered a new trial.

The practical effect of the high court order was to relieve Small from further prosecution. It may be the Tama authorities decided to drop the case. The pioneers did considerable moving around. Perhaps the necessary witnesses were no longer available.

Small, who had been under heavy strain for years, didn't last long. He had an attack of "nervous prostration" and died three weeks afterwards. Says one historical account: "He was a man of excellent character and is sincerely mourned to this day by all surviving friends."

What happened to Simmons isn't known. Apparently he was never tried. The blacksmith seems never to have been arrested.

A third Bunker brother was caught in Des Moines. He also was accused of stealing horses. He was hanged to a tree in Union Square which was at East Thirteenth and Walker streets on the east side.

This Bunker didn't die, however. The report said he was "choked" until he made a full confession. He was lowered to the ground, given a horse and told to leave the country, which he did with alacrity.

The Stars Are Gone

O nly eight stars remain in an old American flag in the State Historical Building in Des Moines. The hand-sewn flag of the Civil War originally had thirty-four stars, one for each of the states of the nation at the time. Each of the other twenty-six stars was taken off the flag and buried with a soldier when he died during the 1861–1865 war.

The old flag was the banner of Des Moines' Company D of the famed Second Iowa Infantry. Women of the city proudly presented the flag the day the company marched off to the war.

The flag is silent evidence that twenty-six members of the company lost their lives in that bloody conflict. The deep emotion of the Civil War period in Iowa is hard to imagine now. It was a time of fervent patriotism, of elation and grief, of pride and anxiety, and of growth and prosperity.

Cannons were fired in town to celebrate Union army victories. Huge bonfires were lighted in downtown streets. Des Moines men hastened to join the "Sawbuck Rangers," an organization formed to cut wood for families of absent soldiers. (Wood was used to cook meals and warm houses in those days.)

Veterans without arms or legs became a common sight on Des Moines streets. So were military funeral processions, with comrades sometimes carrying a coffin on their shoulders. Bodies frequently were shipped home from battlefields by stagecoach. (The railroad had not yet come to Des Moines.)

Commodity prices were high and farmers came to town with "big rolls of bills" in their pockets. Butter was 35 to 40 cents a pound at various times during the war; sugar was 18 to 25 cents a pound; lard, 10 to 12 1/2 cents; potatoes, $1 to $1.25 a bushel. But beefsteak was only 10 cents and pork only 12 1/2 cents a pound.

Eggs were not to be had at any price late in the war. Coffee sometimes was unobtainable and the use of burned sorghum molasses was recommended as a substitute.

Polk County, of which Des Moines is the county seat, had a population of 11,625 in 1860, a little under rural Guthrie County's 1980 figure of 11,983. Des Moines, 1860 population was 3,965, a little larger than the 3,860 of county seat town Cresco in 1980.

Yet Polk sent more than 1,500 men to the Union army, some 12 percent of the 1860 population. Nearly one-fifth didn't return. Said one writer: "Two hundred and eighty lost their lives, either from wounds received in battle or sickness contracted in the camps or on the march."

The war took the lives of thirteen thousand Iowans, as many as both World wars and the Korean War combined, and maimed thousands of others.

Polk and Des Moines were proud of their three brigadier generals, five colonels, six lieutenant colonels, ten majors, and forty captains of the Civil War.

Here's one measure of the casualties: The Second Iowa listed 1,247 men in its ranks. A total of 258 died and 321 were wounded; in other words, 46 percent of those on the original roster died or were wounded in the service.

Deeds of the Second Iowa are legendary. It was credited with having made "the most reckless and gallant charge of the war" at the battle of Fort Donelson. Company D had two men killed and seventeen wounded in that battle.

A feeling of joy swept through Des Moines February 25, 1862, at the report of the Fort Donelson victory. *The Register* said: "The news of this great success was announced to the legislature about noon yesterday! The effect was like an electric shock!

"Cheer after cheer went up until the very rafters seemed to feel the inspiration. Adjournment for the day was moved and carried unanimously.

"All over the city, at the hotels, in the streets, everywhere—men stopped to shake each other's hands and express the joy they entertained. All this enthusiasm was, of course, clouded by the knowledge that some of our brave Iowa boys had been in the thickest of the fight and had fallen. But there are thousands yet in the state to make good their places, should the progress of the war make it necessary."

Six hundred Iowans were killed or wounded at Donelson.

Incidentally, the celebration at the statehouse was marred that "Victory" afternoon by an explosion which severely injured Butler Sells, young son of the Iowa secretary of state. Some prankster put fire into a basket of cartridges the boy was carrying to fire salutes in a gun.

The war dragged on and casualties mounted as the years passed. The number of wounded needing care after the horrible battle of Shiloh in Tennessee was so great that free stage travel was offered to get doctors and nurses to go to the battlefield.

Drums and marching feet were regular sounds in Des Moines streets. Iowa companies streamed through the state capital. A Chariton company marched the fifty miles from home to Des Moines in twenty-four hours.

For some reason, Polk County looked upon the drafting of men into the service as disgraceful. Leaders pleaded with men to volunteer so that a draft could be avoided. Such old-timers as "Uncle Tommy" Elliott volunteered. He was sixty years old, had five sons in the service.

Des Moines businessmen pledged ten thousand dollars to be paid out as bounties at the rate of fifty dollars to the family of each man who enlisted.

In 1864 a notice signed by forty-one married women appeared in the newspapers. The women offered to serve as substitutes in the jobs of "all patriotic men who will enlist and hasten to the support of our glorious husbands, sons, and brothers in arms."

Unmarried women got into the act, offering to serve as job substitutes. If men did not volunteer in sufficient numbers, the maidens threatened to march on each place of business and tell the men to "go!"

"The young ladies were not compelled to make that call," said one authority. "A few days later appeared another card stating they were spared that task by the prompt response of patriotic young men. . . ."

The desperate effort to avoid the draft altogether was almost successful. Only about fifty men had to be drafted in Polk to meet the county quotas by the war's end.

The draft did cause a number of able-bodied men to decide in 1864 that Iowa was "a good state to emigrate from." These men planned to hunt for gold in the west and then perhaps come back to Iowa after the war was over. Governor William Stone was irked. He issued a proclamation prohibiting Iowa citizens from leaving the state before the March 10, 1864, draft deadline. Said the governor: "Those who have so far avoided the stern demands of patriotic duty and now attempt to skulk away, can not be allowed to leave the state until the obligations to the general government are fully and honorably discharged."

Governor Stone declared that any men physically capable of crossing the Great Plains in winter "to delve in the golden mines of Colorado . . . would make excellent material for filling up the wasted ranks of the Union army."

It was a nice try by the governor, but it didn't mean anything. He had no authority to issue such a proclamation. He asked soldiers between Leavenworth, Kansas, and Sioux City, Iowa, to enforce the proclamation. They halted a few emigrants at the Missouri River. But there was no way to blockade the entire western border of the state.

Even if you were drafted, you could still escape service. You could hire a substitute to go in your place if you had the money. The cost of a substitute was $500 early in the war, and went up to $1,500 later. Tempted by the money, some discharged soldiers went back into service as substitutes.

Meanwhile, the problem of caring for families of soldiers grew more difficult. Well-to-do men such as James Callanan assumed the responsibility of supporting one or more families. Also, money raised by private subscription provided from ten dollars to twenty-five dollars a month for seventy-nine separate Des Moines families. There were no federal allowances for such families in the Civil War.

Des Moines' spirits soared in 1864 as Union victories foretold the approaching end of the conflict. Batteries of cannon were fired in the city every time a report was received of a major Union triumph. Thirty-six cannon thundered at the confluence of the Des Moines and Raccoon rivers when Union troops captured Atlanta, Georgia, in September.

Richmond, Virginia, the capital of the Confederacy, fell April 3, 1865. Des Moines celebrated by blasting 136 cannons. The jubilant city was "lighted up that night." The Savery House was a "blaze of light," with 375 lighted candles. (Electric lights were still many years away.)

The surrender of Confederate General Robert E. Lee ending the war touched off a wild celebration. Again, 136 cannons were fired, 100 by order of the governor and 36 by order of the mayor. "The cannonading smashed many windows but that was a slight affair," said one report.

While the thrill of victory was still pulsing through the hearts of the nation, an assassin's bullet took the life of President Lincoln April 15, 1865. The people were appalled.

"On that Saturday, business was generally suspended [in Des Moines]," said one report. "Men gathered in groups around newspaper offices and hotels. In subdued voices they talked of the great calamity. ... Many wore crepe, desiring to express without words the sense of loss they felt."

Sunday afternoon silent thousands gathered in the courthouse square. It was a sad throng from throughout the county. All joined in the singing of hymns and the saying of prayers. General James A. Williamson, one of Polk County's leading soldiers, told how he stood at Lincoln's side March 4, 1865, when the president was inaugurated for a second term.

The war was terrifically costly, as wars usually are, but it did bring prosperity. Population boomed. Polk County's population increased more than 25 percent in five years, from 11,625 in 1860 to 15,244 in 1865. Des Moines grew from 3,965 in 1860 to 5,722 in 1865, a gain of more than 45 percent.

One historian reported that, as the war progressed, "money became more plentiful and labor was in demand. . . . Not only did new people come in with the intention of becoming permanent citizens, but many new business enterprises were initiated, new buildings projected and built, new farms opened, and on every hand was seen evidence of prosperity."

She's A-Comin'

The throng at the brand new railroad station was tense that summer afternoon. Des Moines had never seen such a crowd. Merchants, farmers, lawyers, workers, public officials—they were all there with wives and children dressed in their Sunday best. Everybody strained their ears in the near-quiet. The only sound at first was the occasional stamping of a hoof or neigh of a horse harnessed to a parked buggy. Dozens stood on the track, staring to the east. A far-off

She's a-comin'! (Frank Miller/George Mills)

low and mournful whistle was heard. A thrill ran through the packed thousands. "She's a-comin' !" Then, puffing grandly into the station at East Fifth and Market Street, rolled the first train ever to reach Des Moines.

Gaily decorated with flags, the train had come from Keokuk over the newly completed Des Moines Valley Railroad. Aboard were 300 happy southeast Iowa notables from Keokuk, Burlington, Fairfield, Oskaloosa, Ottumwa, and other cities and towns. The date was August 29, 1866.

Des Moines has had some great celebrations in its time. But it is doubtful whether any produced the wild enthusiasm per capita that greeted the first train.

A city absolutely had to have a railroad to get anywhere in the last century. Des Moines' population was about 6,500. The city had spent seventeen heartbreaking years trying to get a railroad. It had been a state capital without a rail line for nine years.

"When the train came in sight," one news report said, "as far down the track as could be seen there was a wilderness of handkerchiefs, hats, and hands waving from the windows. On the crowded platforms could be seen men waving their hats and shouting their greetings."

A continuous roar of cannons fired on capitol hill lasted from the time the train passed Four Mile Creek until it stopped in the station.

"If we were to live one thousand years," *The Register* said, "and acquire every day of that period more or less qualification as a reporter for the press, we would never be able to do justice for the great celebration of yesterday.

"There were 20,000 people at the depot. Not a man or woman less or a baby less. We will stand by that estimate until we die. It looked as though the whole valley from Des Moines to Keokuk was crowded with a swaying and hurrahing mass of human beings. We may have been mistaken, but never until Iowa shall have the population of China do we expect to see such a sight again. It beat the army of Xerxes considerably if not more."

The train had taken nearly seven-and-a-half hours to come from Keokuk, slow indeed by modern rail standards but a vast improvement over traveling by stagecoach which took three days.

"There were speeches," a report said, "but [only] one-third of the crowd heard them. They were too happy to listen. . . . Many had never seen a train. . . . The crowd was the jolliest ever seen in Des Moines. And the women were there in great numbers, for where the men are, the women will be also."

The shouting and singing crowd paraded from the station through gaily decorated streets to the old Savery House (where the Kirkwood Hotel now stands). Some citizens did not go to bed at all that night. One jubilant father was reported to have named his new son "Valley Road."

"If that story isn't true," *The Register* commented, "it ought to be."

The frustrating battle for a railroad from the east into Des Moines had started in 1849. The first big barrier was the depression of 1857 which halted rail building. Then the Civil War of 1861–1865 slowed down and stopped construction. In describing the rail disappointments of the pioneers, one speaker at the 1866 celebration said: "They waited for its coming, they prayed for its coming, they talked of its coming until their tongues grew eloquent with the theme, but they died and were all in their graves before their eyes saw the glory of this latter age.

"Now it is here. All doubts have fled. The great triumph has been achieved. The promised train is here today. The sun shines in a clear firmament. . . . The final hour of victory has come."

It is hard to understand now how vital railroads were to Iowans 120 or more years ago. There were no automobiles for travel then, no trucks, no buses, no airplanes, no highways as we know them.

When you went anywhere, you jolted along at a slow pace in a stagecoach, wagon, or on horseback. Sometimes you could travel by river boat, if the river ran where you were going (and it wasn't frozen over, or too low). Or you journeyed on your own two feet. Rail service was badly needed to ship farm produce to eastern markets and industrial products as well, if you were going to have any major industry.

There was a happy lilt in *The Register*'s step-by-step story of the long battle to get the Des Moines Valley. "The railroad has left Eddyville and is on its way to Oskaloosa," the newspaper reported. "It has come to Oskaloosa! . . . It has come to Pella! . . . It has come to Monroe! . . . It has come to Prairie City! . . . The train will be here today! Israel's God has interposed in behalf of his people."

Keokuk, then a metropolis of ten thousand, was just as eager as Des Moines for the railroad. Keokuk was called the "Chicago of the Valley," and as such was the commercial and distribution center for southeast Iowa.

Arriving aboard that first train were at least three Keokuk notables: Justice Samuel Freeman Miller of the United States Supreme Court, Civil War Gen. W. W. Belknap, and an "S. Yownker," probably a misspelling of "Younker," Des Moines and Iowa's most famous department store name. The original merchandising Younkers did come to Des Moines from Keokuk.

The train returned to Keokuk the next day. The engine bore two banners saying: "Keokuk-Des Moines, the gate open to the capital" and "DMVRR, the link that unites us."

Despite the original enthusiasm, the Valley line didn't prosper for long. A new company took over by mortgage foreclosure in 1873. The route was absorbed into the Rock Island system. That railroad, by the way, first reached Des Moines on an east-west route from Davenport in 1867, the year after the Valley line arrival.

Des Moines boomed as a railroad center in the following generation. One enthusiast advertised in the 1890s that Des Moines was served by "fifteen lines and ninety trains daily." That would be an average of a train every sixteen minutes around the clock. The city had a population of more than fifty thousand by then.

As recently as 1957 Des Moines had about twenty passenger trains a day. The population had increased to above two hundred thousand. But by 1987 the city had no passenger trains. Passenger service had come to an end throughout Iowa in the auto-plane-bus era except for some trains on federally subsidized Amtrak.

Many small railroads have come and gone in central Iowa and other parts of the state. Usually they were absorbed by larger roads. How many of these old-time railroad names do you know?

Albia, Knoxville, and Des Moines; Chariton, Des Moines & Southern; Des Moines, Adel & Western; Des Moines & Fort Dodge; Des Moines, Indianola & Missouri; Des Moines & Knoxville; Des Moines & Minneapolis; Des Moines, Osceola & Southern; Des Moines, Winterset & Southwestern; St. Louis, Des Moines & Northern.

A real treat in the early days was to take a moonlight excursion train from Des Moines to High Bridge in northeastern Dallas County. The outing to the old bridge was highly popular with young Iowans in the 1880s. Sitting in the dark holding hands with your girl while the cars clicked over the rails through the moonlight was described as "great sport." Inexpensive too, by modern prices. A ticket cost fifty cents per person round trip, or one dollar per couple. Excursion trains handled as many as thirty-five hundred persons a day (and night) over the July 4 holiday.

Goodbye Bridge

A drove of 200 big horses clumped along unpaved Walnut Street in downtown Des Moines toward the Des Moines River. Passersby stopped on the wooden sidewalks to watch. There was no hint that a spectacular accident was about to take place. The year was 1869.

The wooden Walnut Street bridge was the only above-the-water link between the west and east sides of the city. The bridge was built and opened to traffic three years before in 1866 amid gala ceremonies. The honor of driving the first horse and buggy across the structure went to Colonel S. F. Spofford, early Des Moines hotel man.

One of the big problems of pioneer Des Moines was maintaining traffic communication between the east and west sides. Grand Avenue, then named Sycamore Street, and Locust Street had no bridges. Court Avenue had had one but a flood washed it away.

The horses belonged to A. H. Cummings of Des Moines. He had driven the animals up from Texas. He would be selling them to farmers. Horses were a vital part of farm operations in those pre-tractor days. The horses had been in a pasture on the south side of town. Cummings decided to take them to a pasture on the east side. He was warned to divide the drove before crossing the bridge. He paid no attention.

Riders on horseback herded the drove on to the structure.

"The foremost 100 moved along in a shambling trot or fast walk," *The Des Moines Register* reported. "The weight of 100 horses is immense, and shuffling around uneasily as they were, it became almost double and would strain the strongest bridge in the country."

The bridge began to sway. A loud cracking of wood was heard. Supporting timbers broke like match sticks. The whole east span gave way. Panic-stricken horses scrambled wildly to keep from falling. They had no chance. A "great entangled" mass of horse flesh spilled into the flood-swollen river.

(Frank Miller/George Mills)

Approximately 100 horses fled to safety off both ends of the bridge. The others dropped screaming into the swift current.

Horses with broken legs, horses with gashed sides struggled to reach the banks. Some were carried blocks downstream before they could climb out. Fugitive horses ran loose for hours on both sides of the river.

Cummings counted the casualties when the pandemonium died down. Two horses were killed outright. Nine others had to be destroyed. Dozens were treated for injuries.

Cummings was mighty unpopular around Des Moines. Loss of the bridge was a hard blow for the city of under twelve thousand population. *The Register* said of Cummings: "Many spoke harshly of his action which brought such an inconvenience upon our people and upon the business of the city."

The city council sued Cummings for damages. He in turn sued the city for the loss of horses. Whether either side ever won anything isn't known.

The Walnut Street collapse was only one of a number of bridge misfortunes in the early years of the city. Originally, of course, there were no bridges over rivers at all. The only way you crossed the Des Moines was by wading at low water levels or by ferry.

One thing for sure: the earliest pioneers didn't know how to build bridges. They all came to a bad fate. The first was a pontoon bridge, built in 1850, about on a line with the present Grand Avenue. A flood carried it away two years later, in 1852, known as a wet year in Des Moines annals.

A trestle bridge was built at Market Street in 1858 and it was carried away the next year, in 1859. That bridge was rebuilt immediately, only to be destroyed by high water in 1861.

A bridge completed at Court Avenue in 1858 weakened badly in 1866 and was rebuilt only to be smashed by a flood in 1869, the year of the Walnut Street horse disaster.

Des Moines was particularly proud of the original sparkling new 1858 Court Avenue bridge. The *Iowa Citizen* newspaper, predecessor of *The Register,* commented: "The splendid structure stands out in its beautiful proportions to attract the eye and to accommodate the necessities of the people. It is an honor to the builder, the company and the city." But it came to the same disastrous end.

Destruction in 1869 of the Walnut bridge was a good break for the ferry enterprise. The ferry carried passengers and also pushed barges with freight back and forth across the river. The ferry transported 3,000 passengers, 212 wagons, 421 horses, and 75 cattle in one day after the Walnut breakdown. The Walnut bridge was soon repaired but gave way again and had to be replaced altogether in 1871.

A Raccoon River bridge also collapsed in those early Des Moines days, just before the arrival of an overcrowded stagecoach. The stage was a little late, for which the passengers were deeply thankful.

Since bridges were such a costly convenience, the city at times collected tolls from all users. That led to a lot of complaint in 1858 when members of the Iowa Legislature were assessed along with ordinary citizens. The outcry stopped when the lawmakers all received free passes.

A pitched battle ensued in 1871. The city ordered collection of tolls on a Raccoon River bridge near the present Des Moines baseball park. Angry Bloomfield Township people reminded the council that

that bridge was supposed to have been forever toll-free.

The council refused to back up, declared the bridge unsafe, and ordered it torn down. City employees started to take the bridge apart. That was too much for the southsiders. Says one news report: "A small army of irate Bloomfield Township residents charged the bridge. They chased the workers away and relaid the floor."

The objectors won that battle but lost the war. The old bridge was torn down the next year, a new one built, and it cost to cross that bridge whether the customers liked it or not.

Few if any Iowans ever came closer to death in a bridge failure than the Dennis Lowry family of Des Moines. The Lowrys were driving across the Sixth Avenue bridge in Des Moines when a large section of it caved into the Des Moines River. The chunk that fell was 100 feet long and up to 20 feet wide. Dozens of lives undoubtedly would have been lost if the collapse had happened on a busy day. The bridge carried an average of 13,000 to 14,000 vehicles daily. But traffic was light at three o'clock on that Saturday afternoon April 18, 1965.

Goodbye bridge, 1965 (*Des Moines Register*)

In the Lowry car were Dennis, his wife, and their two small children, Tammy, three, and Stacy, eleven months. "I was driving south in the center lane," said Lowry. "A pickup truck was about half a car length ahead of me in the right lane by the bridge railing. Suddenly I saw this bridge collapse. The fellow in the pickup—he was alone—swerved to the left in front of me over to the east side of the bridge. I don't know that I could have turned in time if his action hadn't forced me to. And if there had been any oncoming traffic in that lane, we all would have been done for."

Lowry jumped out of his car at the bridge end and waved the traffic to stop. Another driver blockaded the traffic with his car. The police were called by amateur radio and the bridge was swiftly secured.

Who was driving the pickup was never learned.

Larry Lawtron, a Western Union employee, drove over the bridge about an hour before. He said he could feel the movement at that time. "You could feel it going up and down," he said. "But there wasn't much play in it. I thought the motion was normal."

Two weeks of high flood waters apparently had weakened the bridge supports and they gave way. What was left of the 1907 structure was demolished and a new bridge was built at a cost of about eight hundred thousand dollars.

What bothered city officials and the people most was the fact that engineers a few weeks before had reported the Sixth Avenue bridge in the best condition of four that were inspected. Which caused many to wonder if they risked their lives when they crossed other Des Moines bridges.

Rascals and Republicans

Black Diamonds

Palatial Terrace Hill was dark on a June evening in 1873. Banker B. F. Allen had gone to bed but wasn't asleep. He heard the clop clop of horses' hooves and the sound of carriage wheels coming up the driveway.

He lighted a kerosene lamp and went down. There was his friend Wesley Redhead from the east side.

"We've hit fine coal!" Redhead exclaimed. "Look at this!" Allen examined the lump in the flickering light. "How thick is the vein?" he asked. "At least four feet six inches," Redhead replied. "All I want is your backing."

The vein had been located after months of fruitless drilling near the Seventh Street bridge south of the Raccoon River within the city and maybe a mile from downtown.

Redhead told how three inferior veins had been found on the way down. Then the drill struck flint rock. For four weeks, day and night, the drill bit slowly into the tough rock. Some days only three inches of progress were made.

Redhead had to pay both a day and a night shift, each of eight men. He had eight thousand dollars tied up in the project at that point, and no worthwhile coal to show for it. Then, without warning, the drill broke into the thick vein of coal 125 feet below the surface.

Allen liked the prospects. He invested thirty-five thousand dollars. Before long the mine was producing seventy-five tons of coal a day. It was the beginning of a large scale coal mining industry in Des Moines and Polk County. The industry long since has vanished but more than 150 mines operated in the county over the span of nearly a century.

In 1910 a total of 4,040 men made their living from coal mines in the county. Of this number 2,943 were miners. The city's population was eighty-six thousand then, less than half its size in the 1980s. Any industry that generated four thousand new jobs would be treated with utmost respect by any city today.

Polk County's output of coal used to be tremendous. County production exceeded 1 million tons a year in all the early years of the twentieth century. The 1910 production was a whopping 1,736,000 tons. Polk County frequently was second and third highest in coal production in the state, and may have been first occasionally.

Deep under the streets, buildings, and farms of the county are still rotted timbers, water-filled tunnels, and other vestiges of a once-prosperous mining industry. Nearly all the ancient passageways have been filled in long since. Once in a while, however, the old diggings have caused settling and cracks in buildings. For years, no large and heavy buildings were constructed in parts of the city until maps were checked to see if mines once operated in the area.

There was some real "relaxing" in east Des Moines on mining paydays in the old days. Miners packed Billy Asherd's saloon, Gus and Pat's, the Blue Ribbon, and other taverns.

Redhead sold the coal from his Pioneer mine under the Black Diamond label. The Pioneer was the largest mine in the county for a time. The last mine in the county was so small it employed only four men; it closed more than a generation ago.

Yet coal is still plentiful under Polk County; estimates place the untouched deposits at 600 million tons. But mining long since became unprofitable. Most productive areas were worked out long ago. (One early mine had a vein eleven feet thick.) In addition, other fuels such as oil and natural gas, and superior coal from other parts of the nation captured the market.

The trend hasn't been all loss. In the old days, when every household and every business burned coal for heat, a heavy pall of smoke pressed down on Des Moines in the winter. Smoke pollution isn't that much of a problem any more.

At one time railroads were big users of Polk County coal. So were brickyards. It is said that Polk County produced more than 23 million bricks a year in the late 1870s.

Prices and wages were low in the old mining days. The average selling price of coal at the mine was $1.61 for a two-thousand-pound ton in 1890. The miner got 88 cents a ton for his pay. Records indicate Iowa miners earned an average of $31.66 a month in 1882, somewhat more than $1 a day.

Death lurked in those early mines. About thirty miners a year died in accidents. Scattered through mine statements are reports of deaths due to "powder explosion," "fall of slate," "fell down chute," "caught by car," and "kicked by mule."

An explosion some eighty years ago at the New Riverside mine on Harding Road north of Euclid in Des Moines killed several men who were sinking a new mine shaft. One report said lightning struck the shaft and detonated a stock of dynamite. Another story had it that the men were foolishly thawing out a keg of frozen blasting powder on a stove.

At one time or another, mines were to be found about everywhere within the city of Des Moines. One mine was on Second and Center; another at Sixth and School; another on Fourth north of Keosauqua Way; at least four north of Euclid near Harding Road; two south of Greenwood Park; and one at Sixty-third and Grand. There were six mines north of University Avenue between East Fourteenth and East Eighteenth, a number of others east and south of the statehouse, and several out in the country east and north of town.

As recently as 1927, a big argument developed over whether a mine should be started in the exclusive "south of Grand" residential section of Des Moines. The mine would have been only a quarter mile south of Salisbury House, once the home of millionaire Carl Weeks and more recently headquarters of the Iowa State Education Association. Nearby property owners vigorously protested and the project was abandoned.

Redhead's Pioneer mine wasn't his first. Nor was he the first mine operator in Polk County by any means.

Generally the first mines were small. Coal was mined from a bluff southeast of the site of the statehouse as early as 1843, before there was a Des Moines. The mine at Second and Center was producing coal in 1856. Then there were the Watson, Eclipse, Cipher, and Eureka mines east and south of the statehouse in the early days.

Redhead made a lot of money from the Pioneer mine, and just about every other business venture that he tackled. He bought out Allen and others interested in Pioneer.

Redhead built up his coal sales by adding an "economizer" to each ton. The substance was supposed to induce the coal to give more heat, and to prevent large chunks called "clinkers" from forming from the ash.

The "economizer" was a patented formula which consisted of bicarbonate of soda, saltpeter, bicarbonate of ammonia, resin, Epsom salts, common salt, and coal dust. Whether it really was effective is not known.

Redhead also once thought he had found silver in east Des Moines. A sparkling ore showed up in the digging of a well at his home at 1757 Dean Avenue. The ore was reported to have assayed at $258.50 a ton, an amazingly rich find. No silver rush developed, however. Either it really wasn't silver, or no more was found.

Redhead also attracted a lot of attention by proposing that a couple not be permitted to apply for a marriage license without providing evidence of ability to support themselves and any children they might have. He introduced a bill to that effect while serving in the Iowa House of Representatives in the late 1860s. The bill didn't pass.

Redhead was so highly regarded as a businessman that he was elected vice president of the Equitable Life Insurance Company of Iowa when it was organized in 1867. He was the leading bookseller and stationer and was one of the town's early postmasters. He was one of the principal founders of Asbury Methodist Church (which started in his barn). He died in 1891 and is buried in Woodland Cemetery in Des Moines.

The Redhead home on the east side was just as much a city landmark in its time as Terrace Hill was and is on the west side. Before it was razed a generation or more ago, a number of ancient and withered floral pieces were found hanging in the attic. They were believed to have been from the Redhead funeral.

Redhead, by the way, didn't have red hair. The origin of the family name is not known.

The mob overpowered jailer Wise. (Frank Miller/George Mills)

Courthouse Lynching

Two men left the Polk County courthouse in downtown Des Moines about midnight on a cold December night. They walked down dimly lighted and deserted Fifth Avenue toward the Raccoon River. They anxiously scanned the empty streets, peering in between buildings. At the river they turned and trudged over to the quiet east side.

They had heard rumors that a mob was forming. They spotted no one on the streets, however. The date was December 15, 1874. The men were Polk Sheriff Dan Bringolf and his friend, attorney Dan O. Finch. Convinced the rumors were incorrect, they went home and to bed at 1:30 A.M. The sheriff took the precaution to station six special guards in and around the courthouse.

Jailer B. Wise slept soundly in his bedroom under the county jail, which was in the courthouse in those days. Prisoner Charles Howard, however, was awake and uneasy in his cell.

Howard, a bartender and banjo player by trade, had been convicted of murdering John Johnson, a Des Moines tailor. Howard was given life. He was to be taken to the Fort Madison penitentiary in several hours.

Howard's wife Annie also was in jail. She had been arrested as an accomplice. Johnson's body had been found in Second Street near

51

Walnut Street, close to Annie's house, which was a questionable place. Johnson reportedly had been hit in the head with a wine bottle, perhaps in a brawl.

After Bringolf and Finch departed, the street light on the northeast corner of Fifth and Mulberry went out. Someone may have put it out.

At 2:30 A.M. the sound of shuffling feet was heard at the east door of the courthouse. Lanterns flickered in the gloom. Between 100 and 200 men pushed into the building. Their faces were blackened or masked. Some carried revolvers.

The mob moved past the guards, marched downstairs and overpowered Wise. One man swung a hatchet threateningly at the jailer, who fought back and caught his assailant by the throat. Wise thereupon was flattened. One man put his knee on Wise's chest and pointed a gun at the jailer's head. They took his keys.

"All seemed to be large men and handled me lively," the jailer said later. "They didn't talk much. The man who talked to me did so in a coarse voice. They seemed to be stern and were very cold and sober."

A number of the men barged into the jail, grabbed Howard and tightened a rope around his neck while he was still in bed. He pleaded for "a minute or two to see my wife." She was screaming. One story said she threw herself on her husband in a vain effort to protect him.

Howard, wearing only an undershirt, was dragged up the stairs into the main corridor, thence downstairs and out of doors. Probably already choked into insensibility, he was pulled along the ground in the dark to a lamp post at Fifth and Mulberry.

Quickly the body was swung from the post, with the feet only inches off the ground. In a matter of minutes Howard was dead.

A number of shots were fired for some reason, perhaps as a warning to possible interferers. One bullet went through the windows of the empty county auditor's office.

Abruptly the mob scattered. Some went south on Fifth Street, others east on Court Avenue. Several had horses tied up a few blocks away. The streets were again empty when officials cut down the body. The mob action is believed to have been the only case of murder by lynching ever to have taken place inside the Des Moines city limits.

Residents were horrified and incensed. Citizens' groups meeting in the courthouse the next two days demanded strong action by law enforcement authorities. One resolution said those responsible for the "heinous crime" deserved "the strongest reprobation of this community." Another resolution demanded the authorities take "all necessary steps for the apprehension and punishment of those guilty of this base and most infamous offense."

The mystery of the lynching was never solved. Members of the mob never were identified. Why did they take Howard's life? Why did presumably ordinary peaceable citizens do such a thing?

The most likely explanation is this: The people were impatient for action. There had been six unsolved murders in Polk County in four years. Three had been committed in ten weeks that year. No arrests had been made. Justice moved slowly, if at all.

Johnson was slain June 14, 1874. A woman name Ella (or Ellen) Barrett was beaten to death on August 27 in her apartment. She lived above McFarland's small dry goods store at Seventh and Walnut, where the Financial Center is now. She was twenty-eight or thirty years old.

On or about that same night a bachelor named Mailand was shot to death in his home in Camp Township in the southeast corner of the county.

The police arrested no one for several weeks in the Johnson slaying. Then Howard and Annie Groves were taken into custody. They were not married at the time of the crime. Howard was known as a frequenter of her house.

Officers made the arrest in the belief that Johnson had been killed in her house and the body had been placed in the street afterward.

Des Moines was startled some days later at the news that Howard had married Annie. He was a rather handsome man and younger than she was. Suspicious individuals reasoned that Annie compelled Howard to marry her by threatening to disclose how Johnson died.

Howard was found guilty after a trial of three weeks. He was sentenced on December 14 to life imprisonment for second-degree murder. When he heard the verdict, he exclaimed: "You have convicted an innocent man!"

The judge added to the tension by his comments. Indicating his belief a death sentence would have been justified, the judge said: "The very air seems tainted with rapine and murder."

There was talk around town that afternoon of mob action. Angered citizens pointed out that no arrests had been made in the Barrett and Mailand slayings. And here was Howard getting only a life sentence!

Lawyers of Des Moines held a dinner that evening in the Savery House (which was located where the Kirkwood is now). The lawyers heard the rumor that a mob planned a raid on the jail. That rumor was a reason for Bringolf and Finch stirring around in the streets late that night.

There is some doubt to this day of Howard's guilt. The killer of Mailand never was found. Two persons, however, were convicted of killing Mrs. Barrett. One of those convicted is said to have confessed on his deathbed in Fort Madison that he killed the woman.

Robbery was the motive in the Mailand killing but no one knew for certain why Mrs. Barrett, who purported to be a dressmaker, had been slain. The killer took no valuables but ransacked her trunk. It is believed he may have sought some compromising letters in her possession.

The coroner did find a number of such letters in her apartment. These letters, says one authority, "would have caused trouble and grief in a number of homes had they been published." The coroner "prudently" kept them secret and finally had them destroyed.

A Fabulous Meal

Perhaps the most fabulous meal ever served in Des Moines was spread before a President of the United States. President Ulysses S. Grant came to Des Moines September 29, 1875. He and other distinguished Civil War generals took part in a stirring reunion of the Army of the Tennessee. Many Iowans served in that northern Yankee army which had a brilliant record in the 1861–1865 war.

It was said that fifty thousand veterans of the Army of the Tennessee took part in an impressive march down Walnut Street in downtown Des Moines during the reunion. The reunion banquet was held in the old Savery House, located where the Kirkwood Hotel is now at Fourth and Walnut streets in the loop.

The old *Iowa State Register,* predecessor of *The Des Moines Register,* said the banquet was "unquestionably the grandest and most complete affair of its kind ever known in the state." Here was the menu:

Soups—Green turtle and oyster.
Fish—Blue fish, wine sauce; white fish, a la pointe Shirley.
Hot—Filet of beef, larded with mushrooms; roast prairie chicken, venison, steak with jelly; blue-billed duck; English snipe; roast partridge; mallard duck; redhead duck; roast quail; fried oysters; golden plover; escalloped oysters; oyster patties.
Cold—Roast turkey; boned turkey with jelly; sugar-cured ham; lobster salad; smoked tongue; chicken salad; Russian salad; hardtack and sowbelly; pork and beans.
Vegetables—Sweet potatoes; mashed potatoes; stewed tomatoes; fresh green peas; lima beans; succotash.
Relishes—Worcester sauce; horse radish; nabob sauce; pickles; English mixed pickles; Chowchow; piccalilli; celery; olives; sliced tomatoes.
Pastry—English plum pudding, brandy sauce; ladyfingers; macaroons; coconut drops; pound cake; delicate cake; fruit cake; claret wine jelly; charlotte russe; Swiss meringue.

Ices—Neapolitan ice cream; lemon ice; vanilla ice cream; lemon
ice cream; pudding glace; raspberry ice; tutti frutti.
Fruit—Grapes; pears; peaches; apples; oranges.
French coffee; oolong tea; hyson tea.

The accounts do not say exactly what "Russian salad" was. The
"hardtack and sowbelly" and "pork and beans" undoubtedly were
served as a gag. Union troops ate a lot of that kind of food in the field
during the Civil War.

In addition, there were fourteen toasts, each accompanied by a
speech.

The dinner started at a fashionably late hour, 9:30 P.M. The guest
list was limited to 200. Besides the President, those present included:

William T. Sherman, one of the great Union generals of the war
and a brother of Hoyt Sherman of Des Moines; W. W. Belknap of
Keokuk, the Iowa general who was Grant's secretary of war; General
John A. Logan, who started Memorial Day; General Jefferson C. Davis
(this Union general is not to be confused with President Jefferson Davis
of the Confederacy); and Iowa Governor Samuel Kirkwood.

All the army officers wore resplendent blue uniforms. The St.
Louis arsenal band played such rousing Civil War pieces as "Tramp,
Tramp, Tramp, the Boys are Marching" and "Marching Through
Georgia."

"The ceilings were hung with ropes of evergreens caught up at
intervals over a cluster of flags," a newspaper account said. "The
handsome chandeliers were wreathed with the national colors. . . .
Around the walls were portraits of distinguished generals. Fifty Chinese
lanterns [hung] from the ceiling."

General Ulysses S. Grant
(Iowa State Historical Department)

It must have been well after midnight when the gorged gathering broke up. Each of the fourteen toasts was accompanied by music, cheers, and, toward the end, by loud noise as the effect of drinking so much alcohol became apparent.

The glory and blood of the Civil War still were fresh in veterans' minds in 1875. After all, the war had been over only ten years. Emotions still ran deep.

The first toast of the evening was to "Our Country—One and Indivisible." A General M. M. Bane responded with an impassioned patriotic speech fifteen minutes long. Toasts were then drunk and speeches given on these topics: the President of the United States; the State of Iowa and her volunteers; the March to the Sea; the Society of the Army of the Tennessee; the regular army; the navy; the Army of the Tennessee; the Army of the Cumberland; the Army of the Ohio; our volunteer army; our judiciary; the signal service; and the patriotic women of America.

The crowd was downright boisterous by the time General H. N. Eldridge responded to the toast to the "patriotic women." His comments were not recorded. The report only says he made "some felicitous remarks bringing forth hearty applause."

Des Moines was intensely proud of entertaining the President for two days and of being host to such an important reunion. Describing the scene in the Savery, *The Register* said: "The President of the United States and the conqueror of the rebellion rising and acknowledging the compliments and congratulations, the immortal Sherman himself telling of the march to the sea, was a picture which the older Des Moines of coming years will treasure even more proudly than the people of the present Des Moines."

It is a matter of fact, however, that knowledge of the Army of the Tennessee long since has faded from the memories of all but professional and amateur historians. And few Iowans of this day know there ever was such a thing as a big Civil War reunion in Des Moines.

President Grant, who served in the White House from 1869 to 1877, came to Des Moines by special train over the Rock Island lines. He had headed the Army of the Tennessee before taking command of all Union forces in the final years of the war.

Iowa had brilliantly uniformed local military organizations in those days. The Des Moines groups included the Olmsteds, the Zouaves, and the Sarsfield Guards. They were drawn up in grand array on Fourth Street near the depot to greet Grant on his arrival.

Through some misunderstanding, the President and his party got off the train a block east and came uptown via Third Street. This caused the "boys very much regret since they had got up in the early morning for this especial purpose."

Des Moines went all out in decorations. Two big "arches of honor" were erected, one over the street on Walnut at Fourth, the other over Court Avenue at Fourth. Public buildings, stores, factories, offices, and residences were gaily outfitted with flags, bunting, and evergreens.

Hoyt Sherman, a major in the Union army, did an elaborate job of decorating his home at Fifteenth and Woodland. (Now the west portion of Hoyt Sherman Place.)

The President was housed at the beautiful "Colechester" residence of Judge Chester Cole on Fourth Street, several doors north of Keosauqua Way. This was one of the finest homes in the state.

Grant went on at least one quick sightseeing carriage drive. He visited the grave of General Marcellus M. Crocker in Woodland Cemetery. Crocker, a Des Moines attorney before the war, had an outstanding record in the Union army. In his autobiography, Grant said of Crocker: "He was fit to command an independent army."

Those words were carved along the bottom of the original impressive monument over the Crocker grave. Vandals destroyed that monument decades ago. The grave went unmarked for many years before members of the Civil War Roundtable organization in Des Moines arranged in the 1980s for a new marker.

One highlight of the 1875 reunion was an address by the president delivered to twenty-five hundred school children in Moore's Opera House on the southeast corner of Fourth and Walnut. And Grant held two receptions. He shook thousands of hands at the post office but "not a fifth of those who wished to do so" were able to greet him. Another reception attended by at least five thousand took place in the old state arsenal located on the south side of Grand Avenue west of the Des Moines River.

"Hundreds of soldiers shook the President's hand with the old army-like cordiality," a newspaper report said. "Many had a word to say about the battles they had been in under his command. 'Vicksburg' was the word most frequently heard."

An organization known as "Baker's Battery" fired a deafening salute of twenty-one cannons for the President and thirteen each for Sherman and Belknap.

All the notable visitors took part in the session of the reunion held the first night in the opera house. The session was a fanfare of music, color, and crowds. "Thousands stood about the outer doors unable to gain admission," a news report said. "They surged about the streets, noisy and good humored, finding faint pleasure in the occasional notes of the band or the ring of applause that found outward passage through the windows."

One veteran on the program recited the poem "Sheridan's Ride" in a manner that "electrified the audience." (General Phil Sheridan was a top Union hero of the war.)

A final reunion event was a ball at Aborn House, then a leading hotel on the southwest corner of Court and Fourth. The event was a "brilliant affair . . . attended by 200 couples."

President Grant did not dance. The newspaper report said he had his "Methodist boots on." The Methodist church forbade dancing in those days. But General Sherman, the "hero of Atlanta, enjoyed the mazes of dancing as hearty as any who were there."

Membership in the Society of the Army of the Tennessee, prominent in the reunion, was limited to officers. A move to make privates eligible was voted down at the Des Moines reunion. Officers wanted the society to continue to be their own exclusive organization. The by-laws attempted to keep the society going permanently by permitting the officers to will their commissions to their sons, grandsons, and so on. The society seems not to have survived, however. The Library of Congress says it has no information on the existence of such an organization. The plan for immortalizing it didn't work. Like all human endeavors, the Society of the Army of the Tennessee has faded away with the relentless passing of the years.

Train Disaster

Little Four Mile Creek is a quiet stream that ordinarily causes no trouble. After meandering through eastern Polk County, Little Four Mile flows into Big Four Mile Creek.

There was nothing ordinary about the tributary stream in late August 1877. For thirty-six hours, heavy rains poured unceasingly down on the countryside. The swollen stream became a torrent. The storm increased in violence early in the morning of August 28. The prairie was covered with water. Jarring thunder and sheet lightning added to the wildness of the night.

The Rock Island railroad tracks crossed Little Four Mile on a bridge nine miles east of downtown Des Moines and a mile and a half southwest of Altoona, Iowa. The bridge was a sturdy structure with stone supports five feet thick. The east bank rose ten to eighteen feet above the creek bed.

A locomotive pulling freight cars passed safely over the bridge about 1:30 A.M. Shortly after 2:30 A.M., while the storm was at its height, the Rock Island mail-and-passenger train from Chicago came chugging along about 30 miles an hour.

The train, well-filled with passengers, was on time. It was due in Des Moines at 3:30 A.M. The train consisted of seven cars, including a Barnum and Bailey circus advertising car en route to Des Moines, a smoking car, a baggage car, two passenger coaches, and a sleeper.

Engineer John Rakestraw of Stuart, Iowa, slowed the train on a downhill curve near the bridge. He wasn't able to see the track more than a few hundred feet ahead. He was reassured when the bridge came into sight. The steel rails and ties looked all right. There was no way for him to know that the raging flood had torn out the stone bridge supports. He opened the throttle.

Suddenly the locomotive lurched downward. The track gave way under the engine. The big iron machine rammed into the west bank where it half-buried itself into the mud and water. Cars carrying dozens of passengers toppled after the locomotive into the creek. Rakestraw was crushed to death. The only way his body could be freed later in the day was by amputation of both legs.

Fireman Abram Trucks was miraculously thrown clear on the west bank. He was dazed and bruised but otherwise uninjured. He staggered away in the rain for help.

The sleeper was left standing on the track. But all the other cars tumbled into the roaring creek. Some passengers from the sleeper ran back to Altoona to seek help. Others struggled in the rain and darkness to dig out groaning victims.

Seventeen persons were killed outright in the tangle of steel and wood. Thirty-eight others were injured. Three died later, bringing the death toll to twenty. The tragedy was the worst railroad wreck in the history of the Des Moines area, though not of the state.

The circus car was demolished. Seven employees of the circus died. The car, loaded with posters for The Greatest Show on Earth, was coming to Des Moines to prepare for a show September 9 and thence on to Atlantic, Iowa, September 10.

Thousands of brightly colored posters were plastered helter-skelter on the wreckage and strewn around on bushes and trees all over the countryside, creating a weird effect in the flooded area. There were torn posters of huge elephants, of the triumphant "Golden Street Procession," of spangled women performers, of monkeys, of those two "Super Eminent Bareback Riders"—Charles Fish and Martin Lowande, and of the "Tattooed Greek Nobleman Captain Costentenus."

Charles Browning of the Barnum crew was found several hours after the wreck clinging to a tree downstream. He had been badly scalded by escaping steam from the engine. He apparently survived.

The mail and express car had been catapulted upward. It landed on top of the Barnum car, "grinding it to matchwood." The two passenger coaches plowed ahead and were so badly broken up that

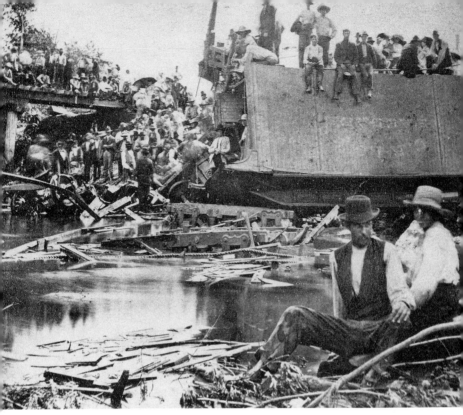

Train disaster

rescue crews were not certain at first whether they were working with one or two cars.

In one flattened car there were passengers who drowned. The creek was an estimated twenty feet deep in places. One of the victims was a seven-year-old Boone, Iowa, girl, Allie Bolt. Her father, a Boone druggist, also was killed, but her mother survived.

At least two other bridges in the area were washed away in the same storm. One was nearby on the old Des Moines and Keokuk railroad line. A train was due at about the same time on that line. Had that train been on time, it too would have been wrecked. And another Rock Island bridge nearer Des Moines was washed away as well. Thus, the train with the Barnum car probably would have been wrecked that night even if the Little Four Mile Creek bridge had been intact.

Drs. F. E. English and W. H. Booth of Altoona were the first physicians to reach the wreck scene. There were also two physicians on the train. Neither was injured to any extent.

Dr. George P. Hanawalt of Des Moines took care of many of the victims in Cottage Hospital, which was Des Moines' first hospital of any size. The thirty-bed hospital was established in 1876 on Fourth

Street in the neighborhood of the present Mercy Hospital. (There is a school in Des Moines named for Dr. Hanawalt.)

Between two thousand and three thousand circus tickets for the Des Moines show were lost. More than four thousand curiosity seekers visited the scene in the next few days. Can you imagine what happened to many of the tickets?

Those who figured on seeing a free circus were disappointed, however. Phineas T. Barnum, owner of the show, announced that the color of tickets good for the Des Moines circus had been changed. The old tickets were not accepted. (The price of admission was fifty cents.) Barnum himself came to Des Moines. He was so appreciative of the help and work of Des Moines people with wreck victims that he delivered a "benefit lecture" September 8, probably at the old Grand Opera House on Fourth Street south of Locust in downtown Des Moines.

The lecture raised a reported twelve thousand dollars, a huge amount for the times. The money was given to Dr. Hanawalt to be used for the benefit of Cottage Hospital.

Barnum lectured that Sunday night on the evils of drinking. Local preachers canceled their church services—there was church every Sunday night as well as morning in those days—so that everyone could hear the noted circus man. Barnum, who was a strong teetotaler, talked for an hour and a half.

"He believes in pledges and local temperance effort," a local report said. "He expressed his faith in the power of women to save men from the evil habit of drinking alcoholic stimulants and especially in the influence of young ladies over their companions and sweethearts. He declared his belief in the power of Christianity to unlock the fetters of the inebriate."

Which was the kind of speech not usually expected from a spokesman of the rough and tumble circus business. Barnum said little about the wreck.

Downtown Gumbo

Levi Wells was irked. His hacks kept getting mired in the mud of the unpaved streets in downtown Des Moines. Wells was Des Moines' best known operator of hacks in 1878. The hack was the taxi of its time. It was a small carriage drawn by horses. The auto had not yet been invented.

Levi J. Wells

Walnut Street, Locust, and Sycamore (now Grand Avenue), all were messes in wet weather because the city council refused to vote paving. Wrote historian L. F. Andrews: "At certain seasons, the wet, heavy, sticky clay rendered the passage of light vehicles difficult and of heavy loads nearly impossible. It was ruinous to fine carriages and wearing on horseflesh. . . . To get heavily loaded wagons stalled on Walnut Street out of the mud with jacks and hoists was a common occurrence."

Wells' hacks had a sorry experience on one dark night carrying passengers to events. Hack wheels sank to the hubs and horses fell in the gumbo at Fourth Street and what is now Keo Way. "All that could be done was to extricate the passengers, get the horses clear and abandon the vehicles," Andrews said.

Another major problem developed in getting people to the statehouse: "In struggling up the Locust Street grade, the horses got as far as East Ninth Street and quit from sheer exhaustion. They were removed and the hacks left. During the night the mercury suddenly dropped and the hacks were frozen fast in the earth, to be chipped out or left to the radiant rays of the sun."

Still, the council remained obdurate until Wells resorted to angry ridicule. One day when "the streets were simply sluggish rivers of ooze," Levi drove into Walnut aboard a "large flat bottom boat drawn by four fine large horses."

An individual in front of the boat carried a big pole with depth markers on it. As he jabbed the pole into the mud, he shouted in a deep voice: "Four fathoms . . . three fathoms . . . two fathoms." Wells saw to it beforehand that everybody and everything—the horses, the boat, the men—were covered with mud. The boat carried a sign saying: "For passage apply to the city council."

The demonstration was called "a masterly production of satire and [it] brought results." The council ordered a paving program to begin forthwith.

One Wife at a Time

A Des Moines man had the delicate job of limiting each Mormon husband in the territory of Utah to one wife at a time.

Another Des Moines man saw the British burn the White House and the national capitol in Washington, D.C., in 1814.

A third was reputed to have been the world's first locomotive engineer.

A fourth Des Moines man was so important in American railroading that special trains brought notables to his funeral from New York, Chicago, and St. Louis.

The history of Des Moines is filled with reports about spectacular but now largely forgotten persons. They come to life again when dusty old books are opened or yellowed pages of ancient newspapers are scanned.

Colonel George L. Godfrey must have led a lively existence for the ten years that he fought polygamy in Utah. He was a Des Moines attorney and Civil War hero. He was the father of Mrs. Grover Hubbell.

President Chester Allen Arthur appointed Godfrey to the Utah Commission in 1882. Godfrey became highly unpopular among the Mormons.

"That was understandable," said Mrs. Hubbell. "My father put so many Mormons in jail."

Polygamy (the practice of a man having two or more wives at a time) was not universal among the Mormons in that western territory. It was said that three-fourths of Mormon men had only one wife. Nevertheless, the Mormons believed in polygamy as a matter of "divine revelation.

The rest of the nation seemed to be deeply concerned. Said one authority: "Should this practice [of polygamy] be even tolerated anywhere in the United States, it might one day become a serious menace to the institution of monogamy [single marriage] which the world has come to consider the most important factor for the advancement of civilization anywhere."

Congress passed a law making polygamy a crime. Polygamists were barred from voting and holding public office.

The Mormons charged violation of religious liberty. Mormon church leaders went into hiding. At one point a flag was placed at half staff in Salt Lake City as an expression that religious liberty had been destroyed.

One judge agreed that the Mormons had a right of religious liberty. But he said they did not have the right to engage in a practice which the American people, through the laws of the country, "declare to be unlawful and injurious to society."

An 1884 report said 196 males and 263 females had entered into polygamous marriages. There were 330 convictions in 1888. Usually the judges paroled the defendants on promise of good behavior.

As chairman of the five-member Utah Commission much of the time, Godfrey was in the forefront of the battle. He recommended that the federal government "take no backward steps" in the conflict. He fought with a Mormon newspaper.

Yet one report bearing his name as chairman praised the Mormons as a "kindly and hospitable people. . . . In matters of religion they are intensely devotional, rendering a cheerful obedience to their church rules and requirements. They possess many of the elements which under wise leadership would make them a useful and prosperous people."

In 1890 the Mormon church issued a statement dropping polygamy as a fundamental belief. The action cleared the way for the admission of Utah to the union as a state.

Godfrey later was collector of federal customs in Des Moines. He died in 1915.

David Norris lived long before Godfrey. It is likely that Norris was the only person in Des Moines' history who saw the British burn the White House and other major buildings in Washington during the War of 1812.

The capture of Washington took place long before the founding of Des Moines, of course. Norris was a thirteen-year-old boy in 1814. He lived in his native state of Maryland. He was big for his age, and he was driving an ammunition wagon into Washington when the British army appeared.

Norris saw President James Madison and his wife Dolly fleeing the city. They were not captured nor was Norris. The boy joined bucket brigades which worked hard in putting out the fires set by the enemy.

Norris came to Fort Des Moines in 1845. He opened a butcher shop in 1847 at Second and Vine, then the heart of the business district. He was a jolly 250-pounder who lived to be ninety-six years old. He died in 1897.

Edward Entwistle lived about the same time as Norris. He was an apprentice in 1833 in the factory of George Stephenson in Newcastle, England. The Stephensons built the world's first high-speed steam locomotive, called the "Rocket." It had a top speed of twenty-nine miles an hour and would average fourteen miles an hour.

The fifteen-year-old Entwistle went along on the trial trip. On the

David met President Madison fleeing the city.
(Frank Miller/George Mills)

return trip he was given the throttle. For two years after that he was engineer every day on trips between Liverpool and Manchester.

Entwistle came to America and in 1858 arrived in Des Moines. He was engineer for twenty-one years in a flour and woolen mill on the Des Moines River bank between Locust Street and Grand Avenue.

He also worked as an engineer on a steamboat operating on the Des Moines River between Keokuk and Fort Dodge. While living in retirement a century ago, he reminisced: "I never was sick a day in my life and I never was drunk, though you could buy whisky in those early days for thirty cents a gallon and it was much better than the stuff you pay three dollars a gallon for now." (Three dollars doesn't even come close to paying the federal tax alone on a gallon of 1990 whisky.)

One of the most famous Des Moines men of his time was Herbert M. (Hub) Hoxie. He helped build the Union Pacific Railroad. He was general manager of the Missouri Pacific Railroad in the last century.

Hoxie died in 1886. To his funeral came special trains bearing leading railroad and businessmen from the financial citadels of New York, Chicago, and St. Louis. Newspaper accounts of the time said the men who gathered around Hoxie's grave in Woodland Cemetery represented an important share of the nation's wealth.

He is a completely forgotten personality now.

Dynamite in Distillery

Don't go near the big distillery! They've found dynamite on the pipes! Somebody's trying to blow up the place! That exciting warning spread like wildfire around Des Moines on November 14, 1882.

The warning was no idle rumor. Considerable dynamite HAD been planted in the International Distillery. It was reputed to be the largest producer of alcohol in the world at the time, with a capacity of twenty-five thousand gallons a day. The big red building was located in the East Eighteenth Street area north of the present Iowa Packing Company.

The plant was not blown up. But there were several anxious days and nights around town. The mystery never really was solved. It was highly likely that disgruntled associates of the company management were responsible. But nothing was ever proven.

Few Des Moines or Iowa people of today know there ever was a distillery in the capitol city, let alone one of that caliber.

Alcohol production appears to have been Des Moines' largest industry in the 1880s. Besides International, there was a smaller plant called Atlas. The two plants had a combined output in 1884 valued at $3.4 million, a lot of money in those times.

International employed about 100 men. (It was said that some workers took home their lunch coffee bottles filled with alcohol every night.) The distillery used as much as six thousand bushels of corn a day, thereby providing a good corn market for central Iowa farmers.

The plant cost an estimated four hundred thousand dollars to build and equip. The equipment included five kettles ten to twelve feet in diameter and three stories high. There were seventeen fermenting tubs, each with a seventeen thousand gallon capacity.

"We pay about ten dollars a day taxes to the government," a New York official of the company said in describing the plant. The distillery's

Dynamite in the distillery (Frank Miller/George Mills)

leftover refuse was sufficient to provide feed for up to three thousand cattle at a time.

The alcohol was shipped to other states and to Glasgow, Scotland, and Marseilles, France. The product was used in the manufacture of liquor, wine, and perfume. It was assumed that some of it went into the making of Scotch whisky.

No alcohol was distilled for a number of days during the dynamite scare. People gave the building a wide berth. A newspaper reporter took out a three thousand dollar accident insurance policy before he entered the building to get the story.

Distillery Manager John Kidd was having a quiet Sunday morning at home when the crisis developed. He lived at 1425 West Locust Street, no longer a residential area.

A fearful employee came to Kidd's door with a note that had been delivered by a small boy. "There are 50 pounds of dynamite in the mash room," the note said. "It will explode at 140 degrees Fahrenheit, or a slight jar will explode it. . . . This is no child's play. We mean business. If you follow instructions, there will be no danger." There was no demand for money, no instructions.

Kidd hurried to the plant. Almost immediately, a dynamite cartridge seven inches long and eleven inches in diameter was found attached to a steam pipe. In the next few hours, 16 more cartridges were found on the pipes.

Several additional notes showed up in the building. One said that "this machine is loaded with dynamite. . . . Interference will make it explode." Another note said 150 cartridges had been hidden around the building, but only 60 were found. The officials vacated the plant.

Voicing the general alarm, *The Register* said: "If the dynamite had exploded, all the factories in the city would have blown down and indeed the eastern part of the city might have suffered seriously."

Although he never said so, Kidd might have had an understanding of the situation. There had been bitter arguments at the distillery. The

The distillery before the explosion
(Paul Ashby Collection, Iowa State Historical Department)

plant had been using newly converted machinery installed by two men, William Babbitt and George Woosley. They had placed the machinery in the plant under an arrangement by which they would receive half the alcohol produced above sixteen quarts per bushel. Thus, if the output were twenty quarts on the average, they would each receive two quarts. They planned on recovering their sixteen thousand dollar investment, and getting a good profit in addition.

The production, however, didn't even reach the sixteen-quart level in the fall of 1882. Babbitt and Woosley weren't getting anything. They were unhappy. They believed their machinery wasn't being used properly. Babbitt filed a fifty thousand dollar suit against the company. He also accused the management of processing inferior corn.

Babbitt and Woosley naturally became number-one suspects. Babbitt's name was on some of the notes. But whether it ever was verified that he wrote them was not reported.

"The whole plan looks like a plot to stop the distillery and force a compromise or settlement," *The Register* said.

Babbitt was arrested in Chicago. He returned voluntarily to Des Moines. He declared the explosives were a "ruse on Kidd's part to excite sympathy for himself and to stir up prejudice against me." Babbitt's attorney even hinted that his client may have planted the dynamite. The attorney said if "Babbitt did the work it was merely an attempt on his part to demand that Kidd pay the amount due him."

An expert confirmed that the cartridges were dynamite but said he didn't believe the heat of steam in the pipes would have touched off an explosion. But he said any "violent concussion" might have done so.

Halting the plant operations caused unexpected trouble in the cattle-feeding program.

"These cattle have been fed on malt and other refuse for six months," *The Register* said. "It would be impossible for them to eat corn because their mouths and teeth have become tender by eating soft malt." Soft feed had to be bought elsewhere.

The dynamite excitement died down, apparently without anyone going to jail.

The controversy came at a time when Des Moines was entertaining hopes of becoming the key distillery center of the nation. International had built the plant because of the plentiful supply of cheap corn nearby. (The price in 1882 was sixty to sixty-five cents a bushel, not particularly cheap for the times.) International officials predicted Des Moines ultimately would replace Peoria, Illinois, as the top producer of alcohol in the nation. Instead major troubles lay ahead for the industry in Des Moines.

Iowa had been a "dry" state all along. That meant the sale of liquor and beer was prohibited anywhere in the state. The "drys," who were in the majority, bitterly opposed alcohol distilling operations in Des Moines. They maintained the law forbade not only the sale of alcoholic beverages but the production as well. Some "drys" expressed shame over the Des Moines operation. "Other states get the drinking and we get the proceeds," wrote one dry editor. "Other states suffer the ills of intemperance and we make money out of it."

In response to an action started by the "drys," the Polk County district court ruled that alcohol could not be made for beverage purposes in Iowa. The state supreme court upheld that verdict.

The big distillery closed its Des Moines doors forever.

Mob vs. *Register*

In these computer days when the polls are scarcely closed before the winner is declared, it is fun to recall that the early *Des Moines Register* once refused to concede the outcome of a presidential election for two weeks. A mob gathered and threatened to burn the newspaper building even after the paper gave in.

Up in the building tower, the paper's two brother-owners waited with guns. James (Ret) Clarkson and Richard Clarkson were ready to fire should an attack occur. The rock-ribbed Republican Clarksons simply would not recognize the victory of Democratic Grover Cleveland over Republican James G. Blaine in the presidential race of 1884.

Des Moines supporters of Cleveland were enraged at the long delay. They gathered in front of the old *Register* building on the southeast corner of Fourth Street and Court Avenue to vent their anger.

As it happened, the throng made a lot of noise but didn't charge the building. Thus, no pitched battle took place between the gathering outside and the armed owners (and probably loyal employees) within. Few if any papers ever have held out against the facts of an election as long as that *Register* did.

The Clarksons, who published the paper from 1870 to 1902, went all out in backing Blaine. Newspaper editors were red hot partisans in those days. There were few neutrals in the political arena.

Cleveland won a hard-fought and dirty campaign in which religion was a vital issue. Cleveland got 219 electoral votes and 4,875,000 popular votes, to 182 and 4,852,000 for Blaine.

The Clarksons went into the election solidly confident. An election day editorial November 4 predicted "one of the grandest victories in the history of the Republican party." The editorial added: "The tide of Republican success is sweeping over the country with

James S. Clarkson

Richard P. Clarkson   **Old Iowa State Register Building, Des Moines**

relentless power. Democracy is doomed and every lover of his country, every lover of liberty and the rights of man, every lover of moral and material progress, will say of democracy in the language of the Delphian Oracle: 'Let it die!' "

The brothers were radiantly certain as early returns rolled in. The 4:30 A.M. edition of the November 5 paper carried four one-column pictures of crowing roosters. (The rooster was the Republican symbol of victory in those days.) One headline said: "Victory Assured! The Solid South Broken! The North Comes Grandly to the Support of the Republican Ticket!" The paper predicted the pivotal state of New York would go to Blaine by 12,000 votes.

Returns were slow in those days of paper ballots and still primitive communications. On November 6, two days after the election, *The Register* said bravely in a page-one story: "Sufficient returns have been received to indicate the election of Blaine and Logan [the vice-presidential candidate] in one of the hardest fought contests in the history of the country." But an element of uncertainty appeared in another story which said: "New York without doubt Republican by a small plurality." No more talk of a 12,000-vote margin.

In fact, the unofficial figures indicated that Cleveland had captured New York.

The defiant attitude nevertheless continued day after day in *The Register* columns. The next Tuesday, a full week after the election, the paper declared "the official count will give New York to Blaine." New York had emerged as the deciding state in the contest. On Wednesday the paper declared: "We believe that Blaine is entitled to a plurality of the votes cast in New York, and believing that, we can await the official count with calmness and confidence."

But the outlook for Blaine was anything but good. The Clarkson doubts became more pronounced Thursday but there still was no outright concession. "Whether the Republicans have elected their president or not," the paper said, "they have made the most remarkable gains all over the country."

On Friday appeared the statement: "If the Democratic canvassing boards are willing to give a fair share of votes . . . there is no doubt Mr. Blaine has probably a safe margin of votes in the state [of New York]."

On Saturday, the eleventh day after the election, *The Register* charged fraud in New York. The following day, Sunday, a top story carried the headline "Still Crowing" followed by a rooster picture and a statement claiming "Victory by ballots but may be counted out by the Democratic bulldozers who control the canvassing boards of New York."

Not until Tuesday, the fourteenth day after the election, did the paper finally agree the official New York returns had given the state to Cleveland by a flimsy 1,149 margin. But *The Register* continued to maintain the election had been stolen. "Cleveland Counted In" was the head over the editorial that said: "The people elected Mr. Blaine president. The Democratic returning boards of the State of New York have counted him out and Cleveland in."

Cyranus Cole, a native of Pella and later a Cedar Rapids editor and congressman, was a *Register* reporter in that era. Cole wrote later of the angry crowds that gathered outside the old *Register* building.

"Ret was so reluctant to concede the victory to Cleveland that mobs threatened to burn the building," Cole recalled. "It was said that on a certain night Ret stood in the tower window of the building with a gun in his hand, and back of him stood his brother, who had fought at Shiloh [in the Civil War], with a larger gun, both ready to shoot any man who came with a torch."

Lending support to Cole's account were stories in a rival Des Moines newspaper, the *Leader*. That Democratic daily said crowds did badger *The Register* several nights. On November 6, two days after the election, the *Leader* reported a crowd of "Cleveland men violated the sanctity of the pavement [in front of *The Register*] and vented their joy with cheers." A fist fight broke out that night between a Democrat and a Clarkson employee. The Democrat was said to have flattened his opponent.

Large crowds gathered the next night and two nights later and made a lot of noise, but it was on the night of November 20, sixteen days after the election, that violence came close to developing and possible gunfire was mentioned. "It is fortunate," the *Leader* said, "that no break was made by the armed mob [inside *The Register*]. . . . Had a single shot been fired, the building would now be represented by a smouldering pile of ruins."

Blaine might well have won but for an eastern clergyman-supporter, one Dr. Burchard. In a campaign speech, he linked the Democratic party to "rum, Romanism and rebellion." Opponents thereupon denounced Blaine as anti-Catholic because of the "Romanism" charge and he was slow to repudiate it.

Ret Clarkson wrote that "the foolish remark of Dr. Burchard no doubt stampeded enough Irish-Catholic Republicans" to enable Cleveland to carry New York, Indiana, and Connecticut. Clarkson might have been right in that assessment. The vote in all three of those states was close.

Clarkson also placed some of the blame for the loss of New York on a fellow Iowan, Postmaster General Frank Hatton of Burlington. Clarkson said Hatton refused to close the New York post offices on election day and that kept thousands of Republican carriers and postal clerks from voting. Postal employees were all Republicans in Republican administrations and Democrats in Democratic administrations in those days. Who held the postal jobs was determined by which side won the election.

Clarkson declared those postal votes "would have been enough" to insure a Blaine triumph. (Hatton served as postmaster in the administration of Republican President Chester Arthur, who preceded Cleveland.)

Blaine, however, was not a strong candidate. He carried rock-ribbed Iowa by a margin of only 20,000, on a vote of 197,000 to 177,000. Some nationally known Republicans distrusted Blaine and went for Cleveland. They were assailed as fence-straddlers or "mugwumps," with their "mugs on one side of the fence and their wumps on the other."

The campaign had been merciless. Blaine drew a lot of flak because of his shady reputation. Even children chanted on the streets: "Blaine, Blaine, James G. Blaine, the continental liar from the State of Maine!" The Republicans fired back with this ditty: "Ma! Ma! Where's my pa? Gone to the White House. Ha! Ha! Ha!" The Republican verse was based on the fact that Cleveland had had an illicit relationship with an alcoholic woman who then had a child. Cleveland didn't know whether the child was his but frankly admitted that it could have been. That situation didn't keep him from winning the presidency twice in 1884 and again in 1892.

Another mob menaced *The Register* twelve years later, in the heat of the 1896 campaign.

Thousands of cheering Iowans greeted William Jennings Bryan when he got off the train at the Rock Island station two blocks from *The Register*. Bryan was on his way home to Nebraska after winning the nomination for President at the Democratic convention in Chicago. He attained lasting fame by delivering his famed "Cross of Gold" speech at the convention.

The Register ardently supported William McKinley, the Republican candidate.

After Bryan left, the crowd roared up to the newspaper building, shouting "Down with *The Register!*" The demonstration scared Richard Clarkson (his brother had moved to New York by that time), but no violence occurred.

Despite the Bryan hoopla, McKinley carried Iowa and won the election. Clarkson jubilantly celebrated the outcome by turning on a steam siren he had installed atop the *Register* building and blasting the ears of everybody in the neighborhood.

(Frank Miller/George Mills)

Sledgehammer

An angry and stubborn Iowa state official refused to unlock his office in the statehouse. A squad of troops beat in vain against the door with rifles. A sledgehammer was brought. A tense crowd watched as a husky soldier rained heavy blows against the lock. The splintered door gave way. The troops moved in. The battle was over, temporarily. Auditor John Brown of Chariton had been ousted from his office.

The conflict took place March 19, 1885, in the old statehouse in Des Moines. The new golden-domed capitol was almost finished. The old statehouse, located a few hundred feet south of the present structure was still in use.

Brown, a one-armed Civil War veteran, was one of the "fightingest" state officials ever. Suspended by the governor, he refused to leave office. Not only was his door beaten in, he and his deputy had to be seized and carried unceremoniously out of the office.

In the end the Iowa state senate vindicated Brown and he was restored to his elected position. The struggle lasted more than a year.

Buren Sherman of Vinton was governor. He had been state auditor. Brown was in his second term as auditor. Sherman suspected that Brown had not accounted for all the money he had received, and had collected excessive sums from banks and insurance companies. The governor appointed a commission to investigate.

The commission reported the auditor's actions reflected "disgrace upon the state and are highly censurable." Brown was accused of destroying state records and of failing to use "painstaking care" in running his office.

Brown insisted that he didn't have to account for the money under the law. He pointed out that other state officials had kept corresponding cash for themselves in the past. (The law is clear on that point now. Public officials have to account for every dime.)

Sherman went to Brown's office to examine the books. He couldn't get in. Brown was in the hallway. "Mr. Brown, I desire to enter your office," the governor said sharply. "I demand admission now." Brown didn't move. Sherman couldn't find a janitor with a key. Whereupon the governor on March 3, 1885, suspended Brown for "having failed and refused to produce and fully account for the public funds and property under his control."

Sherman named Jonathan Cattell of Des Moines acting state auditor. Cattell had been auditor from 1858 to 1864. (There is a school named for Cattell in Des Moines.)

Brown refused to make way for Cattell. After some maneuvering in the courts, the governor filed a charge accusing Brown of a misdemeanor by preventing access to his office. The Polk County sheriff arrived at the statehouse March 19 with warrants of arrest for Brown and his deputy, Samuel P. Stewart. The door to an outer office of the auditor's suite was open. The door to the main office was locked.

The sound of marching feet was heard on the stairway. Up came a squad of what would be called national guardsmen today. "I have an order from the Governor directing me to take possession of your office," the commanding officer said. "You are doing an illegal act and we refuse to comply with your demand," shouted the excited Brown.

The officer barked an order. The soldiers advanced. Brown and Stewart stepped inside the open door and attempted to shove the guardsmen back. The officials were "quickly seized by several pairs of strong hands and carried struggling . . . back into the hall."

When the lock wouldn't yield to the butt ends of the rifles, a Sergeant Parker struck a number of solid blows with a ten-pound sledgehammer. Brown broke away from the men holding him and grabbed Parker. Brown screamed at the sheriff: "Preserve the peace! Preserve the peace!" Brown was quickly subdued and Parker battered open the door. Inside were three frightened minor employees.

The guardsmen released Stewart as they marched into the office. The deputy calmly walked through the door and sat down at his desk as if nothing had happened. The guardsmen grabbed him again and hustled him out.

The soldiers cleared the spectators out of the hall. Soldiers with fixed bayonets took control. No one was allowed near the auditor's office. Even Cattell had to get a special order to enter.

News of the battle raced around Des Moines. "People began to gather from all parts of the city," one report said. "They kept crowding into the lower halls of the statehouse and starting upstairs. But those bayonets seemed to bear a potent influence, and they readily turned back with little urging."

Charles C. Nourse, Brown's attorney, hurried to the statehouse. Told of the sledgehammering, Nourse called the guardsmen "criminal housebreakers or burglars before the law. We will see just how far they can go."

Acting Auditor Cattell ran into trouble right away. The Great Seal of the State of Iowa couldn't be found in the office. All the books were missing except the cash book. The safe was locked. Brown refused to open it. A locksmith was called. Nourse and Brown warned him that he would be arrested for burglary if he opened the safe.

"This disheartened the locksmith," a report says. "After picking at the lock for some time, he gave it up and quit in disgust." Another locksmith appeared after dark. He got the safe open by midnight. The seal and the books were there. The office resumed functioning the next day. Thus the skirmish ended with a Sherman victory. But the war was far from over.

Sherman's term as governor ended that year. William Larrabee of Clermont was elected and took office in 1886. Brown's term had one year to go. State officials were not all elected in the same year.

Larrabee had his doubts about the Brown situation. The new governor requested and got an opinion from Attorney General Andrew

J. Baker. The attorney general said the report of the investigating commission did not show "any misappropriation of funds" by Brown.

Larrabee reinstated Brown. Legislators filed impeachment charges against the auditor. Larrabee suspended Brown again and named Charles Beardsley of Burlington temporary auditor.

Brown this time was accused of failing to account for public money and with having retained money paid in for examination of insurance companies and banks. He also was cited for refusing to admit Sherman to examine the books.

As the Iowa constitution provides, Brown was tried before the Iowa Senate. He sat in the Senate chamber for weeks, chewing tobacco as he listened to the proceedings. He was acquitted on all counts.

Larrabee restored Brown to office again July 14, 1886. The feisty auditor had won a complete victory.

Bankrupt Track

D es Moines built a horse track in 1892 with great fanfare and at heavy cost in what is now Waterworks Park. The track went broke after only four days of racing because of poor attendance. It was an unhappy situation for civic boosters who had hoped to build the city into a major racing center.

Scarcely five thousand persons total went to the races in the four days. At one dollar admission, that was far from enough to meet expenses. But name horses and a promised one hundred thousand dollars in purses couldn't pull in the crowds.

The track was located on 112 acres in the north part of the present park, at the foot of Twenty-eighth Street and just south of the railroad tracks.

Even the usually magic touch of wealthy Frederick M. Hubbell failed to save the sponsoring Des Moines Riding Park Association from insolvency. Hubbell took $60,000 of the $75,000 stock issued by the association. About 125 others bought the rest in small amounts, mostly $100 each.

It appears that, except for Hubbell, all the rest lost their investments. Hubbell, who was a railroad, insurance, real estate, and public utilities magnate, paid for his stock with ninety acres of land which was part of the racing park. He got the land back when the project collapsed. He may not have lost any money.

Reports of the bankruptcy ran wild around the city. A large and excited crowd gathered in front of the old Youngerman building on

Fifth Avenue south of Walnut, where the riding association had its offices. Making the loudest noises were more than fifty racehorse owners demanding their money. They didn't get much.

F.M. Hubbell

Des Moines and all Polk County hoped in the late 1980s that history wouldn't repeat itself in the big new racetrack near Altoona, Iowa. The new track, a much more elaborate setup, had at least one advantage over the old one. Pari-mutuel betting was allowed under the Iowa law. That was out of the question in the 1890s. Betting of any kind was illegal, period.

Apparently few people from out of town came to the 1890s track. But what angered the promoters most was the refusal of Des Moines' residents to patronize the track. "Des Moines is much more of a camp meeting town than a sporting city," said an unhappy stockholder. (Camp meetings were pioneer religious revivals, often held out in the woods.)

There were probably several reasons for what *The Register* called the old track's "bad failure." The racing dates of August 15 through August 20 may have been too close to the state fair, which opened August 26, the next week. Also, the one dollar admission was too high. That's all some workers made a day in wages in the 1890s.

Other forms of entertainment were less expensive. The cost of a round trip on an excursion train from downtown Des Moines to High Bridge in Dallas County was only fifty cents. And for seventy-five cents round trip, you could ride another train to see the natural gas well being bored at Redfield in the same county. (The well proved to be a dud.)

The one-mile racetrack was not the usual oval, such as at the state fairgrounds, but was "kite-shaped" in a figure 8, with an intersection where horses could collide if one or more were that far behind the leaders. The most famous "kite-track" in Iowa was at Independence, long a racing capital.

Des Moines was a growing city of about fifty-two thousand in 1892, somewhat larger than one-fourth its 1990 size. The track was a community project involving big local names even if they didn't risk a lot individually. Younker Brothers invested $300, as did banker Simon Casady and Supreme Court Justice C. C. Cole. The Savery House was in for $400 and Albert Cummins, later governor and United States senator, for $200. More typical were $100 investments by Isaac Brandt, I. E. Tone, C. Huttenlocker, and Henry Liebbe.

It started out as a high-class venture, with high expectations of putting Des Moines on the map as a center for trotter and pacer racing. That kind of racing, where horses pull drivers riding in sulkies, was popular around the country then, and was still in many places in the 1980s.

The association and Des Moines newspapers staged a lively campaign to arouse interest in the weeks before the racing meet. The association bought large ads trumpeting: "STAKES $100,000 . . . $10,000 STALLION RACE . . . $5,000 PACING RACE . . . $10,000 FREE-FOR-ALL-RACE. HALF FARES ON ALL RAILROADS." Those were huge purses for the times and as the association found out, more than it could handle.

News stories painted a rosy picture of what a great meet it would be and how much the track would help Des Moines.

"It is one of the greatest attractions Des Moines has ever had and will draw immensely," said one story. "There has been nothing done by our citizens that will do more to advertise our city than the building of this splendid mile track. . . . Many thousands of new faces will be seen on our streets, who will come here to attend the races."

Another story predicted: "The city will be over-flowing the coming week. There will be thousands here to witness one of the grandest events ever to take place within her borders. The new track is the wonder of our enterprising city."

Sponsors drew praise as well: "Our citizens should feel proud of the energy and pluck of some of our well-known citizens who have long felt the need of such an attraction and hastened at once to gratify the public."

Another story sought to entice readers into going to the track with this tantalizer: "The sight of a beautiful horse in motion is one of the most inspiring in human experience. He who is not thrilled, whose blood does not run faster at the race track, is wooden-nerved and dull-witted."

But disaster was in the offing. The sponsors got a chill Monday, the first day of the meeting, when only 421 paying customers passed through the gate, far below the break-even point. Tuesday was a little better with 792 admissions, but that didn't help much. Wednesday produced 1,196, still woefully short.

Association directors held an emergency meeting Wednesday night. Some wanted to shut down right then and there. But a majority hoped against hope there would be an outpouring Thursday when many businesses closed to enable their employees to attend. But that attendance reached only 2,863 and the jig was up. The directors met again Thursday night and canceled the final two days.

The next day, Friday, was hectic. First, somebody suggested the horses race for the gate receipts as prizes. The owners said nothing doing.

Unaware of what had happened, some fans boarded the train at the Union Station at Fifth and Cherry and went to the track in the early afternoon. (You traveled by train or horse and buggy from downtown in those days to such "remote" places as the track or the state fairgrounds.) The fans found the races were off and hastened back to town where rumors were rife about the association's troubles, and most of them were true.

The race cancellations had saved the Riding Park from going any deeper in the hole. But what about the $65,000 in debts, and no money in the bank? That question came to a head in a hurry in the clamoring crowd outside the Youngerman building.

Enraged horsemen displayed association checks that had bounced. The horsemen not only had not collected at least twenty thousand dollars in prize money but were out their entry fees as well. An individual described as a "well-known attorney" appeared with a list of recorded claims against the track, including a $15,000 mortgage held by the old Des Moines Savings Bank. Also on the list were numerous mechanics' liens, including one for $5,254 due lumbermen J. H. and W. H. Gilcrest, another for $3,571 due J. H. Queal & Company, and still another for $9,169 due the Chicago Lumber Company.

Representing his father during the crisis was Frederick C. Hubbell, twenty-eight-year-old son of Frederick M. The elder Hubbell was in London on business. Frederick C. told the Riding Park stockholders that the Hubbells would assume two-thirds of the debts, about $43,000 if the other stockholders would pay the other $22,000. They declined.

Young Hubbell mollified the horsemen somewhat by writing his own personal check for $4,000 to refund their entry fees. That especially helped those horsemen who were broke.

The excitement died down but the embarrassment remained. Said one editorial: "We will be made the laughing stock of the west."

You would think the sponsors would have had enough of trying to make good on the track. But no. Hope springs eternal, and another meet was scheduled for October. The ads said young Hubbell was in charge as "lessee" of the track.

He drastically scaled down the operation. Admissions were lowered to 50 cents, half the previous figure, and prizes for nearly all races were reduced to $250 each. (In actual practice, some races were run for $100.) Hubbell quieted the apprehensions of horsemen by promising the prize money would be paid on the spot at the end of each race, and it was.

Once again, however, the attendance was poor, even counting women who got in free. Overall attendance figures were not released, but a news story said the turnout one day "did not touch the two thousand mark." Another day "possibly a thousand people" were present. Another report commented: "The attendance has been discouraging, as it has every day so far."

News coverage dropped off to little or nothing by the end of the week. Frederick C. Hubbell had another flop on his hands. It was the end of the road for racing at that location.

The riding park has been long gone. What happened to it is not easy to ascertain. It is unlikely that any major horse racing was held there in the next few years, especially since the deep depression of the 1890s gripped the nation. The state fair itself was almost canceled in 1893. The track was used at times for bicycle racing, a leading sport of the times.

In 1897 a big Raccoon River flood inundated and damaged the park and grandstand. Historian Ashby believed that's what finally did the riding park in.

Was rigid enforcement against the sale of beer in the park at least partly responsible for the track's failure? The *Democratic Leader*, a Des Moines daily, thought so. Statewide prohibition against both beer and liquor was in effect. Said the *Leader:* "People from other states will not come to a city where the chief duty of the police force seems to be an eternal search for beer. The patrol wagon is used ten to twelve times a day to haul beer kegs to the station. . . . It grates harshly on the sensibilities of strangers unused to spectacles of this character."

Kelly's Army

An "army" of two thousand wet and miserable men limped into Des Moines on a soggy Sunday morning. The army had marched in heavy rains all night from Van Meter, seventeen miles west in Dallas County. Leading the procession into town was "General" Charles T. Kelly astride a big bay horse.

This was the famed Kelly's Army, moving from the West Coast to Washington, D.C., to demand that Congress give them jobs. The date was April 29, 1894. The United States was in the throes of a deep depression. A similar army got to Washington and thus is better known in American history. The other group was Coxey's Army, which walked a much shorter distance from Ohio to the national capital.

Kelly and his ragged men had arrived in Omaha aboard a Union Pacific train they had seized in the West, but faced a tense time in Council Bluffs across the Missouri River from Omaha, because the National Guard had been called out to prevent the army from moving into Iowa. As the guardsmen approached them, Kelly's men fell on their knees and started praying and singing hymns. That stopped the guardsmen in their tracks. They retreated and left. One of the Kelly troops was Jack London, who later became one of America's top writers. He was then eighteen years old and out of a job.

Des Moines police met the hungry army on the Walnut Creek

Kelley's Army passing Terrace Hill on West Grand Avenue
(Frank Miller/George Mills)

bridge on West Grand Avenue. The marchers were turned into a nearby pasture where a camp was set up.

The almost penniless army became an immediate major worry for Des Moines' people. The city then had a population of 55,000, considerably less than a third of its size in the 1980s. Thus, having 2,000 bedraggled and jobless strangers come into town all at once constituted a serious problem. The city didn't need a lot of jobless to add to its already heavy load. Besides, these men had been sufficiently desperate to seize a train. Who knew what other violence they might commit?

The newcomers made it clear they were in no hurry to leave. For one thing, they didn't want to walk any farther. The overnight ordeal from Van Meter had been too much.

Des Moines residents didn't go to church in great numbers that first Sunday morning. A traffic jam developed on Grand Avenues as the curious drove out in carriages to see the army's encampment.

Kelly delivered a speech to them near the creek bridge. He called his men "a living petition" to Congress. "I tell you we are going to Washington," he declared. "We are going in spite of all the forces that may oppose us, to ask for a chance to earn a living. We are going to urge Congress to give employment to those who can't get it otherwise. We did not bid our little ones goodbye to falter now."

The Des Moines reception was not warm. The *Register* report said: "The army had expected to make a triumphant entry after leaving Van Meter about nine o'clock Saturday night. It started to rain and the walking was pretty miserable. Kelly himself was in a carriage accompanied by two women. They got lost. Where they were during the night is not known.

"Kelly mounted a horse, not looking heroic but trying to act so. He wore an unmistakable look of disappointment."

The army did get a lift from a haranguing speech delivered to them by General James B. Weaver, a Civil War hero who had been the Populist candidate for President in 1892. "You are a fine looking body of men," declared Weaver, a Des Moines resident. "Keep on and get work. When you get work, that is all you want. These laboring men are not traveling of their own free will. They didn't drop their shovels to go. They had their shovels taken away from them."

Kelly pleaded for gifts of food and clothing. He had a little money. He used $178.22 to buy 222 pairs of shoes.

The Populist party in Des Moines joined forces with a laboring men's trade committee to procure food. That Sunday they collected considerable quantities of bread and coffee, a little meat, a few vegetables, "some milk and delicacies, potatoes and biscuits."

To his credit, Kelly instructed the men not to go begging around town. As a matter of fact, the whole army was well behaved throughout its stay in Des Moines. But the city didn't know what to expect, especially after Kelly served notice that the army would remain until given transportation. That announcement inevitably led to a rumor that spread like wildfire: The army was planning to seize another train! The Great Western Railroad demanded, and got, police protection.

The railroad workers' union denied a strike would be called because the army had been balked in getting transportation. The teamsters offered ten teams of horses to carry the men eastward out of town. But Kelly wouldn't budge. He insisted on traveling by rail. It finally became necessary in the wet and chilly weather to put the men in an old stove works building on the east side, north of the intersection of Easton Boulevard and the railroad tracks.

Later the men marched in formation to the east side, passing the Terrace Hill mansion of Frederick M. Hubbell on the way. Capitalist Hubbell wrote in his diary: "Kelly's army of tramps passed our house today."

While civic leaders debated what to do, news reporters interviewed army members. The Democrats were in power in Washington in those depression years of the 1890s. President Grover Cleveland was criticized by Kelly's men in the same way that Republican President Herbert Hoover was assailed in the 1930s. One Kelly marcher said he had been a Democrat "but no more." A machinist was sorry he had voted for Cleveland. Another marcher said half the men "have changed from Democratic to Republican." The army sang a parody entitled "We'll hang old Grover to a sour apple tree."

Drake University students questioned the men and found the average marcher had been out of work for six months. Most said they would accept employment for one or two dollars a day. One man declared he would rather "work a 15-hour shift in a mine than make such a march as we had from Van Meter."

The two women who came with Kelly excited talk around Des Moines. They were Mrs. Ada Harper and Miss Anna Houton of Council Bluffs. They had helped Kelly during those tense hours in Council Bluffs and decided to go east with him. So far as is known, they stayed with him for some time. The deeply religious Kelly said he couldn't turn them away. "They have lost their positions and their friends," he commented. "They are ostracized by their families and warned not to return. All I can do is let them go along, only requiring that they stop at respectable houses and deport themselves well."

In an effort to raise money, Kelly delivered a series of lectures, probably in the Grand Opera House then on Fourth Street south of the Savery Hotel. The box office receipts totaled $250, but expenses ate up nearly all the income. The rent was $125. The band cost $92, and the profit was only $16.41. Part of the program consisted of songs, by an army quartet, such as "Where is My Wandering Boy Tonight?" and "Nearer My God to Thee." A temperance lecture circulated among the men and got nearly all of them to sign pledges not to drink.

There were two professional baseball players in the army. They organized a team and played the Des Moines All-Stars. The Stars won a well-played game, 6-5, before a paid attendance of 350.

Several days went by and even Kelly's best friends lost their enthusiasm. General Weaver and a citizen's committee were reported to be getting "very tired of the job of feeding 1,400 men." If that number was correct, Kelly must have lost some 600 marchers from his group of 2,000 while in Des Moines. (One marcher got a job in a Des Moines restaurant and was given an "honorable discharge" from the army.)

Weaver also became impatient over Kelly's demands for rail transportation. Weaver said he could "march across the state and never get a corn (on his feet). These men can do the same." In an argument with Kelly over food, Weaver declared: "I have stood this abuse as long as I can. It has cost this city not less than $500 a day to take care of you. We have done everything in our power for you. I have neglected my correspondence and devoted myself to this task and so have many others who could ill afford to do it."

Mayor Hillis reached the point where he served notice on Kelly and his army to "get out of town." Kelly retorted that the law said the army could remain a week "before we can be arrested for vagrancy." The mayor said he didn't want the army to disband and "become competitors with the Des Moines workingmen."

It so happened the Des Moines River was high because of the heavy rains. Somebody suggested that the army build flatboats and float down the river to the Mississippi. Both the men and the townspeople greeted the idea with enthusiasm. Work started at once. A "navy yard" was established on the bank of the Des Moines River below the mouth of the Raccoon River.

The army marched in formation down to the river, singing "John Brown's Body," "Marching through Georgia" and "Only One More River to Cross." Gilcrest Brothers lumber yard provided the wood for 150 flatboats at cost, between $600 and $700. M. H. King donated the use of tar buckets and caulking irons. Paving tar was used to seal the cracks. Numerous Des Moines carpenters worked as volunteers helping build the boats. There was much hammering and sawing for several days. Work went on by night by the light of fires.

Thousands of spectators gathered at the scene. The hat was

passed at least once and yielded a collection of $100 for the men.

Each flatboat was 18 feet long, 6 feet wide, and 1 foot thick. A boat drew about 6 inches of water with 13 men aboard.

On May 9, after ten days in Des Moines, the army took off down the river in 134 boats. The men waved American flags to the large crowds on the banks. Farmers drove in from miles around to watch. "Kelly is actually gone," *The Register* said the next morning. "The boats rendezvoused just below the packing dam. It was much fun at first." (One boat was decorated with wild crabapple blossoms.) There were also caustic comments from sight-seers such as: "If you want tobacco, work for it. That's how I got my chawin'."

It was an anxious day for one Joe Hansen. He mournfully reported his wife had gone with the army. He rode up and down the bank trying to find her. It isn't known whether he was successful. Several other women were taken off the boats downstream, however.

It took those who got there about ten days to reach the Mississippi. Towns along the way were very wary of providing too much hospitality. Keosauqua, for example, wouldn't allow the army to land but did provide 600 loaves of bread, 100 pounds of coffee, and a "fat beef." Some boats became stranded on sandbars and the men of necessity got off and walked. They begged handouts from farm families, which provided food to get rid of them.

Few marchers were reported to have reached the Mississippi. Fewer still reached St. Louis and those who did so got there by lashing flatboats together. Kelly is believed to have reached Washington on July 12, but with few or any of his army. The bulk of the men scattered behind across the continent. Congress did nothing for Coxey or Kelly or other similar demonstrators.

Some Drake faculty members as well as students spent time with the army during the Des Moines stay. Drake President Barton O. Aylesworth seems to have been sympathetic with the Kelly cause. He never said he favored the march, however. He declared himself in favor of more control of monopolies and corporations, and he said the establishment of an income tax would help cure the nation's ills. (The federal income tax was still nineteen years in the future.) Aylesworth also advocated free trade in necessary articles and commodities. His ideas were advanced thinking for his time.

Aylesworth never was reprimanded so far as is known. The university, however, did issue a statement saying: "In view of the chance connection of the name of Drake University with the Kelly army, and the possible misinterpretation of its attitude toward such political uprisings, we deem it advisable to make a plain statement of the relationship of the university to this and similar demonstrations. . . .

The university is not now, nor has it ever been, an advocate of fads or faddism, or an exponent of any new social schemes which enthusiastic dreamers seek to foist into general acceptance by the use of an honorable name. We believe most profoundly in the old tried and homely virtues of industry, economy, integrity, honesty, and loyalty, and these are taught with no uncertain sound by every member of our faculty."

The statement went on to urge the faculty "to face boldly every problem of the age, to investigate every principle and measure proposed for the amelioration of society, and to champion moral reforms recognized as such by the Christian conscience of the nation, and in consistence with loyalty to government and its laws." The statement concluded: "We do not understand it to be the mission of a university to engage in current crusades to test this or that proposed special theory for the correction of the ills of society, but to study broadly all the great questions from all sides, and especially to build a well-rounded manhood and womanhood that can cope successfully with all issues and conditions."

Steel, Love, and Murder

T his is a story of Damascus steel and of love and the murder of a groom on his wedding day. All of which happened in Des Moines in 1895.

S. R. Dawson was a big, bearded inventor who lived over the old Grand Opera House on Fourth Street between Locust and Walnut in downtown Des Moines. The Dawson abode was notable for two reasons: It was a workshop where he was said to have invented an exceptionally hard metal of the Damascus-steel type, and it was the home of his pretty seventeen-year-old step-daughter Cora.

Dawson worked night and day perfecting his variety of Damascus steel, a substance that had been a mainstay material for hundreds of years in making cutlery, swords, and daggers. Dawson had high hopes of making a fortune from his steel, and he very much wanted a marriage of distinction for Cora.

A problem developed with Cora. A handsome and breezy young man named Walter Scott had come into her life. Walter's parents didn't have much class. They operated a small eating joint at East Sixteenth and Grand Avenue. They were well below the aristocratic level that Dawson had in mind.

Walter, however, was magnetic and slangy. He didn't have any money, but he had guts. He spieled for circuses when they came to town. He sold merchandise on the street. He had two goals in life: To make a fast buck and to marry Cora. He brushed aside Dawson's disapproval of him. "The old man's a crank," Walter said. "Cora's my style and I'll get her if I have to steal her." And that's what he did, three times. It must be said that Cora relished being stolen by Walter. She wasn't swayed by Dawson's distaste of the young man.

Dawson took drastic action, presumably with the approval of his wife, who was Cora's mother by an earlier marriage. Dawson sent the girl into what he thought was hiding in an Indiana boarding school.

Scott discovered the plan ahead of time. It was said he did so by eavesdropping at the Dawson keyhole. It is more likely that Cora spilled the beans to him.

"Here's where I smash the ethics of good breeding," Walter said. To Indiana he went. As few students were strolling around the boarding school grounds one evening, a guy dashed from behind a tree, grabbed Cora and vanished. It was a case of kidnapping by Scott, with Cora probably the delighted kidnappee.

Walter hid the girl in the home of friends and dared Dawson to find her. The furious step-father hired two private detectives who did locate her. Back home willynilly came Cora.

Dawson proposed not to lose her again. This time he sent her to Missouri under even more secrecy. But Walter couldn't be balked, especially since Cora undoubtedly was on his side. He found her and again hid her away. The enraged Dawson put the detectives on her trail once more. Sure enough they again were successful and Cora was returned a second time.

Dawson hid her a third time at an undisclosed place, and the tireless Scott located her once more. This time he had what he regarded a surefire idea. Cora celebrated her eighteenth birthday on December 24, 1895. She had come of age and Walter reasoned: Why not just go and get married? That very day Walter took her to an east-side parson and they became man and wife without the knowledge of the Dawsons.

Scott went to the police station, told the chief about the marriage and asked for a policeman to come with him to the Dawson apartment to get Cora's clothes. The chief assigned Patrolman Duvall to provide protection. An expressman named Wyatt went along to carry Cora's trunks away.

Dawson answered Walter's knock at the door. Walter broke the news of the marriage and said he had come for Cora's trunks.

"Dawson was fairly beside himself with rage at this culmination," a detective said afterwards. "He grabbed the gun, fired point blank at Scott twice and banged the door shut." The patrolman proved no protection at all. He left to get help.

Detectives found Scott's body in a crumpled heap by the door. They peered through the keyhole and saw Dawson sitting on a sofa in the center of the room, holding a .38-caliber gun and glaring like a madman straight in front of him.

There were two entrances to the apartment, and one detective got in behind Dawson's back and disarmed him before he could shoot again. He was seized, taken to the station and locked up.

"In the meantime Cora became aware of the tragedy," a story in *The Register* said. "Widowed on the day of her wedding was tragic enough, but to have the killing done by [Dawson] was a double shock. She went to the home of relatives and sank into a semi-torpor of grief.

"Dawson had killed in the heat of rage. But he had not intended to yield himself to easy capture." Two wicked-looking daggers were found in his clothes when he was searched at the station.

Dawson was tried and convicted of second-degree murder. He was given a sentence of ten years in the state reformatory at Anamosa. He served several years before being pardoned by Governor Leslie Shaw around the turn of the century.

While Dawson was in prison, Cora recovered from the shock of Walter's death. Ultimately she married a young Canadian and moved with him to his country.

"Dawson served his time behind bars," *The Register* said. "Then he applied himself to his brain-child." A company was set up to manufacture and sell his Damascus steel but failed. When last heard of, Dawson was living in Pennsylvania.

Grave Robbers

What's inside the cemetery fence?" Mrs. George Wheeler asked her son Bert. "Looks as if somebody lost an overshoe."

It was a cold day in January 1896. The Wheelers were driving in buggy and horse past the Saylorville cemetery. The cemetery, on Sixth Avenue north of Des Moines, now is known as Pine Hill. They stopped the horse, and Mrs. Wheeler went to the fence to investigate. The object was not an overshoe but a woman's slipper. Puzzled, she went into the cemetery. Almost immediately she came running out. The Wheelers drove as fast as they could to the home of George Townsend. "Your mother's grave!" she gasped. "It's empty!"

Mrs. Rachel Townsend had died at the age of seventy-three. She had been buried ten days before. The slipper was hers. The news spread swiftly through the Saylorville community. Residents flocked to the cemetery. They found not one empty grave but two.

The body of Sandy Bell, a coal miner, also was gone. He was killed several days earlier by falling slate in the Oak Park mine in north Des Moines.

George Townsend went to the Des Moines police station, six miles away. Detectives McNutt, Hardin, and Johnson solved the mystery in a hurry. They found both bodies in the Drake University Medical School. The school was on an upstairs floor on the north side of Mulberry Street between Fifth and Sixth avenues, opposite the Polk County courthouse in downtown Des Moines.

The officers also found two other bodies at the school—a James Muldoon and a Mr. Anderson. Both had been buried a few days before at the Polk County poor farm. "To all questions whence the bodies came, students and [faculty] were dumb as the proverbial oyster," says one report at the time.

The whole county was in a ferment of excitement. Seventeen students and a janitor were arrested and released on bonds of $300 each. No cases of grave-stealing could be developed against anyone personally, however, and the cases were dismissed. The bodies were reburied.

How the robbers happened to leave the graves open never was explained. Perhaps they were scared away.

Drake had a good medical school. (It was discontinued in 1913.) But procuring bodies for medical study was difficult. Commenting on the stolen-bodies cases, the *Iowa Medical Journal* said: "Under existing circumstances and law, grave-robbing has become practically a necessity. The necessity demanding it is neither a mean or a low one.

"The sole purpose for which graves are robbed is the acquisition of that knowledge of the structure of the human body without which neither medicine nor surgery can be intelligently practiced, and their inestimable results given to a suffering human race.

"Only by careful dissection of the dead can such knowledge be obtained. The motive, then . . . has in view the greatest good for the living generations on earth."

The Register proposed in an editorial that medical colleges arrange to meet future needs by buying bodies while individuals were still alive. Since there was such a shortage, the editorial commented, "physicians, surgeons, medical students and medical editors" should have been willing to arrange to give their own bodies after death to medical schools. (The practice of individuals willing their bodies to medical schools became commonplace in Iowa in the latter part of the twentieth century.)

Grave robbers (Frank Miller/George Mills)

The Saylorville cases also brought to light the activities in 1896 of a ring that had been stealing bodies in Omaha. The ring shipped the bodies to Drake, which reportedly paid fifty dollars for each one. The bodies were taken from such Omaha cemeteries as Mount Hope and Forest Lawn.

Three years earlier, in 1893, police held a ghostly vigil in Woodland Cemetery in Des Moines. Cab driver Nathan Freeman told officers he had an order to "drive a party of men to Woodland because they were going to rob a grave."

Freeman didn't want to lose his job of driving a horse-drawn cab. But he didn't want to get mixed up in a grave robbery either. The police promised to protect him. They told the driver to go to the northeast corner of the cemetery at midnight, as he had been directed.

It was cold and eerie as the police crept silently through the snow toward the cab outlined dimly in the cemetery lane. Bundled against the cold, the cabbie sat motionless on the box. The ghouls were away at work.

"Suddenly Police Captain Morgan stepped up to one side of the cab and pointed a loaded revolver at the cabbie's head," a news report said. The cabbie was ordered to hold up his hands "and not one word if you value your life."

Morgan crouched down beneath the cab. A sergeant secreted himself next to the horses.

"Soon they faintly heard footsteps. . . . A man, John Sloan, emerged and climbed up upon the cab with these words: 'Hello, we did the job up fine.' " Sloan was ordered to hold up his hands and to keep quiet.

Half an hour later, John W. Schaeffer and a man named Martin slowly approached the cab. They were dragging a body later identified as that of William Case, a recently buried Civil War veteran. "Hands up and don't make a sound!" Morgan ordered the men. He frisked the three suspects and found all were carrying loaded revolvers. The officers put the body and the men into the cab and drove to the police station.

Again the action was traced to Drake. Arrested was Dr. John Overton, a Drake faculty member. He posted bond but apparently never was tried.

Schaeffer, described as an instructor at a U. S. Signal Service station (wherever that was), was found guilty of grave robbing. He appealed to the Iowa Supreme Court. His lawyers maintained the prosecution had to prove that he didn't have a permit to disinter the body.

The high court, however, ruled that the defendant had to show that "he had a lawful permit from the state board of health. . . . Having failed to show that he had a permit, it should be presumed that he did not have any."

Schaeffer seems to have disappeared before the supreme court decision. At least he hadn't served any sentence up to the time the Saylorville robberies took over the headlines. Guards were posted around Woodland Cemetery for a long time after the 1893 theft.

Such robberies were not limited to Des Moines. The grave of Amanda Hanna was robbed at Vinton in 1896. That touched off a fifty-thousand-dollar damage suit by her relatives. It isn't known whether they ever collected.

Grave robbing long has been a major offense under Iowa law. The penalty for such a crime, or for assisting in the performance, is up to two years in the penitentiary or a fine of two thousand dollars, or both.

Bare Breasts of "Iowa"

Probably the biggest battle over a monument on Capitol Hill centered around the bare breasts of "Iowa." The partly nude feminine figure seated on the Civil War monument is a depiction of Iowa as a young and beautiful mother offering "nourishment to her children." She is holding both her breasts. The monument, largest on the capitol grounds, pays tribute to Iowa soldiers and sailors of the 1861–1865 war.

Straight-laced Iowans were appalled nearly a century ago at the first sight of feminine "Iowa." Was there no shame? What had happened to decency and modesty? Complaints poured in demanding that "Iowa" be suitably "dressed."

But that was not to be. The monument commission decided in 1896 that "Iowa" should be left as is. And she has been, for more than nine decades now.

"After all the worry and bother," said a contemporary newspaper report, "poor, dumb 'Iowa' is not to get enough duds to keep the rays of the boiling sun off, to say nothing of the winter's blasts.

"It is a victory for the nude in art, as it were, and the supporters of calico fell down in their attempts to hold up sufficient garments to shield Iowa's busts from curious gaze of the pilgrim to the shrine set up on Capitol Hill for Iowa's honored soldiers. It is expected that a howl will go up from the dispensers of dry goods."

Harriet A. Ketcham, Mount Pleasant sculptor, designed the

monument. She didn't live to see it built, dying in 1890.

Strife over the monument wasn't limited to modesty. Civil War veterans were furious over where it was placed south of the statehouse. The veterans felt it was over-shadowed by the golden dome. The legislature voted generations ago to move the monument to a spot east of the capitol but the state hasn't ever gotten around to doing that.

Dubuque residents were angry over the fact that Major General Francis Herron of that city wasn't shown on horseback on the monument. Herron was a worthy Union general and probably deserved that recognition. But there are only four corners and the commission decided to so honor Generals Grenville Dodge of Council Bluffs, Marcellus Crocker of Des Moines, John Corse of Burlington, and Samuel Curtis of Keokuk. And that's the way it was and is.

Among other things, the monument carries a tribute to "the patriotic work of Iowa women during the war of the rebellion. Unsurpassed in every excellence."

Also, on the monument is this stirring message: "Iowa, her affections, like the rivers of her borders, flow to an inseparable union." The latter words are inscribed on the Iowa stone in the Washington Monument in Washington, D.C.

Dawn of a New Century

Women Vote? "No!"

We women don't want the right to vote."
A fashionably dressed Des Moines woman made that statement before a committee of the Iowa legislature.

Legislators looked at each other in amazement. They had been under all kinds of pressure from women seeking the right to participate in elections. Now here was one saying her sex wasn't interested.

The woman opponent was Mrs. Henry Foster, wife of a coal company official. She headed a delegation of upper-crust Des Moines women against woman suffrage. The year was 1897.

Appearance of the delegation was a controversial highlight in Iowa's battle of a half century over whether women should be allowed to vote the same as men. The exciting and sometimes bitter conflict became hot and heavy in 1870 and didn't end until 1920. That was the year the federal constitutional amendment providing full voting privileges to women everywhere in the nation went into effect.

The Iowa state constitution, however, technically didn't grant such privileges for another fifty years. Not until 1970 was the state constitution amended to get rid of the male-only provision. That ban on women voting was meaningless in the intervening half century, however, because women could and did vote under the federal amendment.

In 1897 Mrs. Foster assailed women "reformers pushing for suffrage."

"They as a rule have no families to care for and to keep them at home," she said. "If this matter could be put to a vote of women alone, the result would be an overwhelming no." She maintained that "contented wives and mothers" didn't want to be "bothered with politics."

The numerous so-called "suffragettes" were enraged at that kind of talk.

"The best wives, mothers, cooks, and housekeepers are in the suffrage ranks," declared Mrs. Evelyn Belden of Sioux City. Angry Mary Coggeshall of Des Moines said "every drop of our blood boils at the thought that we are not free women." And Carrie Chapman Catt, once of Mason City and Charles City and an internationally known suffrage leader, commented: "We women are part of the nation. We

Mary Coggeshall, with her husband John Milton Coggeshall
(Iowa State Historical Department)

obey its laws and we pay our taxes. We are entitled to a part in making the laws that regulate our welfare."

Some of the tactics used in the struggle were not very polite. Suffragettes were charged with being "radicals and socialists." One anti-suffrage pamphlet carried the title: "Women should mind their own business."

Other opposition reasons for denying women the right to vote sound strange today. Here are a few:

• The scriptures command women to be silent and under obedience, and teach that women are inferior to men.

• The polls are not a fit place for wives and mothers.

• Women are too emotional to understand politics.

• The demand for the right to vote comes only from unhappy and unmarried women.
• Chivalry will cease when women become politicians.
• Women's sphere is in the home. Equal suffrage threatens the family with dissolution.

The Iowa suffragettes fought a never-say-die battle against heavy odds for generations. They were completely at the mercy of men on this issue. Women could get the right to vote only by masculine consent. Only men voted at the polls, of course, and only men served in the legislature, which had the sole power to pass state election laws.

Also, women themselves didn't present a united front. Such groups as that headed by Mrs. Foster got into the headlines by opposing suffrage.

Opponents used ridicule as a weapon. "My children would come home crying from school," recalled one old-time activist. "Other kids said we ate only baked beans at our house because I was always away working on 'votes for women.'"

What may have galvanized women into action was granting the right to vote to blacks. That amendment to the federal constitution was approved in 1869 and 1870. The women asked: Former slaves get the right to vote, why not us? That embarrassing question was not answered. The women thereupon resorted to the national and state suffrage associations.

The topic of "free love" provoked an angry discussion in the first state suffrage convention in 1871 in Des Moines. ("Free love" was the term given to sex outside of marriage.) Mrs. Nettie Sanford of Marshalltown proposed the convention "denounce the doctrine of free love, believing that marriage is sacred and binding on all the good men and women of Iowa." Mrs. Amelia Bloomer of Council Bluffs, the state president, objected. She said even considering such a topic would constitute "an insult to this convention."

Mrs. Anna Savery, wife of the famed Des Moines hotel operator, agreed. She said "a woman will not abandon her home and children once she gets the ballot." The Sanford resolution was killed.

Mrs. Bloomer, incidentally, attained permanent fame by having feminine bloomer pants named for her.

The women shook the state before 1900 by flying an American flag with only one star on it. Above the star was the name "Wyoming," which was the only state in the union where women were permitted to vote. The flag was flown defiantly over the suffrage cottage at the state fair.

Women did acquire limited voting rights in 1894 in Iowa. The legislature approved feminine voting on questions of increasing tax levies for schools and municipal governments. Women assailed the concessions as "only a crumb." When such issues did appear on the ballot, mothers streamed to the polls carrying infants. "We held each others' babies while we voted," said one old-timer. "We did that to show 'em having children wouldn't keep us from voting."

Meanwhile the women activists were bombarded with criticism. State Senator Shirley Gilliland of Glenwood said in a 1911 legislative debate: "We do not need in politics this new element of ornamental coal skuttle or hobble-skirts. . . . We do not want women tearing around in politics. We want them to rear the population. . . . We want women to rear boys who will be real men and not the kind that make ninnies and sissies.

"The people of Iowa ten, twenty and fifty years from now will not be better for women suffrage. . . . Let them get down the old Bible and learn what true womanhood and true manhood are."

State Senator Horace R. Chapman of Bennett declared the Creator never intended women to vote. "May the Lord save the day when we have mannish women," he said.

An Association of Men Opposed to Women Suffrage was organized in the state. Former Governor Frank Jackson of Des Moines was president. Members of the executive committee included Clyde L. Herring of Des Moines, later governor of Iowa and U. S. senator, and Oscar Strauss, longtime widely known Des Moines attorney. The group sent out a letter in 1915 saying: "If you believe in the conservation of womanhood, if you believe in the present exalted position of American women, if you would free women from politics and public office for which nature did not design them, sign the enclosed application for membership and mail at once."

Herring retained some of his opposition to women voting even after he became governor in 1933, although he didn't talk about it much then. Women were voting in large numbers by that time. The gallant Herring (and he was gallant) did say on one occasion: "We lost something when we brought women down to the level of men. We lost something when it became no longer the thing to do for a man to rise and give his seat to a woman on a streetcar or bus."

On the other hand, the suffragettes had some impressive masculine names on their side in Iowa. They included Dan Turner of Corning, who later became governor; Horace Towner, also of Corning, and Hubert Utterback of Des Moines, both congressmen; George Cosson of Des Moines, Iowa attorney general; James Good of Cedar Rapids, onetime national secretary of war; editor Harvey Ingham of *The Register;* capitalist Frederick M. Hubbell of Des Moines; and Governor George Clarke of Adel. "There is no sex line in patriotism any more than there

A women's suffrage delegation meets in the Martha Callahan home at Twenty-eighth and Woodland in the late nineteenth century.
(Paul Ashby Collection, Iowa State Historical Department)

is a color line in patriotism," Ingham wrote. "Nor is there a sex line in intelligence, courage, sagacity, public spirit. . . . Little by little a hundred of these absurd sex limitations of a barbarous age have been abandoned.

"Women have equal property rights, equal rights in their children, equal rights in employment. There remains but one marked division on the sex line and that is the division of citizenship. It is an illogical division and it is bound to go."

In rebuttal, the anti-suffrage forces gave wide circulation to a statement by Federal Judge O. P. Shiras of the northern Iowa district. He said the suffrage movement "already is injuriously affecting home life, the relation of husband and wife, of parent and child."

Mrs. F. A. Millard of Burlington was president of the feminine state association opposed to equal suffrage. She sent out a letter saying "all the radical and extreme elements . . . the socialists . . . are strongly for woman suffrage."

"Government is masculine while the fine delicacies of the home are feminine," her letter said. "Men are not fitted for women's work, so women are not fitted for men's. Neither work is greater or more important than the other, but they are equally high and honorable."

A common theme of opponents was that women didn't want the right to vote. A petition against suffrage circulated before 1900 in Shenandoah and Essex in southwest Iowa indicated a lot of them didn't. Of 489 approached in Shenandoah, 421 signed. In Essex 240 signed.

Most frustrating of all to the suffragettes was the record of the Iowa legislature. Beginning in 1870, an equal suffrage resolution was filed in every session for two generations. The resolution sought to amend the state constitution to extend voting rights to women. Never once in that period did the women succeed in getting the required two successive legislative sessions to approve the resolution.

In 1913 Harvey Ingham and Governor Clarke spoke in thirty cities in behalf of equal suffrage. Whether those speeches had anything to do with it, the resolution did pass both houses of the legislature that year and again in 1915. Those actions sent the proposed suffrage amendment to the men-only voters for final approval in the June 1916 primary election.

The women were happily confident that victory was at hand. They believed the men voters would give them what they had been denied for more than four decades. They were wrong.

Iowa's harshest battle ever on the suffrage question took place that spring. A strongly negative farm campaign was waged. A red-letter headline in a farm magazine advertisement said: "Woman Suffrage Means High Taxes." The ad declared suffrage "means doubling the city vote in Iowa," with the result that city women "with axes to grind" would have "easy access" to the polls and would push up farm taxes.

The ad also said city and town women wanted to use voting rights to pave highways "so they might drive automobiles into the country." Numerous farm-taxpayer leagues had been formed around the state to fight hard-surfaced highways as an "unjustified extravagance." Iowa was still a mud-road state, and many Iowans wanted to keep it that way. Thus those against paved highways also opposed suffrage.

What apparently hurt the women's cause the most, however, was a struggle going on at the same time over liquor. The Republican candidate for governor was Lieutenant Governor William L. Harding of Sioux City. He was believed to be a "wet"; that is, he was regarded as favoring the legal sale of alcoholic beverages, illegal statewide at the time. The Democratic candidate was E. T. Meredith of Des Moines, the founder of *Better Homes and Gardens* and *Successful Farming* magazines. Meredith was an ardent "dry."

Many Republicans feared that women would vote "dry" and for

Meredith in the 1916 fall election if they were successful in getting the right to vote.

Thus, a lot of Republicans voted against suffrage. So for the most part did voters of both parties in the "river" counties on the state's east and west borders. They were mostly predominantly "wet" in sentiment and they didn't want feminine "drys" monopolizing future elections.

The outcome was a stunning defeat for the women. The suffrage amendment was beaten, 173,000 to 163,000, an edge of only 10,000 but still enough. Three eastern "river" counties, Dubuque, Clinton, and Scott, piled up a combined majority of 9,000 against suffrage. The Dubuque vote alone was 6,963 against to 2,605 for.

Anna Lawther of Dubuque, state suffrage president, probably kept the "river" vote from being even worse than it was. Other leaders in the unsuccessful campaign included Flora Dunlap of Des Moines and Mrs. James A. Devitt of Oskaloosa.

A prominent Republican reportedly said of the amendment defeat: "We had to do it in self defense." In the fall general election, Harding easily whipped Meredith in a one-sided election. President Woodrow Wilson appointed Meredith secretary of agriculture a couple of years later.

The suffrage issue returned in a big way in 1919 when the legislature was called upon to take action on the federal constitutional amendment to give women the right to vote. The Iowa climate was much different this time. The women prevailed on Governor Harding to summon the lawmakers into special session to vote on whether to ratify the amendment.

The Iowa Senate voted unanimously to ratify. The House did also on an 86–5 vote. The assembly "no" votes were cast by Representatives E. H. Knickerbocker, Linn County; T. J. O'Donnell, Dubuque County; W. H. Vance, Madison County; and C. A. Quick and George A. Smith, Clinton County.

Iowa thus finally joined the parade of states supporting woman suffrage. The amendment was ratified nationally and women came into their own and voted in the 1920 elections.

The forty-eighth and last annual convention of the Iowa Suffrage Association was held in 1919 at Boone. The association "happily dissolved" by a unanimous vote.

"The State League of Women Voters was at once organized with Miss Flora Dunlap of Des Moines chairman," said one account. "The old workers faced the new task of making political suffrage for women the privilege and blessing they always believed it would be."

Not all the old-timers were happy with the subsequent results. Mrs. Margaret Richter of Des Moines expressed disappointment decades later with what she called the failure of women to prevent the sale of alcoholic beverages. She was a onetime president of the Des Moines Equal Suffrage Club and a strong "dry." "Honestly, I don't think things are very much better since women got the right to vote," she said. "The results never did reach our hopes. When you are engaged in a hot [anti-liquor] fight like that, I guess you expect too much."

Jeanette

She didn't want the location of her business to look shabby. She had the place painted and refurbished. Then she put on a special event celebrating the improvements. Lots of men came to the place at Elm and Fourth streets and south of the loop.

All went well except for one thing. A reporter sat on the front steps and wrote the names of all who entered. They included two members of the Iowa legislature.

It was said the reporter got punched around plenty during the uproar that followed at the statehouse.

Which was not surprising since the woman was Jeanette Allen and she operated one of the most prosperous whorehouses in Des Moines' notorious White Chapel district. The time was around 1900.

The police did all they could to reduce the embarrassment suffered by the two legislators. The police said there had been a mix-up on names; the legislators were not there. Whether anybody believed that was doubtful.

Jeanette was known as the "Queen of Pelton Street," a street since absorbed into an industrial area.

That "red light district" had flourished as early as 1887 and probably before.

Historian Cyrenus Cole was a *Register* reporter in '87. He visited the district on an inspection trip late one afternoon.

"There sunset was sunrise; the day began with the darkness," Cole wrote years later. "The denizens of the place were getting ready for the orgies of the night that was falling. Musicians were trying out their squeaky pianos, for vice has its own music and it is apt to be ragged as its devotees."

Cole said "painted women were beginning to exhibit themselves in upper windows. Beardless boys and bewhiskered relics of what had been men were already prowling about the streets." (Another report said the area drew "silk hatted dandies in carriages" as well. These were pre-auto days.)

On street corners "stood policemen with billy clubs and guns.

They were there to protect the nefarious business of the place, not to interrupt it." Cole said Des Moines licensed houses of prostitution in those days and "it was whispered that one respectable man paid his pew rent in a fashionable church out of rents he received from buildings in the red light district."

Jeanette was a vigorous woman. She reportedly went to Alaska in the gold rush days a little later and returned with a lot of the precious metal. Whether she got it plying her trade or digging for it isn't known.

The Burlington railroad subsequently pretty much wrecked White Chapel by buying up properties for use in expanding its switching facilities. Prostitution had to move up on Cherry Street and to East Walnut and Court Avenue on the east side.

The last vestiges of the White Chapel era disappeared in 1931 when the city had the final two blocks of brick tenements on Fourth Street and Pelton torn down as uninhabitable.

A Close Call

A feeling of dread swept over Des Moines. The statehouse was on fire! The beloved golden-domed capitol of which all Iowa, and especially Des Moines, was so proud!

It was no little piddling fire either, as the thousands of worried spectators could see. Huge clouds of smoke poured out of the north wing where the chamber of the House of Representatives is located. The north attic was a mass of flames.

First alarm was sounded at 10 A.M. on January 4, 1904. Virtually the entire Des Moines fire department responded. By noon the outlook was grim.

"Unless we succeed in keeping the flames from extending to the senate chamber (in the south wing), the building is doomed," said Fire Chief Burnett.

State Architect Henry Liebbe also feared the $3 million structure couldn't be saved. He advised state officials to get ready to evacuate all books and records.

State Treasurer Gilbert Gilbertson sought to mislead possible thieves. He had a truck backed up to the ground floor window to carry away his documents. He said the load consisted only of books and records. Actually, the most important part of the cargo was twenty-five thousand dollars in cash which was taken to the Capitol City Bank.

The fire mystified as well as alarmed the officials. "They had not supposed it was possible that the building, supposed to be fireproof,

Fire at the statehouse, 1904

should have burned so extensively," said *The Register*. "The inability of the firemen to stop the [fire's] progress, was heart-rending."

A major part of the problem, a newspaper said, was this:

"The distance of the building from hydrants rendered the use of high water pressure impossible without bursting hose, and the water merely ran out of the nozzles. . . . The hill upon which the building is located is one of the highest points in the city, while the height of the building added to the difficulty." (A booster pump was installed in the basement after the fire to take care of the pressure problem.)

Also handicapping the firemen was their unfamiliarity with the statehouse and not knowing where to go to get at the flames.

There was no question as to where the greatest damage was being created. The fire, of unknown origin, had started somewhere in the back of the house chamber, probably in the ceiling of the committee room next to the speaker's office. Before long the chamber itself and the attic above were a shambles. The north gallery fell to the chamber floor level.

The entire false ceiling above the chamber crashed to the floor, along with the chandeliers.

F. J. Elbert, an electrical foreman, was in the attic trying to stem the flames when he fell to his death through the ceiling to the house floor.

By 2:30 P.M. the beautiful law library adjoining the house appeared ready to go. The east wall kept getting hotter despite constant streams of water where hoses could reach. Governor A. B. Cummins, wearing high rubber boots and a rough coat, ordered as many of the library's one hundred thousand volumes saved as possible.

Books from the library's upper stacks were sent down chutes to the porch and thence by other chutes to the ground. More than twenty thousand volumes had thus been handled when the immediate crisis eased late in the afternoon and the book-rescue operation was stopped.

Three men were credited for halting the spread of the fire. They were a Mr. T. H. Rattenbury, a consulting engineer named Lindley, and an unidentified electrician. They went up to the burning house attic. Groping through the heavy smoke while holding hands, they succeeded in closing the doors connecting the house and senate attics.

"This shut off the fire," the news story said, "and rendered it possible for the firemen to get to the part of the building that became free of smoke. They were thus enabled to keep the fire from invading the Senate."

By nightfall the conflagration was over but plenty of smaller blazes kept firemen busy that day, and into the next couple of days as well. In fact, a stubborn wisp of smoke continued coming out of the north small dome for several weeks before stopping of its own accord.

Though the danger of total destruction was past, the after view was an unhappy one. Next morning's *Register* said: "Last night the beautiful structure on Capitol Hill presented a scene of desolation. The outer steps were covered with ice while within lighted candles and lanterns, the only means of illumination, were flitting fitfully about. Water dripped down the marble walls and rushed in torrents down the staircases.... The chamber of the House ... is a mass of charred and smoldering ruins."

Damage was estimated as low as three hundred thousand dollars and as high as five hundred thousand dollars, probably comparable to several millions today.

Electric wiring was being installed in the House chamber at the time. Officials said the current hadn't been turned on, however, and the electrical workers were absolved from blame.

The chamber was sufficiently cleaned up in the next several days so that the House was able to convene in regular session the following week. But it wasn't easy. For one thing, the roof had been burned through in spots and tarpaulins were installed to plug up the holes, and openings in the ceiling as well.

The chamber wasn't a symbol of cleanliness either. House members said they often had to take baths after each daily session because of the ever present soot. The chamber wasn't permanently repaired until after the session ended that spring.

Mulberry Street

Mulberry Street never slept in the early decades of the twentieth century. Player pianos and billiard and pool halls operated all day and all night on the street on the south edge of downtown Des Moines. Nearly a dozen saloons thrived in the four blocks between Fifth Avenue and Ninth Street.

Many Iowans came to the state fair by rail in the pre-automobile days. They got off trains at the old Union Station south of the courthouse. Hundreds made a beeline for the joints on Mulberry Street a block away. Some never got to the fair at all.

Two uniformed police constantly patrolled the street during fair week. They were joined by plainclothesmen, some imported from other cities, who mixed in the crowds nabbing pickpockets. Careful celebrants gave their money to friendly bartenders for safekeeping while they "did the town." Prostitutes plied their trade in two smaller hotels as well as on the street.

At least one railroad ran shuttle trains frequently from downtown to the fairgrounds. A saloon on Cherry Street under the Seventh Street viaduct did a land-office business selling big picnic bottles of beer in straw carriers to take to the fair.

Food wagons selling chili and sandwiches lined Mulberry. Shouting newsboys from nearby newspaper offices descended on the crowds. The old *Des Moines News* was located at Seventh and Mulberry; the old *Capitol* was a block away at Seventh and Walnut; *The Register* was in the vicinity at Fourth and Court. The newsboys picked up extra change selling sheet music to customers. Some newsboys played the tunes on hand organs for prospective buyers.

One of the city's first movie houses before World War I, the Dreamland, was on Mulberry between Sixth and Seventh. From the streetcar waiting room on the northwest corner of Sixth and Mulberry, you could board a car for any place in town.

Rob King's saloon at 513 Mulberry, across the street north from the Polk County Courthouse, was a key spot for politicians and political plotting. That building had an unusual combination of occupants. On the second floor above the King saloon was the King Ying Low Chop Suey Restaurant, and on the third floor was the Drake University Medical School, where students dissected bodies.

Two liveries where you could rent a horse and buggy were close by: the John Rocell Stables at Sixth and Cherry and the London Stables on Ninth just north of Mulberry.

Hustlers were thick in the pool halls, waiting for overly confident young men from the country wanting to bet on their cue prowess. Sometimes hundreds of dollars were bet on a game, with the hustler usually the winner.

Big-name Americans frequently shot pool on Mulberry. Frank Gotch of Humboldt, the world heavyweight wrestling champion, played in Frank Wegner's place between Sixth and Seventh. Bill Robinson, the famed black dancer, liked to come to the street to play when he was in town on the vaudeville circuit, as did Eddie Leonard, the well-known minstrel.

The old Mulberry Street pizzazz had all but faded out by 1940. About all that was left was Billy Galvin's tavern on the site of the King saloon. There's a bank lot there now.

Tall Corn Song

Iowa's "Corn Song" didn't come from a farmer or even a rural county but straight out of the chamber of commerce in Des Moines. Chamber secretary George Hamilton wrote the song in 1912 with help from band leader John T. Beeston. The tune was taken from the song "Travelling."

Hamilton was a member of the Iowa delegation which went to a big Shriners' convention that year in Los Angeles. The delegates wanted a "rousing song" for the convention, "to advertise the chief product of the state: Corn." Hamilton and Beeston put the song together.

There were a lot of verses originally but only the chorus has survived and that has gone through several revisions. Here's the way it is mostly sung now:

> We're from IOWAY, IOWAY,
>> Best state in the land,
> Joy on every hand,
>> We're from IOWAY, IOWAY,
> That's where the tall corn grows!

The Iowa delegates enthusiastically sang the song while marching in Los Angeles and started the practice of pushing their right arms skyward on the last line.

Some Iowans have regarded the song as too corny in recent years and it has been boycotted often by bands at sports events. But old-timers still like it and look upon it as a good signature song for the state, even though the tallness of corn has become unimportant from a production standpoint.

The "Corn Song," incidentally, is not the official Iowa state song. That song was written in 1897 by Major S. H. M. Beyers and is sung but rarely. It is set to the German tune of "Der Tannenbaum."

Early Eyesore

Time was when an eyesore neighborhood occupied much of the present statehouse grounds in Des Moines. A 1913 account says the area around the golden-domed capitol square consisted largely of "old shanties with broken windows; tumbledown outbuildings; unkempt yards; closets with doors left open; unpainted shacks one or two stories high, with decayed foundations; discarded clothing doing the service of window panes; billboards directly in front of the capitol advertising beer and underwear. . . ."

In the wintertime the heating plant north of the building belched "continuously every hour of the day a cloud of smoke and soot." The account said it was embarrassing that such a sight should be the first to greet the eyes of passengers arriving in Des Moines on trains at the rate of 1,000 a day.

It was an intolerable situation that couldn't last, and didn't. Under pressure from Governor George W. Clarke of Adel, the legislature voted to acquire upwards of sixty acres of adjoining ground and to clear out some twenty blocks of buildings. Said the governor: "We will have Statehouse grounds equal to those of any capital in the Union, and I am not excepting the grounds in Washington. The people of Iowa have come to realize that state pride is a factor in the upbuilding of a commonwealth."

But the goal wasn't easy to achieve. Clarke found himself the target of harsh attacks from newspapers around the state. "Two Million Dollar Land Grab Railroaded Through Assembly!" shouted a headline in the old *Iowa City Republican.* "Legislature Saddles Big Debt on State to Please Des Moines Boosters and Speculators. Add 21 Blocks to Capitol Grounds."

Slums in the shadow of the statehouse

Besides delighting in sniping at Des Moines, what irked the editors and others was the decision to finance the improvement with a state property tax levy of one-half mill for at least two years. Further arrangements were made for future smaller levies up to eight years if needed.

Editor John W. Rowley of the *Keosauqua Republican* took direct action. He and four others brought suit to have the law declared unconstitutional. Rowley said there was a "great uprising of sentiment . . . sweeping across Iowa in protest against this enormous proposed outlay of $2 million with more millions to follow." (Those were the days long ago before millions of dollars became peanuts in governmental discussions.) Rowley also said Des Moines individuals "coaxed, cajoled, and urged the Legislature to commit an unlawful act."

The lawsuit came to naught. The Iowa Supreme Court upheld the constitutionality of the act.

Undeterred, Rowley made it a political issue. He declared his candidacy for the Republican nomination for governor against Clarke in the 1914 Iowa primary. Rowley got no results there either. Clarke won easily with 86,000 votes, with one C. G. Lee in second place with 37,000 and Rowley a distant third with 19,000.

Over the next few years the state bought 300 properties, including homes and apartments where 1,400 people lived. L. A. Jester, the agent who handled negotiations for the state, said purchases totaled a little over 40 acres. The city of Des Moines donated 20 acres of streets, most of which were torn up.

The acquisitions increased the size of the statehouse grounds from the 11 acres in the two-block-square statehouse site to 62 1/2

Rooming house near the soldiers' and sailors' monument, Des Moines, early twentieth century

acres. (The state already had owned 2 1/2 acres consisting of the site of the historical building and a now long-gone dairy and food regulation building southeast of the capitol.)

The result left the grand old capitol on a park-like sward stretching from near East Seventh to East Twelfth and East Thirteenth streets east and west, and generally from Des Moines Street south past Court Avenue to the railroad tracks.

Not all the objectives of the drive were realized. The statehouse was badly overcrowded in 1913, and officials planned to put up a state office building on the northeast corner of East Ninth and Grand Avenue as part of the program. Not until the 1950s was the Lucas building, the first office building on the complex constructed, and then not in that location.

One of the properties bought in the purchase program was the large Jack Byers residence on Des Moines Street. That was preserved and turned into the governor's mansion. Only one governor and his family lived there, however. He was Governor William L. Harding (1917–1921). His successors avoided the place, and it was later a state board of health building.

Most interesting was a housekeeping chore that the state never did get done.

One of the needs in the 1913–1914 period was a place to put a planned sixty thousand dollar monument in memory of U. S. Senator William B. Allison of Dubuque. Allison, who served thirty-five years in the Senate in Washington and eight in the house, is a legendary figure in Iowa lore.

The monument finally was located straight out of the south door of the statehouse and on the south side of Walnut Street. The only trouble with that site is the fact that the monument is awkwardly placed in a spot adjacent to the southeast of the big 1894 Civil War monument.

The legislature and state officials realized that that was a bad situation. A bill was passed to move the Civil War monument to a site on East Twelfth Street straight out of the east doors of the statehouse. But passing the bill was one thing and doing something about it was another.

For more than three generations, the state of Iowa has allowed the two monuments to sit in strange positions in relation to each other. The planned change has long since been forgotten.

Foe of the Devil

They came by the thousands, day after day, night after night. All kinds of people. Lawyers, farmers, carpenters, single girls, housewives, merchants, judges, preachers. Young, middle aged, old. The days stretched into weeks. Still the throngs kept coming to the huge, shed-like building made of pine lumber.

They were drawn by a thick-bodied little man with a powerful and penetrating voice. He did something to them in their hearts. Some who came to scoff remained to pray.

They sat on hard benches and watched him charge around the platform. He shouted. He jumped up and down. He tore off his coat, vest, and tie. He laughed. Sometimes tears streamed down his cheeks. He punched at unseen foes, and never missed. He shook his fist at the audiences. He slammed chairs against the floor. He pounded the pulpit. He jumped up on a chair or table.

The man was Billy Sunday, preaching the gospel of Jesus Christ to Des Moines in his own earnest and exciting way.

The year was 1914. The place was a temporary tabernacle built on the old baseball ground on Fifth Avenue between Grand and Keo, now partly occupied by the State Commission for the Blind building.

The seven-week revival conducted by The Reverend William A. Sunday was a tremendous event in the annals of Des Moines. Total attendance was an outstanding 550,000. Des Moines had a population of scarcely 100,000.

The aisle leading to the pulpit was covered with sawdust and shavings. At the end of each sermon, Sunday called upon his listeners to come forward on the "sawdust trail" and pledge themselves to Christianity. Some 13,000 persons did so in Des Moines. While the choir sang the hymn "Just As I Am," Sunday said: "Come clean for

God. Get in line for Jesus Christ. Come on, ushers, singers, everybody who wants to consecrate or reconsecrate himself to God."

They came over the sawdust by the hundreds some days, 1,250 the last day.

Twenty-five Des Moines mail carriers marched up carrying a large American flag (editor Harvey Ingham of *The Register* and H. W. Byers, former attorney general of Iowa, traveled up also). One hundred attorneys, including judges, rose to answer the call. They asked for the singing of the hymn "Yield Not to Temptation." A group of bricklayers requested the hymn "How Firm a Foundation." One sawdust trailer tossed a long black cigar up on the platform and said: "I guess I'll come clean all the way through." Another surrendered his briar pipe and sack of tobacco to Sunday.

Through the years Des Moines saw and heard all the old-time topflight evangelists, the great Dwight Moody, J. Wilbur Chapman, and white-robed Aimee Semple McPherson.

But possibly the greatest of them all was Billy Sunday. Perhaps he was the Billy Graham of his time, although much noisier and more theatrical.

Sunday was a native Iowan (born at Ames in 1863) and he spent part of his boyhood years in orphan homes at Glenwood and Davenport. He was born after his father, William Sunday, was killed in action in the Union army in the Civil War.

Billy was a great baseball player at Marshalltown as a young man and a success as well as a member of what is now the Chicago Cubs in the National League. The speedy Sunday circled the bases in fourteen seconds.

He quit baseball when he was converted and became an evangelist known the world over. He estimated that he preached to 100 million persons in his time.

Sunday delivered a hell-and-brimstone sermon. He loved to lambast the devil and saloon-keepers (liquor-sellers) in language the man on the street could understand.

"And now, devil in hell, you've walked the streets of Des Moines long enough!" Billy shouted. "We know your dirty, dastardly work. We know how you've caused thousands of girls to lose their virtue, how you've sent men home and made them strike down their wives. We know it, devil, and you'd better sink back in your darkest pit where you'll soon be wearing a bandage around your head!"

Sunday changed abruptly.

"Oh Jesus, Let the angels descend to help the good people of Des Moines. Send legions of angels, Lord. Come on, Lord, to the help of your people, will you?"

Billy threw all restraints to the winds when he railed against liquor. This was when he slammed chairs against the floor.

"The wets are the worst gang of cutthroats this side of hell!" he roared. "If I were God for fifteen minutes, they wouldn't be this side of hell either. I'll fight liquor as long as I live. I'll kick it. [He kicked.] I'll punch it. [He punched.] I'll butt it as long as I have a head. [He butted.]"

He shook his fist at anyone in the audience who might have signed a petition in favor of opening saloons. "I'll skin you alive before I get through!" he shouted. Eighty-six saloons reportedly had been closed in Des Moines at the time.

There were no public address systems in 1914 but Sunday's booming voice could be heard clearly at the rear of the long "temple." Sometimes his voice would be hoarse but he had a way of making even his grating whisper heard in the far reaches of the building.

Rousing, full-throated hymn singing was a major Billy Sunday weapon. The handsome, trombone-playing Homer Rodeheaver was his choir director and business manager. Rodeheaver's choirs set the mood with the vigor and intensity of their singing.

"Brighten the Corner Where You Are" was the Sunday theme hymn. But he also reveled in such robust songs as "The Brewer's Big Horses." Beer deliveries to saloons were made in wagons pulled by big horses in those days. One verse of the song went:

> Oh the brewer's big horses
>   Comin' down the road
> Toting all around old Lucifer's load,
>   They step so high and they step so free,
> But the brewer's big horses can't
>   Run over me.

Billy preached a stern old-time religion. "I believe in hell, old-fashioned hell," he said. "The preachers of today ought to hold the people over the pit and let them smell the sulphur fumes."

But he preached a happier brand of salvation as well. "I pity anyone who can't laugh," he told his Des Moines faithful. "There must be something wrong with their religion or their liver. The devil can't laugh. God likes to have a little fun. . . . Nowhere in the Bible do I read 'thou shalt not laugh.' The Lord doesn't want you to go around with a face long enough to eat oatmeal out of a churn. That's not religion, that's colic."

He disliked formal rehearsed prayers. "If I tried to pray by formula," he commented, "my prayers wouldn't get as high as the gas jets." (Gas lights were still being used for illumination in many buildings then.)

He couldn't stand noise in the audience, except applause. A

crying baby brought him to a dead halt. He said nobody could preach against that noise. He asked the mother to take the baby to the tabernacle nursery.

Perhaps the liveliest of all the 1914 revival meetings was the occasion when ten thousand college and high school students and other young people came together. The first part of the meeting was boisterously non-religious. Said *The Register:*"School colors were everywhere, on the white posts throughout the immense structure, fluttering gaily from the canes of pretty coeds, hanging from the lapels of thousands of coats and middles."

A college band struck up the tune "Hot Time in the Old Town Tonight" and was followed by organized cheering. "E-A-S-T rah rah rah!" roared the big East High School delegation. Cheerleaders brought forth a loud yell from North High rooters. More cheers came from students of Capital City Commercial College, Still College of Osteopathy, Drake University, Highland Park College, and Des Moines College (the latter two are long since gone). Then everybody cheered: "Rah rah rah College! Sunday! Sunday! Sunday! Wow!" (Whoever has heard of student yells at a revival, before or since?)

The students delighted Billy. He promised to go out and see Drake "clean up on Missouri." He complimented the young people on their energy.

"God likes to see men and women with plenty of pep and vinegar and Tabasco sauce," he said, and added: "If you are starting out to succeed, don't leave out religion. It is one of the principal ingredients of success. Don't forsake Almighty God."

Sunday got voluminous coverage in the Des Moines papers, sometimes four and five columns a day in a single paper. He expressed gratitude in his prayers at least once to editors and reporters of *The Register* and *Tribune,* the old *Capital,* and the old *News.*

On the other hand, he threw plenty of barbs at the churches of the day. "There's more fool-headed, hare-brained claptrap nonsense in the church today than almost anywhere else," he declared. "It is degenerating into a third-rate amusement house. . . . I know some sermons where a sinner couldn't find Jesus Christ without a search warrant."

He said some men's religion "is like their property—all in their wives' names."

Many people came in delegations, similar to groups attending ball games in recent years. A thousand Masonic lodge members attended in body. There was a contingent of 375 from the Hubbell building, others from Rotary Club, Randall Lumber Company, Jewett Lumber Company, Sheuerman Woolen Mills, Evergreen Woolen Mills, Hawkeye Transfer, and Farmer's Cooperative Produce Company.

Offerings were occasionally a problem. A dish pan was passed in every row. There was a "ten-cent night" and "dollar night." Sunday was sometimes disappointed in the contributions, although he got none of the money until the last night.

"I have to nag and pull at you to get enough money to pay the Lord's little debt," he said. The tabernacle cost more than nine thousand dollars to build and finally eight hundred dollars to take down, and there were numerous other expenses. Collections for the entire revival totaled thirty-four thousand dollars, apparently sufficient to meet expenses. The thirty-four thousand dollars was like four hundred thousand dollars today.

The amount dropped into the pans for Billy on the final day and night exceeded thirteen thousand dollars and Billy apparently didn't complain about that. He said he didn't know why he shouldn't be compensated. "I have as much right to get something for my work as the hellhounds who slander my name," he said.

That final day and night were a colossal tribute to Billy. The turnout in four sessions reached an estimated forty thousand. The tabernacle seated only seventy-five hundred. And 1,250 streamed down to the front to bring the"sawdust trail" number for the entire revival to 19,941. Des Moines was proud of the fact that this topped the results of Sunday's revival in Denver by more than 1,400 people.

Sunday and his wife (he called her "Ma") hated to leave Des Moines. His eyes were wet and "Ma was crying openly" as the choir sang "God Be With You Till We Meet Again." Thousands gathered at the Rock Island station to bid the Sundays goodbye as they boarded a train for Chicago. The crowd sang "If Your Heart Keeps Right," "Since Jesus Came into My Heart," and the inevitable "The Brewer's Big Horses." There was a glow about the city for some time afterwards. "Ten thousand people could not have been held on benches week after week if there had been nothing more than eccentricity and primitive doctrines," said a *Register* editorial. "Great practical truths urged with intensity upon the consciences of men and women, turning thousands into better walks of life, are the real measures of the work."

Saturday Spree

H alf the city last night seemed engaged in a contest over who could consume the most liquor."

That's how *The Register* described a wild spree which took place on a Saturday when all eighty-six Des Moines saloons had reached their last day in business. The city council canceled every saloon license as of February 13, 1915. It was a time when anti-liquor forces were powerful in Iowa, even in Des Moines.

Drinkers congregated by the thousands to get plastered just one more time before the deadline. Fights broke out all over the business district and elsewhere where there were saloons. Injured battlers were brought to the police station to be patched up by police surgeons. The department had its own surgeons in those days.

Two men were fatally injured but it wasn't known if the tragedies were liquor-connected. L. Moser of Des Moines died after being struck by a street car at Ninth and Pleasant streets. Pat Murphy of Fort Dodge was beaten to death. He was found dying on Crocker Street between Fifth and Sixth.

Half a dozen drunks were hit by automobiles but not seriously injured.

Fifty men were arrested for intoxication by morning, not an unusual number for a Saturday. But that may have been because the police were overwhelmed with other calls and problems and didn't have time to pick up everybody seen reeling in the streets.

One happening that drew special attention was the arrest of two women for intoxication. Almost never was a woman found in such condition in those days. A lady never went into a liquor place under any circumstances, and if she did she wasn't a lady.

A saloon in nineteenth-century Des Moines
(Paul Ashby Collection, Iowa State Historical Department)

At the bar (Iowa State Historical Department)

Calls came in so fast after dark that the day police force had to be summoned into emergency service to help the night men. Seventy officers in all struggled to suppress disorder. "Paddy wagons" and ambulances "scurried about the city with hardly a pause for hours."

The spree started Saturday morning and by noon men staggered in the streets "laboring under heavy loads. At sundown the streets were crowded," *The Register* said. "The sidewalks were jammed with— except in a few instances—good-natured men going from one saloon to another. The walks in front of the thirst parlors were almost impassable and in front of the bars dry humanity stood three deep." Every saloon employee "able to pull a cork or operate a syphon" was pressed into service.

One man was almost kicked out of a Fourth Street bar for ordering a cocktail. He "should have known better than to ask for a mixed drink when patrons were standing in line for even a whiff of straight liquor." It was a record day (and night) for Des Moines saloons.

The bars also did a tremendous business selling liquor by the bottle. Saloon proprietors feared getting caught with large inventories as the zero hour approached. They advertised bottled goods at reductions of 25 to 40 percent. Buyers, some from out of town, came with suitcases to lay in supplies for the dry era ahead. One observer said: "In the apartment where I live, there has been enough booze carried in in the last week to sink a battleship."

It was early, nine o'clock in the evening, when exhausted bartenders shouted in hoarse voices: "All out, boys." The barkeeps had had it, and so had the drinkers.

Incidentally, the term "liquor" included beer in those days. Not until the 1930s was beer placed in its own separate beverage category.

It so happened that the saloons really didn't have to shut up shop that Saturday night. Because of a technicality, they were permitted to operate the following Monday before quitting altogether. But there was no replay of the Saturday night binge, maybe because Monday was a work day which in many cases meant ten or twelve hours on the job. The eight-hour day was not yet in sight. The 1915 working man apparently didn't have the energy and time anyway to go salooning again Monday night.

Thus departed the legal saloon from Des Moines, forever, the drys hoped and believed. But not so. Patrons could again buy beer legally over the bar beginning in 1933 in Des Moines and Iowa. Sale of beer to take out from grocery stores and other retail establishments also became legal at the same time.

Legal sale of "hard" liquor by the bottle returned to the state in 1934 but only in state liquor stores. Legal sale of liquor by the drink didn't return until 1963 although plenty of alcohol and booze was sold in one form or another by bootleggers and in "speakeasies" in the intervening years.

With all those imbibers jamming the Des Moines streets that fateful 1915 Saturday, it would seem the city should have been wet politically, that wet voters would have outnumbered the drys at the polls. Evidently that was not so because the city council wasn't afraid to eliminate the saloons. Anti-liquor forces were sufficiently strong to elect a majority of public officials around the state at the time.

It seems that it would have taken a lot of gumption to close down eighty-six ongoing retail businesses at one time. An estimated 800 saloon employees lost their jobs, not to mention the losses suffered by the proprietors and by owners of the real estate occupied by the bars. But the drys had the power to do whatever they wanted, no question about it. Drinkers who thought they could flee to Valley Junction (now West Des Moines) to have a few were balked. The Valley council closed that town's saloons at the same time.

The Des Moines council's closing action drew a happy comment from Iowa-born Billy Sunday, the fire-eating evangelist who was an implacable foe of liquor. "I am as proud of Des Moines as a boy with a new pair of boots," he said in a message to *The Register* from somewhere on the evangelical circuit. "I think the old capitol city can flash up as fine a sentiment for civic righteousness and moral reform as any city I know of. It must stagger the liquor element because I believe they figured Des

Moines would be the last city in Iowa to be torn from their grasp. The action of the council sees her go free and puts her on the honor roll of American cities that are saying goodbye to booze. May God bless her in my prayers."

The teens and 1920s were the heyday period for Sunday who was born in Ames. That was also a period when dry crusader John Hammond burst on the Iowa scene. He had been a Centerville, Iowa, coal miner earlier. He acquired a tempestuous reputation when he wrecked a drinking joint with wild swings of a chair in the rural community of Bunker Hill near Centerville.

Hammond headed state liquor law enforcement in the state's Prohibition years of 1917–1918, which was the World War I period for the United States. Hammond took out after druggists who had been selling alcohol and liquor illegally in their back rooms to drinkers. Druggists were permitted under the law to sell such products only to patients by prescription. That law was widely violated. As a Polk County deputy sheriff, Hammond reportedly cut the number of druggists licensed to dispense liquor in the county from 430 to 12 in 1922.

Hammond took over as Des Moines police chief in 1923. He heard rumors that his liquor squad was selling booze from the police department steps. He fired them all.

The Blue Laws

A Des Moines merchant was arrested for selling pop on Sunday, contrary to law.

Three men, including a member of the Iowa legislature, were charged with the misdeed of opening the Fort Dodge city library on Sunday.

Eighteen persons working on a Waterloo newspaper were hauled into court one Sunday morning.

A Council Bluffs storekeeper was arrested for selling ice cream on Sunday; others were accused of staging a baseball game on the Sabbath in Des Moines; still others in Des Moines were charged with selling groceries on the Sabbath.

An attorney declared his intention of prosecuting ministers in Winterset for getting paid for preaching on Sunday. (He didn't do it.)

The whole situation could well have been named "the Iowa Comic Opera of 1917." That was the year Attorney General Horace Havner began enforcing the state's long ignored "blue laws."

Those laws forbade "buying or selling property" or "any labor

Horace Havner, Attorney General
(*Iowa Official Register, 1917–1921*)

except that of necessity or charity" on Sunday. To do such things on Sunday was called "desecration of the Sabbath." The penalty for violation was a fine of one to five dollars or jail for non-payment of a fine.

The blue laws got their name from the fact that they had been printed on blue paper in colonial New England from whence they came. The laws had their origin in the Bible, which sets aside a day of worship and rest. The laws had been in the Iowa Code for generations but had not been enforced.

Havner proposed to end that ridiculous state of affairs one way or another. He served notice on the legislature to fish or cut bait. Repeal the blue laws or he would begin enforcing them.

The legislators conceded the laws were meaningless. But the lawmakers feared repeal would upset church-going Iowans who might then vote against the repealers in the next election. The legislature went home without taking action. That opened a zany period in Iowa history.

In May of 1917 Havner sent orders to local officials throughout the state to start enforcing the blue laws forthwith. The Des Moines *News* tried to prepare its readers for what was about to happen. "Next Sunday," the newspaper said, "you can not legally go to the ball game; go to any theater, movie or legitimate; buy a cigar, box of candy, or a coke; a dish of ice cream unless it is part of a meal; drink in a temp [non-alcoholic] bar; go to an amusement park; listen to a band concert; buy flowers except for a funeral; have your shoes shined, except at home by your son; buy gasoline for your auto."

But you could legally "play golf if you are a member of a club; ride on a streetcar; take a cab or a trip about town in the family automobile; eat in a bona fide restaurant. . . ."

Officers arrested hundreds of "violators" around the state that first Sunday. More than 100 were issued summonses in Council Bluffs, including telephone operators, newspaper people, newsboys, theater workers, fruit stand and ice cream parlor proprietors, all for working on Sunday.

Another 100 were arrested in Des Moines, including the 37 for helping stage a Sunday ball game, 6 theater proprietors, and numerous small businessmen, including J. A. Spatton caught selling pop at the southeast corner of Seventh and Locust streets. (Whatever happened in the Spatton case isn't known.)

Still another 100 at Sioux City included workers at such additional businesses as bowling alleys, florists, and pool halls.

In Waterloo, Constable Frank Graf arrested eighteen newsmen and mechanical workers of the old *Times-Tribune* at 12:30 Sunday morning. They all were released on $25 bond each, after which they returned to the plant to finish putting out the Sunday paper. They were not bothered further.

Not so lucky were owners of two establishments in Centerville. Arrested there were F. Mulany and J. Countess for selling candy on Sunday. Both posted $50 bonds, went back and reopened their stores, and were arrested again. This time Mulany took a whack at Sheriff Elgin and a brief free-for-all followed involving the sheriff, two deputies, and the storekeeper. Mulany and Countess were released a second time on $100 bonds.

One J. J. Ryan filed the charge of opening the Fort Dodge library against State Representative C. V. Findlay, Democratic Chairman M. F. Healey, and E. H. Williams.

The Des Moines *Register* pointed to a potential problem. "Druggists were besieged with (Sunday) calls for prescriptions," the newspaper said, "but refused to fill any save on instructions from a physician saying the case was one of life and death."

Druggists in an unnamed Iowa town sold cigars and chewing tobacco only on prescription.

In Eldora shoe shiner Steve Panagoupolos stayed out of trouble by refusing to shine a shoe. (Even smaller cities had professional shoe shiners in those days.) Not so fortunate was an Eldora candy shop man who was fined $5 and $4.85 in costs by Mayor Emeny for a Sunday sale.

Two Des Moines businesses, the Piazza confectionery in the Shops Building and the W. C. Clemens drug store at 323 Fourth Street, were each fined one dollar and costs.

Attorney General Havner was a bulldog of an attorney but the situation started getting to be more than he could handle. Even his friend *The Register* commented: "We can not enforce a Sunday law in the spirit in which New England enforced it. . . . The law should not be enforced literally as it is, and yet the Attorney General can not be blamed if, in the absence of legislation, he takes steps to enforce it."

The courts started going against Havner. Justice of the Peace Howard found Louis Tronchetti of the Princess Candy Kitchen in Des Moines innocent of breaking the law when he sold ice cream on Sunday. Howard held that ice cream could be classed as a "necessity" and thus exempt from the blue laws. The justice had kind words to say about ice cream: "Numerous persons, especially in hot weather, do not care for anything for lunch or evening meal except ice cream. To deprive them of this would be a hardship. It has become as much a necessity as many of the staples of life."

Des Moines Municipal Judge Joseph Meyer struck an even harder blow at Havner by ruling Sunday movies and baseball legal. He held both to be "innocent and proper entertainment." Since they are innocent, he said, "then it follows that all who have a wish to attend have a right to do so."

But what about those who have labor jobs such as ticket-takers? Meyer replied: "Whatever may be properly required for their [the spectators] admission, safety and comfort, may be lawfully furnished, even though to supply these may require labor. Hence the selling of tickets, caring for the place, furnishing seats, ushers, etc., come within the term 'necessity.'"

Des Moines Municipal Judge Mershon was even more explicit. He instructed the city police to make no more arrests for Sunday violations.

Other defendants meanwhile were winning victories as well. Grocer Tony Morasco, at 400 Southeast First Street in Des Moines, was freed for lack of evidence. A jury at Dubuque turned a verdict of innocent in the case of Jack Rosenthal, manager of the Majestic Theater. Many cases appeared to have been dropped.

Havner had been pulling in his horns meanwhile as well. He decided newspapers could be produced, sold, and delivered on Sunday. He had these kind words to say about papers in those pre-radio, pre-TV days: "The only method the average citizen has of acquiring the information as to what is transpiring in the country is through the medium of the daily newspaper. The great mass of people inform themselves largely through the reading of the daily newspaper. To deprive them of this right would be to deprive them of one of the necessities which enables them to acquire the information concerning the happenings and doings of the world generally."

As a gesture to church people, Havner pointed out that the editors of the time devoted part of the Sunday papers to "religious teaching." He concluded by saying the newspaper was the "poor man's library."

The attorney general further diluted the enforcement effort by ruling the blue laws didn't apply to garages, churches, railroads, streetcars, filling stations, and Jewish merchants.

Church spokesmen responded differently to the campaign. Said the Reverend H. K. Hawley of the Congregational Church in Ames: "The Sabbath was made for man, and man should have the right to do things he desires to do." Hawley approved taking pleasure rides in cars on Sunday "if they are made so as not to tire those taking them." He also approved a good Sunday dinner "and after the Sunday paper has been read to learn all the current news, a person should not fail to read a portion of a good book or a piece of literature."

The reaction of the Reverend Howland Hanson of the First Baptist church in Des Moines was more stern.

"We can not align ourselves with Sabbath desecration," Mr. Hanson said. He called Sunday a possession of the people and a "public domain" that was being exploited "for both private and syndicate gain."

"The syndicated motion picture industry sells its not too moral products on that day of public domain," he said. "The commercialized theater usurps the people's day for private gain. Our Sabbath is our oldest and holiest memorial. It precedes in point of origin home, school, church, flag, and government."

What brought Havner's campaign to a screeching halt was the attitude of Iowa's county attorneys, as expressed at their 1917 conference. The attorney general appeared at the conference in Council Bluffs and was "effectively heckled."

The attorney general announced no further attempts would be made to enforce the blue laws. They went to sleep again except in a few places and were finally repealed without ceremony by the legislature decades later.

Battle Over One Cent

Should the fare on Des Moines streetcars be boosted from five cents to six cents? That measly proposed increase provoked bitter debate in 1919.

The conflict stemmed from a demand by the carmen's union for a wage hike from a top of forty-seven cents an hour to sixty cents an hour. The streetcar company was bankrupt and couldn't pay it.

A fare of one cent more would have financed a wage boost to fifty-seven cents an hour. But Des Moines voters rejected the proposal by a margin of nearly three to two.

"The people of Des Moines are not now paying for the service they are getting," declared U. S. District Judge Martin Wade of Iowa City. "The truth must be brought home to them."

The case had come before Judge Wade because company affairs were tied up in federal bankruptcy court. The judge ordered cuts in service to save operating costs on the car lines. The service that survived would be regarded as super-excellent today.

On the Ingersoll line, for example, the old schedule called for a streetcar every five minutes in peak hours. Under the new reduced schedule, there was a car every six minutes. That doesn't sound like much saving but it meant a reduction of from twelve cars to ten cars per hour at peak times.

On the Walker line, the peak frequency was cut from a car every six-and-a-half minutes to one every seven minutes, on the Fairgrounds line from four to four-and-a-half minutes, on the East Fourteenth line from eleven to fifteen minutes.

University to Thirty-fifth Street had the best peak period service, a car every three minutes. The new schedule left that three-minute service intact but did reduce off-hours from a car every nine minutes to one every ten minutes.

A summer streetcar in downtown Des Moines
(Paul Ashby Collection, Iowa State Historical Department)

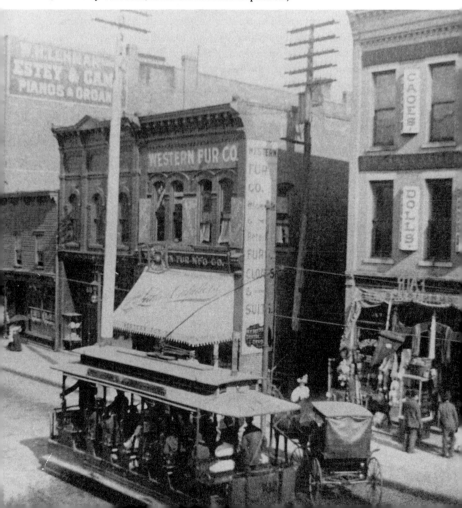

That didn't mean schedules were always followed to the letter. Delays due to bad weather, breakdowns, and other reasons often irritated riders.

City transit problems today are similar to some extent today to those of 1919. For one thing, the streetcar system was broke in 1919; the metro bus system isn't much better off now. Biggest difficulty has been the steady fall in the number of passengers over the generations. Badly needed federal subsidies also have been reduced. It has been suggested the metro might have to go out of business. But nobody expects that to happen.

The principal culprit in the long transit decline is the automobile. People didn't own their own cars to any great extent in the old days. There were only about 350,000 motor vehicles, including trucks, in the entire state of Iowa in 1919, compared with well over 3 million now. Of that 3 million plus, Polk County alone has more than 350,000 vehicles, higher than the number for the whole state seventy years ago.

Thus in the old days you usually couldn't just jump into your car if you wanted to go anywhere in the city or suburbs. You most likely used the streetcar to go to work, or downtown to the doctor, the dentist, to the movies or to shop (there were no big edge-of-town shopping centers), and to visit relatives and friends. Streetcar ridership was enormous compared with the bus patronage of the 1980s.

The revenue picture was different as well. The 1919 fare was 5 cents, against 60 cents now. Wages of car operators were 47 cents an hour early in 1919, compared with $13.97 in the late 1980s, including fringe benefits.

In the 1919 confrontation, the attorney for the receiver argued for holding the top wage to 55 cents an hour. He said that would mean annual pay of $1,500, "as high as the yearly earnings of other laboring men." The union agent replied: "Before the men will work for one cent less than 60 cents an hour, we will tie up the streetcar system for twenty years."

The union went on strike in August and stayed off the job for a week. The men returned to work after the city council agreed to call a special election on the proposed one-cent fare boost. The union and many civic leaders were confident the increase would be approved. It lost, 2,563 yes; 3,720 no.

In the end the union did get the 57 cents.

Judge Wade also arranged for some higher revenues by ordering the fare increased to ten cents for passengers bound to and from Urbandale, Fort Des Moines, and Valley Junction (now West Des Moines). He said the higher cost of serving those suburbs justified the boost.

The order also provided that suburban children under twelve

could ride for 2 1/2 cents, or 5 cents round trip. What the in-city fare was for children is not known.

Des Moines was a city of 125,000 in 1919, considerably under the 1990 population of about 192,000. Even so, the 1919 network of streetcar lines was greater than the bus routes of the 1980s. Here is the list of the 1919 lines affected by the service cuts:

Valley Junction, Ingersoll, Waveland Park, University and Thirty-fifth, Urbandale, Center and Twenty-ninth, West Ninth, Sixth Avenue, East Sixth and Ninth, East Fourteenth, Walker, Douglas Avenue, Fairgrounds, Scott, Sevastopol, and Fort Des Moines.

The Long, Long Trail

The cartoonist studied the finished drawing and frowned. Not good enough, he said to himself as he tossed the sketch on the floor.

It was growing late. Outside the darkness deepened in the wintry evening. A man appeared in the studio door. "We've got to have your cartoon, Jay," he said. "We're right on the deadline."

Jay (Ding) Darling frowned again, leaned over and retrieved the discarded drawing. "Use this one in the first edition," he said. "I'll have another ready later."

It was January 6, 1919. Theodore Roosevelt, onetime great president of the United States, had died that day. Darling had been trying for hours to come up with a cartoon for the front page of next morning's *Des Moines Register,* one that would be a fitting farewell to Roosevelt. The drawing that had been tossed away was headed "The Long, Long Trail." It pictured a shadowy Roosevelt on horseback, waving his campaign hat as he joined the long procession of departed American pioneers winding their way into the distant past in covered wagons.

Register editors weren't enthusiastic about the cartoon but they ran it in all editions because Ding wasn't able to come up with a better one. Never were editors, and Ding himself, more wrong in an evaluation.

Darling's final tribute to Roosevelt, which appeared in more than 100 newspapers nationwide, was received with a feeling of reverence by millions of Americans. "The Long, Long Trail" was used as an illustration in succeeding years in and on an estimated 25 million books and calendars and in deluxe reprints. Every member of the Roosevelt family, into at least the fourth generation, displayed the drawing in their homes and offices.

The Long, Long Trail
(Ding Darling/courtesy Meredith Publishing Company)

For forty-three years Ding's cartoons filled a space all his own in the middle of the front page of *The Register*. (He got his nickname by signing his drawing "D'ing," an abbreviation of "Darling.") He drew more than sixteen thousand cartoons. For twenty-two years his cartoons were syndicated in as many as 120 other daily newspapers.

He could draw what he wanted to on any topic, important or

trivial. Nobody tried to tell him what to do. All that publisher Gardner Cowles asked was that he be honest with himself.

Sometimes his drawings took a position directly opposite to that of *Register* editorials. One day in 1916, for example, his front page cartoon advocated preparedness for war, while an editorial inside expressed the contrary view.

"I do not consult my editorial chief and I never have," he once said. "My convictions may not be worth much to the world, but they are my own, and if I'm going through life expressing anybody's convictions, they are going to be my own."

He twice won Pulitzer prizes, in 1924 and 1943. The 1924 winner showed how an orphan at ten grew up to be president of the United States (Herbert Hoover), how a printer's apprentice became president in later life (Warren Harding), and how a plasterer's son became a great neurologist. "But they didn't get there hanging around the corner drug store," said the caption. Ding never intended to identify the neurologist.

The 1943 Pulitzer was awarded for a cartoon picturing Washington, D.C. buried under piles of government reports and bulletins. The caption said: "What a place for a waste paper salvage campaign."

Strangely, Ding expressed irritation over the fact that he was awarded that Pulitzer prize. "He pointed out several things he thought were wrong in that cartoon," said an associate. "He declared the idea was not plain, the cartoon was not well drawn, and that the idea constituted criticism of the government in wartime, which was something he did not like to do."

Ding told a friend years afterwards: "I think those dimwits [the Pulitzer committee] must have spread out a lot of cartoons and then decided the winner by saying: 'Eeny, meeny, miney, mo.'"

The prize-winning cartoonist got started in his career by accident, and as a result of violence. He was working as a young reporter on the *Sioux City Journal.* The year was 1900 and he was only twenty-four.

"I was reporting a case being tried in district court," he said. "One of the lawyers was a bearish old chap, quick-tempered and important. During the trial he lost his temper and beat his opposing brother with a cane. . . . They were separated, and I hurried back and wrote a big sensational story about it." The *Journal* editors ordered Darling to return to get a photograph of the combative attorney whose name was Treadway.

"I found him still in the courtroom and secretly pointed the camera at him," Ding recalled. "That is, I thought I was doing it secretly, but he caught sight of me."

Treadway let out a "war whoop" and sprang at Ding, who fled with the attorney in hot pursuit. Ding "sailed down the stairs in one leap." Treadway struck at Ding with his cane which didn't land but "breezed" across his neck. Once in the street Ding easily escaped because "my legs were young and his old." But his dignity was "terribly ruffled."

Crestfallen, he told his editor: "I haven't got a picture but I've got a sort of sketch I made of the old fellow the other day, in my desk drawer." The editor chuckled when he saw the Treadway drawing. He liked it enough that it appeared on the *Journal*'s front page.

"That's how I became a cartoonist," Ding said. "They paid me more for making a sketch every day than for running around on my feet all day reporting."

In 1906, when Ding and his bride, the former Genevieve Pendleton, were on their honeymoon in the West Indies, he received a telegram offering him a job as staff cartoonist for *The Register*. He immediately accepted.

But he soon learned that cartooning could have its drawbacks. His very first cartoon for the Des Moines paper got him into a peck of trouble. It involved the heavy pall of smoke over Des Moines in winter. (It's called air pollution today.)

Ding had been told the name "Des Moines" stemmed from the French word for "monk." He drew a picture of a fat monk, labelled Des Moines, smoking a pipe which was billowing out clouds of smoke. On the pipe bowl were the words "soft coal." Iowa Catholics were angered. They said the cartoon was neither sympathetic nor dignified. The reaction dismayed Darling. "I learned not to use the garb of a priest or monk in cartoons, although I meant no reflection on the church or the dignity of the cloth," he said afterwards. "I never transgressed again."

Hard feelings about the cartoon quickly evaporated and Darling became popular around Des Moines.

Five years later, in 1911, Ding quit *The Register*. No one remembered exactly why. Some said he got into a row with editor Harvey Ingham.

Ding went to work for the old *New York Globe* and other papers in a syndicate. His cartoons began appearing in the *Des Moines Capital,* the *Tribune*'s competition—which made *Register* and *Tribune* brass most unhappy. (The *Tribune* was an afternoon paper and sister of *The Register*.)

Less than two years later, Ding returned to *The Register*. He said he wasn't able to maintain contact with the people of America and with nature while in New York. He wanted complete independence in his work and found that he "could not be that kind of a cartoonist" there. For one thing, New York editors wanted him to draw comic strips, which he refused to do.

At least one good thing came from his experience at the *Globe*. Ding always had been most generous in helping budding sketchers. While in New York he met a young cartoonist name Robert Ripley, and helped him get a job on the *Globe*. Ding believed in Ripley's possibilities so much that he offered to pay his salary for the first six months, if necessary. It wasn't. Ripley went on to attain world fame with his "Believe It or Not" cartoons.

But just a year after Ding returned to Des Moines, he began to think he might have to give up cartooning altogether. He slowly began to lose the use of his right hand and arm. At the time he didn't know why. Drawing became increasingly difficult each day.

As the condition worsened (from 1914 to 1916), he resorted to holding the pencil or pen in his nearly limp right fingers and pushing the disabled hand across the drawing board with his left hand. But that was too slow, so he practiced drawing with his left hand, hour after hour, day after day, week after week. In six months he was producing "just as clever work with his left hand as he used to do with his right." The right arm continued to deteriorate, however, and doctors said surgery was the only answer.

New York doctors found that an injury he had suffered more than thirty years earlier was causing the problem. As a boy he had broken his elbow while hunting.

The doctors moved an affected nerve from one side of the arm to the other, and the trouble disappeared. He resumed drawing with his right hand and gained the reputation of being a "double-barreled cartoonist" because of his ambidexterity.

Ding celebrated his recovery by going on another hunting trip. It was a memorable day, October 16, 1916, because it was his fortieth birthday and because the *New York Herald Tribune* offered to syndicate his cartoons. *The Register* consented to the arrangement because the newspaper had no syndicate of its own at the time.

The syndicate contract helped make Ding wealthy. The *Saturday Evening Post* said his incisive brain and eloquent pen earned him $1 million long before he reached the peak of his career. At that peak about 130 papers used his cartoons regularly. He also drew cartoons for *Collier's* weekly magazine for five years.

Even though Ding was widely known and well-liked, he could be a rash individual at times. He sometimes took drastic action if he believed he was on the right side of a controversial situation, and the devil take the hindmost.

He got out of line in the late 1920s over a news story about two little girls who mysteriously disappeared one Saturday morning from the Darling neighborhood in Des Moines. The children hadn't been found by Saturday night. The parents were frantic. Search parties combed the area. The suspense grew.

Sunday morning in Stuart, Iowa, about fifty miles west of Des Moines, a man heard little voices calling from a locked railroad car. The missing children were inside, unharmed. They had climbed into the car, on a siding not far from home. A rail yard worker locked the car, then an engine hooked on and pulled the car to Stuart.

The Sunday Register carried a big story on the missing youngsters, and the editors planned to use pictures of the children in the Monday paper. Ding strongly opposed the pictures, because the parents were his friends.

Nevertheless the engravings were made and put into a page. Just as the paper was ready to go to press, Darling appeared in the composing room and slashed the engravings with a cutting tool. The page had to be made over, the paper was late, and the pictures were not printed.

Such an action would cause all kinds of turmoil in a newspaper office today. Some editors probably would have fired Ding on the spot. But that rashness of personality—individuality if you prefer—was one of the characteristics that made him a good cartoonist, gained him national recognition, and allowed him to keep company with great men of the day, even presidents such as Herbert Hoover.

One day in 1929, Ding received a phone call from Hoover. "Can you come to Washington on a weekend visit?" the President asked. "What was the reason for the invitation," Ding asked. "Did the president want anything special?" "No, I haven't anything particular in mind," Hoover said. "I'd like to know what you're thinking about."

Darling's visit to the White House was the first of several while Hoover was president. "I got the impression," Ding said, "that the invitations came when he got fed up with the yes men around him and wanted a conversation with a free-wheeler from the uninhibited Midwest."

On many occasions Darling played early morning volleyball at the White House, breakfasted with staff members, and occasionally went fishing and horseback riding with the president. Ding was unhappy when Hoover was defeated for re-election in the depth of the Depression in 1932.

"The country crucified Hoover for calamitous circumstances which were not of his making," the cartoonist said. In all the years of their friendship, Ding said, he never heard Hoover express "an ecstatic whoop in victory or a whimper in defeat. . . . I never knew a man so completely void of bombast. . . . [He] was the greatest man I've ever known."

Hoover's successor, Franklin D. Roosevelt, was the subject of a Ding cartoon that *Register* editors refused to print. They turned it down when publisher Gardner Cowles said it was in poor taste. It showed the stealing of a neighbor's privy, which was a common trick for kids to pull on Halloween in early days. "The kids" in the cartoon were Franklin Roosevelt and his lieutenants. The outhouse they were lugging away was labelled "private rights." Peering from the outhouse door was a scared little "ordinary citizen," being taken for a ride. Although the cartoon was used afterwards by the paper, in reprints, Cowles said at the time *The Register* was a family newspaper and should not be portraying outhouses. It was said the privy drawing was the only cartoon in Ding's career that his home newspaper did not use at the time it was drawn. Papers all over the country printed the sketch and got an amused reaction from their readers.

Halloween
(Ding Darling/courtesy Meredith Publishing Company)

All his cartooning life, Ding went after one of mankind's greatest enemies—pollution. He fought a never-ending battle against man befouling the earth. How he would have loved the outcry in recent decades against pollution! Without question his hard-hitting attacks in the first half of the twentieth century helped lay the groundwork for recent public insistence that the environment be restored and preserved.

He said in 1935 that conservation was like "the bow-legged girl of the village. Everybody sympathizes but nobody asks her to the picnic." He added: "When I first saw the state of Iowa [in 1885] it was like a paradise. My father was bringing us from Indiana to settle in Sioux City. Wide prairies, blue from flowers. Even the wild turkeys had not disappeared. Prairie chickens were as thick as English sparrows and black birds. Ducks came down from the north and returned from the south in myriads, and the streams were full of fish. The silt-laden rivers we see running down to the sea may look like nothing but muddy water to you, but they are beefsteak and potatoes, roast ducks, ham and eggs, and bread and butter with jam on it. For there, with the aid of improvident agricultural practices, goes the rich topsoil from American farms at the rate of 25 million acres a year. Some groceries."

Another of his more famous battles, which he eventually won, was "saving the ducks" which came close to disappearing in the 1930s. Ding placed much of the blame on the hunters themselves. "Game wardens have been driven to despair by willful disregard of game bag limits," he said. "Hunters who stop shooting when they have killed their limit are openly rated as poor boobs. . . . They shot before sunrise; they shot after dark and picked up only a portion of their kill. They shot before the season was open and after it was closed. If the bag limit was 15, they killed 15 for each member of the family, including the dog."

More important than the greediness of some hunters, he said, was the "rapid encroachment of agricultural activities on the natural breeding and feeding grounds of our wild game." Marshes and lakes were drained "to make way for the plow," he said. "[There] is no place where a wild thing may lay her eggs and raise her brood in peace."

Then in 1934 and 1936, great droughts struck. Crop yields dropped to disaster levels in Iowa and elsewhere, and the waterfowl population almost disappeared. Annihilation of some species was forecast as prairie potholes and marshes dried up completely in numerous areas, and other water levels sank to record lows. Devastating dust storms hit the Midwest.

The federal government acted, not only with a program of drought relief but also to help conserve wild game. Henry A. Wallace of Des Moines was secretary of agriculture. He appointed Ding to head the U. S. Biological Survey early in 1934.

Darling gave up a reported annual income of one hundred thousand dollars as a cartoonist to take the federal job which paid only eight thousand dollars a year. President Roosevelt approved the appointment even though Ding, a strong Republican, had opposed him in the 1932 election.

One of Darling's first steps was to order a survey of the waterfowl situation. The results showed that less than 3 percent of the normal number of ducks had nested in the northern United States.

Using his slam-bang approach, Ding succeeded in wangling some $17 million (a pile of money in those days) for the cause during his twenty hectic months in Washington. As a consequence, federal game refuges were increased from 33 to 220 in number, and their total area from seven hundred thousand acres to 5.7 million acres.

Ding and other conservationists also worked long and hard for the creation of the first "duck stamp," which originally cost waterfowl hunters one dollar. Income from the sale of stamps was (and is) used for waterfowl protection and development. Ding drew the design for the first stamp in 1934.

The red tape and overlapping federal department functions finally proved too much for Darling's impatient spirit. He resigned late in 1935, somewhat in disgust, and returned to his drawing board in Des Moines. In his final years, he looked upon his role in aiding the waterfowl comeback as perhaps his greatest conservation achievement.

Henry Wallace praised his work but said he was a better cartoonist than economist. Ding replied that things would have been better in the capital if officials such as Wallace had taken the time to read the reports of their underlings. Nevertheless, Republican Darling and Democrat Wallace remained longtime friends.

After resigning from the federal job, Darling had a close brush with death. He became ill of peritonitis, a serious and frequently fatal inflammation in the abdominal area. For a month he lay near death in Mercy Hospital in Des Moines. His condition grew so critical that *The Register* collected statements from top men all over the country mourning his "passing."

But Ding suddenly began to improve, and before long he was on the road to full recovery. He sat in the hospital in a wheelchair and read, with warm appreciation and some amusement, the kind comments that were to have been included in his obituary. In a short while he was again in top form at the drawing board.

"The first thing I observed about Ding was how hard he worked," said Kenneth MacDonald, retired editor of *The Register* and *Tribune.* "Everyone knows he had great talent—talent which few men are privileged to have. Yet the more I came to know him, the more I realized that his working habits, his great concentration, the exacting standards he set for himself were probably more responsible for his success. . . . His talent was great, but in my judgment, his industry was greater."

Ding didn't think of himself as a gifted artist. Far from it. He once confessed that his reflections did not automatically produce good results. The ideas, he said, sometimes were "pretty thin broth."

He doubted, too, if cartoons had any lasting value. Yesterday's cartoons, he said, are as obsolete as "cold potatoes." After his retirement he expressed doubt that he had accomplished very much. "I don't remember any political campaigns that have either been won or lost because of cartoons or cartoonists," he wrote. "I know of no general who won a war, no heathen who became a Christian and no candidate whose successes or failures were seriously altered by the use of cartoons. I don't think they ever moved mountains or changed the course of history. . . . Even rabble-rousers among the cartoonists have never achieved great victories." Later he said somberly: "Looking back, I blush when I think of the times I put my foot on the wrong pedal."

He concluded pessimistically: "Maybe cartoons don't do much good after all." He was wrong. Many of his oldest cartoons are still highly interesting and relevant today, a lifetime or more after they first appeared.

He did his final work, a book called "Ding's Half Century," with his friend John Henry, who at the time was director of public affairs for *The Register* and *Tribune*. In the book are 149 cartoons published during Ding's forty-nine years as a newspaper cartoonist. Ding and Henry arranged late in 1961 to spend from ten o'clock each morning until noon five days a week on the volume. They had completed somewhat more than half the book early in January of 1962 when Darling said: "John, I'm tired as all hell. You can finish the job. I'm going home."

He went home and never returned to the office. He was depressed and ailing and he took his own life. Here's what happened:

Ding and Matthew Johnson, his chauffeur, drove out to the Darling peony farm west of Des Moines. Ding sent Johnson into the building on some pretext. When Matthew returned, he found the cartoonist had shot himself. The shocked Johnson drove Darling to the hospital where he died February 12, 1962, at eighty-five years of age. At his request, there was no funeral service in Des Moines and only a graveside service in Sioux City where he was buried.

Ding had been seriously ill three years before and had drawn a final cartoon to be printed when death came. He recovered , however, and the cartoon was placed in the files. On the morning of February 13, 1962, that last Ding cartoon appeared on the front page of *The Register*. It was headed: "Bye now—it's been wonderful knowing you."

The warmly personal sketch pictured his cluttered studio with his drawing board, his empty chair, and duck decoys and fishing rods behind the sofa. Disappearing out the door and waving his hat in farewell was a shadowy figure of Ding.

'BYE NOW — IT'S BEEN WONDERFUL KNOWING YOU.

(Ding Darling/courtesy Meredith Publishing Company)

Back Before the
Second World War

Moral Twilight

A substantial part of the population of Des Moines found itself caught up with bootleg liquor during Prohibition. That was the era from 1920 to 1933 when it was against federal law to possess or sell liquor. As a result, it was "smart" to drink. A lot of people did it even when it was bad stuff, sometimes produced under filthy conditions. Des Moines *Register* columnist Harlan Miller called it "a social and moral twilight." He told in a 1941 column how Iowans remembered that period, and it was obvious he was remembering in large part his own participation in what went on, both as a reporter and a columnist.

"People in their thirties and forties and fifties remember it with a grimace," he wrote. "The lists of bootleggers' phone numbers; the frantic telephoning just before a party, or on toward midnight when the supply was low; the corruption and the raids.

"They remember the false fashionableness of drinking during the 1920s, which seduced so many reluctant but convivial souls into swallowing the stuff; the plague of female drinking which spread across the land for the first time; the horrible concoctions which had to be swallowed for fear of offending a host."

Miller remembered "the trips into shady slums and down dark alleys in pursuit of the indispensable swill; the guests arriving, each flaunting proudly his bottle of dubious liquid fire; the flasks uncomfortable on the hip; the bulges in overcoat pockets."

Harlan asked: "Or have they forgotten the wheedling of prescriptions from druggists and doctors?" (That was one often used way to get liquor, by pretending illness and a need of, say, a bottle of whisky for 'medicinal' purposes.) "The treasure hunts for 'pure grain alcohol'; the purchase of 'gin drops' or 'bourbon drops' at the neighborhood pharmacy at 6:30 when the guests were arriving at 7."

Knowing that bootleg wares were sometimes made under unsanitary conditions, "some arrogant gentry had their stuff 'analyzed'" and other "fastidious amateurs" used only distilled water in making their own concoctions. And did they remember "the sinister bootlegger who arrived at the back door with a fresh made batch just as the guests knocked at the front door?"

Harlan went on to recall evenings "when everyone brought a bottle though he only wanted a sip, and had to keep at it till all the bottles were empty; the dinners that never were eaten; the glycerine added to make bathtub gin smoother, the murderous headaches.

"Or have they forgotten the hooch barons and the shootings, the gun fight in our own quiet town, and on a peaceful corner of Thirty-first and Ingersoll; the imported Scotch brought by plane from Canada; the 20 percent spiked beer and the Prohibition era divorces?"

The columnist wrote they also "remember the court dockets with bootlegger cases; the corrupt political machines built up with bootleg payments; the bootleg magnates with their catalogues of imported liquors; the $120-case Scotch with the rusty taste."

Numerous Iowans made, or tried to make their own liquor, sometimes with unexpected results: "They remember the home brew exploding in their cellars, and the agents who sold barrels of grape mash, guaranteed to turn into sherry or malaga wine; the bay rum raids on the dime stores" (bay rum often was consumed by down-and-outers) "and the human derelicts drinking canned heat under the bridges and the viaduct.

"Or have they forgotten the smuggling by tourists across the Canadian and Mexican borders, the shooting of innocent people on the highways, the guest cards for speakeasies, the invasion of speakeasies by the ladies, the roadhouses where their daughters rubbed elbows with the underworld?"

Miller concluded with these recollections: "They remember the bellhops who'd bring you a bottle for ten dollars; the white collar bootleggers who'd call at their offices for orders; the high school boys who got the foolish notion that it was smart to drink; the score of acquaintances whose careers were wrecked by the upsurge of Prohibition drinking."

Harlan Miller (*Des Moines Register*)

The Curse of Drugs

At the end of an hour, the young woman opened her eyes lethargically and commenced cursing herself in choice adjectives," the reporter wrote. "She had an abscess on her right leg caused by jabbing the needle through her stocking while in a nervous hurry for an injection. The abscess troubled her and she talked vaguely of going to a doctor but her companion said indifferently: 'Forget it. I've got abscesses all over and it ain't killed me.'"

The reporter was John Spivak of *The Des Moines Register*. The scene was a littered room in a dirty ramshackle tenement in the area of East Fourth and Locust streets in east Des Moines, a few blocks from the golden-domed statehouse.

In the room were two prostitute drug addicts. One was the young woman with the leg sore. She was stretched out on a bed with a cover that once was white. Nearby on a rocking chair sat the other woman, about thirty-five. Each had just taken a shot and was drowsy under the influence of morphine.

This all-too-common sight took place not in the 1980s but in the Des Moines of 1924. The drug problem didn't suddenly burst upon Iowa in the late years of the century as many may suppose. There were an estimated fifteen thousand addicts in the state in 1924. Cocaine and heroin were smuggled in from Germany via Mexico, and illegal morphine as well.

Des Moines was the hub of a dope ring "firmly entrenched in the state, with a network of distributors extending into every important city and sometimes reaching even into small villages and farms." Wholesale distributors forwarded the narcotics from Des Moines "to Davenport, Sioux City, Iowa City, Mason City, etc."

Drug agents battled the flow, just as was the case more than half a century later. They had all kinds of trouble catching up with the masterminds, just as later. The illegal profits were great, just as later. Drugs were described as "one of the great causes of crime," just as later.

It did appear, however, that drugs were more pervasive and the situation was worse in the later years than in the 1920s. Estimates placed the number of addicts in Iowa at fifty thousand in 1986. An added modern hazard was the misuse of drugs supposedly available only for medical reasons, such as tranquilizers and pain killers.

Spivak's 1924 reports in *The Register* said the drug "evil" was a "constant and serious menace to the peace of the various communities harboring the addicts," language that was applicable to the 1980s as well.

One major difference between the two periods: The problem was far more widespread in the later years. In the 1920s the addicts were likely to be concentrated in certain areas, such as sleazy tenements and cheap lodging houses.

One such section was the Des Moines neighborhood around East Fourth and Locust extending two blocks east and one south. Another was First and Locust on the west side and extending two blocks west and one south. A third radiated two blocks in every direction from Tenth and Center streets, where Des Moines blacks formerly concentrated. A fourth active area was the alleys and buildings of "White Chapel," the notorious "red light" district centered at Fourth and Elm streets south of the loop. The buildings and other vestiges of such areas disappeared long since.

Sioux City was the second largest drug center in Iowa, with the traffic described as "largely across the Illinois Central tracks." In Mason City, activity was "especially great in the Mexican quarter." In Davenport the districts were scattered, "but the boldest traffic" was in the "poorer quarters along the river." The business there was "so open that a taxi driver in Davenport can take one to hangouts across the river where dope can be bought," presumably in Rock Island or Moline.

Spivak's 1924 articles were checked for errors by federal officials before publication.

The reports show that the dollar had decidedly different value in those "good old days." Spivak pointed out that the first federal anti-drug law was passed in 1914, or only ten years before. Prior to that narcotics "could be purchased for nominal sums."

"But since the vigorous efforts to stamp out the traffic," he wrote, "drugs have jumped to very high prices. It costs a confirmed addict $5 to $20 a day for the dope he needs." A far cry from the $300 a day the cocaine addict needed in Iowa in the 1980s, and a reflection of the tremendous inflation that has taken place since.

The reporter also described the big markups in drugs as they came to the Iowa addict. In Mexico a one-ounce bottle of cocaine could be bought for "$5 or $6." The value rose to $15 after it was smuggled to the American side of the border. The wholesale dealer in Kansas City, a major center in the trade then, paid $35 to $40 for an ounce. He in turn charged the Iowa peddler $100.

The peddler thereupon sold the cocaine to his addict customers for about $1 per grain. Since there are 437 grains in one ounce, that meant the retail value of an ounce was roughly $450, compared to approximately $2,200 in the mid-1980s.

Spivak observed that it was easier to make big money selling drugs than bootlegging liquor in that Prohibition era. "The possibility of detection is much less," he wrote, "for where a ten thousand dollar liquor shipment would need a large truck, the same value in dope could be transferred in a handbag. . . ."

The reporter was impressed by an "insurance ring" set up in the 1920s to protect the "actual leaders" from detection. Here's how it worked: When a peddler was picked up, the ring provided a lawyer.

"Who pays the lawyer no one knows," the reporter wrote, "and the lawyer can not be made to tell. Good legal counsel thus is supplied, provided the prisoner keeps his mouth shut. Should a conviction result, the prisoner's wants while he is in jail are mysteriously taken care of, and if he has a family, the family wants while he is serving time are also taken care of.

"But if he tells what he knows, he not only faces a prison sentence but loses the attorney and support for his family as well as running the risk of bodily injury or death upon his release from prison."

Spivak said this arrangement "effectively blocked" all efforts to get at the higher-ups. Spivak didn't know, but obviously suspected, that the insurance ring was financed by money set aside from drug profits.

The reporter wormed his way into the confidence of a thirty-six-year-old male addict on the Des Moines east side. "He was exceedingly thin, his cheeks were sunken and his eyes gleamed bright when he talked," Spivak wrote. "It took three hours of convivial fellowship and pool playing before he admitted that he used morphine. In the washroom of the pool hall where he played, he showed me six capsules which he said would do him for a day. In my presence he took a shot [of morphine into his arm]."

He was the individual who took Spivak to the two prostitutes in the tenement. The reporter talked with the women on how they got started on drugs. "The older woman responded with cold replies," he wrote, "but the younger recklessly and in a spirit of bravado told how she had deliberately taken dope after she started on the downgrade. Her whole attitude could be summed up in: 'What's the difference?' "

Spivak concluded one story in *The Register* series with this observation: ". . . the addict lives his precarious existence, a constant menace to orderly society once he has fallen into the depths. The body in time becomes ill and diseased, abscesses accumulate, and one day the desire for drugs is interred in some potter's field where a little cross marks the end of what might have been a useful life."

Thirty years earlier, in the mid-1890s, at least two opium dens operated wide open in Des Moines. A mysterious Chinese named Chung Ling had such a den at 104 East Walnut Street, across from the present federal court building. A *Register* reporter found seven men smoking the narcotic in the den. They paid ten cents for each small pellet. They smoked cigarettes when not smoking opium.

The newspaper carried the story under the head: "Fearful Depravity." Another den operated on Cherry Street west of Eighth on the west side.

An opium den in early Des Moines (Frank Miller/George Mills)

That story may have been instrumental in the 1896 legislature's vote to outlaw both opium dens and the sale of cigarettes statewide. The penalty for operating a den or getting caught in one was fixed at a fine of $500 or six months in jail or both.

The penalty for selling cigarettes, or cigarette papers, was a fine of $25 to $50 for a first offense, and for a second offense, $100 to $500 and/or six months in jail. The anti-cigarette law stayed on the books for twenty-five years, until repealed in 1921. Opium dens have been against the law ever since 1896. The most recent version of the law described them as "places resorted by persons using controlled substances."

Fiery Cross

The "fiery cross" Ku Klux Klan staged a major upset by grabbing control of the dominant Republican party in Des Moines and Polk County.

What's more, Des Moines elected a Klansman as city public safety commissioner and gave many thousands of votes to others on the Klan council ticket; a Klan candidate came close to taking the mayor's office; another Klan-backed hopeful ran a strong second in the Republican primary race for governor of Iowa. Those demonstrations of KKK strength were of brief duration in 1924 but shook Iowans nonetheless.

The "Invisible Empire" Klan was a white-supremacy organization geared to Protestantism in religion while vigorously waving the American flag. Ghostlike in their white hoods and masks, the Klansmen were anti-Catholic, anti-blacks, anti-Jewish, and anti-foreign born. They held secret initiation ceremonies in the woods in southwest Des Moines.

Especially disturbing was the Klan practice of building wooden Christian crosses ten to twelve feet high, dousing them with a flammable liquid and setting them on fire at certain places at night. The purpose was to strike fear in individuals whose ideas and actions the Klan didn't like. Sometimes the crosses were surreptitiously burned at the homes of such persons. Anyone who ever witnessed such a burning knows how upsetting such a sight can be. The Ku Klux organization exists in some areas to this day.

The first KKK terrorized recently emancipated blacks in the south after the Civil War. The second Klan developed in the aftermath of the 1914–1918 World War I when an era of bitter racial and religious controversy set in around the country. The Klan was the product of postwar unrest and a hangover of patriotic fervor and uncertain economic conditions. A sharp economic depression that lasted from 1920 to 1923 accentuated the national malaise.

The Iowa Klan pushed into politics in a big way in the February 1924 caucuses that started the process of naming the state's delegates to the big national conventions. Republican leaders were shocked when the caucuses in Des Moines and Polk County elected a clear majority of Klan delegates to the party's county convention. The Klan claimed fifty-six of the eighty-six Polk delegates were either KKK members or friendly to the organization. The claim was substantially accurate.

Presidential politics don't seem to have played much of a part in the 1924 caucuses, as was the case later in the twentieth century. The Klan's objective appears to have been only to gain power in the Republican organizations of Iowa and other states. Presidential candidates didn't fight it out in the caucuses. Iowa Republicans of all factions supported candidate Calvin Coolidge who was elected.

Klan muscle immediately became apparent when the Republican Polk County convention was called to order. The convention consisted of delegates elected in the caucuses. The custom was to allow the incumbent county chairman to select the convention chairman. Klan delegates forced the election of their own chairman with a loud chorus of votes. From then on it was all Klan.

The next display of power took place in the Des Moines city election March 31, 1924. Klansman John Jenney, a Highland Park grocer and former chief of police, easily won the safety commissioner post by rolling up 26,066 votes to 14,591 for his opponent Frank Harty. No other Klan-supported candidate won, although the vote for mayor was close. Mayor C. M. Garvey was re-elected over former Mayor H. H. Barton on a vote of 21,604 to 19,993. The total vote of more than 40,000 was a Des Moines city election record up to that time. Des Moines' population was 141,000, about 50,000 under the 1990 figure. The Klan tried hard to elect C. H. Kies as parks commissioner but he lost by a substantial margin to J. G. Rounds, 22,130 to 16,781.

Jenney, who liked to ride a white horse in parades, did benefit from a lot of non-Klan support. The anti-liquor forces were strong in Des Moines, and, to a considerable extent, they backed Jenney against Harty who was a liberal and regarded as a "wet."

The highly respected Reverend C. S. Medbury of the University Church of Christ said he supported Jenney "not because he is a Klansman but in spite of it." And many women voted for Jenney because he was dry.

What the Klan wanted to achieve most of all in 1924 was to elect W. J. Burbank of Waterloo governor of Iowa. He was the incumbent Republican state treasurer and a good candidate. But he was competing in a tough field. Other candidates for the Republican nomination included Lieutenant Governor John Hammill of Britt, State Auditor Glenn C. Haynes of Mason City, and Iowa House Speaker Joe H. Anderson of Thompson, plus two minor aspirants.

Burbank polled a respectable 88,304 votes in the June primary, not far behind the leader Hammill with 95,313. Anderson was third with about 75,000 and Haynes fourth with 65,000. Hammill got 27 percent of the vote and Burbank 25 percent.

Since no one polled the minimum 35 percent necessary for a primary nomination, the choice had to be made at the second 1924 state convention in July. That convention was made up of 1,784 delegates from the ninety-nine counties.

Burbank had finished first in a sizable share of the counties in the primary voting. He was tops in Polk County with 9,500 votes, to 5,200 for Hammill in second place. Burbank also led in his home county of Black Hawk and in Linn and Dubuque among the larger counties. The Klan got out a good vote.

Thus it was expected that Burbank would come to the state convention with a fair share of delegates. He didn't, and the regular Republicans were the reason. The regulars backing all the other candidates ganged up and wiped out Burbank in the second set of precinct caucuses and county conventions. The regulars made sure they weren't caught napping a second time.

Des Moines newspapers, all anti-Klan, sounded the alarm early. A *Register* headline said: "Fear Ku Klux Plot 'Packing' of Caucuses. Quietly Lay Plans to Put Burbank Over in Convention."

Polk was the scene of hot caucus battles with record turnouts running as high as 200 voters per precinct. This time the Klan didn't get the job done. Another *Register* headline said: "Polk Caucuses Jolt Hopes of KKK."

The Ku Klux Klan's fiery cross of fear and hate

The Klan did win a lot of delegates in such areas as Highland Park in Des Moines. But the Klan was able to muster only a strong minority in the county convention, and the Republican regulars were merciless. Said *The Register*:

"The regular Polk County Republican organization took every vestige of representation as well as its short-lived power away from the KKK-Burbank alliance. The Klan was well represented both in the delegate section and the lusty-lunged gallery but were without sufficient strength to get even a single motion adopted."

The Polk Republicans agreed to divide their convention delegates as follows: Hammill 35, Haynes 34, Anderson 15, and Burbank none.

A battle broke out as soon as the county convention was called to order. The first issue was who should preside. Anti-Klan George A. Wilson, later a notable governor of Iowa and U. S. senator, was the victor over John MacLennan on a vote of 256 1/2 to 121 1/2.

"From then on the convention was in the hands of the anti-Klansmen," said *The Register*. "Slates picked days before were mulled through. The Klan—defeated, ignored and humiliated by successive defeats—moved on to the central committee, only to again be refused as an integral part of the Polk County Republican organization."

Burbank did not give up hope. He went to the July 23 state convention claiming he still had 400 delegates. But he withdrew his candidacy before the balloting started. He knew the jig was up. Hammill won on the first ballot with 1,153 delegates to 339 for Haynes and 292 for Anderson. Hammill went on to win three terms as governor. The day of the Klan in Iowa politics was pretty much over, although the real decline over the nation didn't start until about 1926. Des Moines Safety Commissioner John Jenney was an exception. He was elected twice more to two-year terms before being defeated in 1930.

Just how many Iowans joined the KKK in the 1920s apparently never was made public. The number might have been as high as 100,000 an estimate based in part on the Klan's voting strength. Nationally the organization peaked at around 4 million, mostly in the South and Midwest.

Besides frequent cross burnings, the Klan maintained a certain visibility through infrequent parades. More than 500 Klansmen marched in full regalia through downtown Perry in June 1924.

There is little question but that the KKK used active terrorism in parts of the nation but there doesn't seem to have been much in the way of violence in Iowa. The battle raged in print, however. It was a type of civil rights conflict that went on for years.

Des Moines churches ended up on both sides of the struggle. The Reverend N. C. Carpenter of the Capitol Hill Church of Christ had been a Keagle (top official) of the Klan locally. A member said Carpenter "wanted everyone who belonged to the church to be a member of the Klan." A row broke out in the church and the pastor resigned.

On the other hand, the Reverend L. H. Griffith, pastor of the Douglas Avenue Church of Christ, resigned from the Klan and said: "I am a believer in the teachings of Jesus Christ. I have a neighbor who is a Jew and another who is a Catholic. I have come to the conclusion that one can not follow the teachings of Christ and be a member and part of an organization opposed to and prejudiced against these people, my neighbors."

The Iowa American Legion opposed the Klan, pointing out that men of every creed, color, and place of origin had been taken into the armed forces in World War I. The approving *Des Moines Tribune* said: "No veteran of the war can stand for the principle that his comrades are to be denied a full share of the government of the nation because of race or religion."

The Klan incident that caused the greatest tumult in Des Moines occurred in September 1924 when the Conference of Catholic Charities held its national convention in the old coliseum.

Late at night somebody placed a Catholic banner on the pole above the American flag on the coliseum roof. A Klan photographer took a flash powder picture of the flags, purportedly to show that Catholic Americans felt closer to the Vatican than their country. The whole thing was obviously a frame-up to embarrass the Charities convention.

In the uproar that followed, the *Des Moines News* carried an angry page one editorial that said in part:

"Honored guests have been insulted who were brought here by the convention bureau of the Chamber of Commerce. The Ku Klux Klan, shining in its true colors, with a callous disregard of the dignity of this great city and its residents, has, by a cheap, gaudy fraud, perpetrated a crime on the civic virtue of this community. The offense has been rendered more flagrant because it was aided and abetted by the police department."

Three Klan-affiliated policemen were fired for having allegedly been involved in the picture-taking incident.

Quality of Mercy

Harvey Ingham

Every morning they waited, eight or ten in a group, on busy Locust Street in downtown Des Moines. Mostly ragged and unkempt men, one a crippled girl selling pencils. Their eyes brightened as they saw him approaching. "Hello Uncle Harvey. How are you? Can you spare a little something for breakfast?"

He could. He gave each a dime or maybe a quarter. The crippled girl got a dollar. He turned none away. The amounts were small compared with the inflated money of the 1980s but were not so incidental in this time of the 1920s. A dime in those days was more like a dollar in modern purchasing power and a dollar more like ten dollars.

Harvey Ingham, editor of *The Des Moines Register* and *Tribune,* whom presidents consulted and the great of the nation sought out, generously handed out cash each morning to down-and-outers in the sidewalks of Des Moines.

His liberality wasn't limited to the street. That was just the tip of his generosity. Pleas came to him by the hundreds in the mail each year. He helped a great many, large and small, and perhaps all.

Lots of people donate money to worthy causes. But probably few could match the volume and diversity of Ingham's gifts. His total ran into many thousands of dollars a year, probably tens of thousands in terms of late twentieth-century buying power.

He contributed to untold numbers of institutions, universities, colleges (at least one overseas), children's homes, international organizations, the National Association for the Advancement of Colored People (NAACP), and institutions for the blacks in the South.

Most touching were the many letters he received in response to checks sent to individuals. A Swea City, Iowa, man wrote in 1933: "I wonder when you wrote that check if you knew how much it meant to us. It guaranteed a home on the place . . . where every tree and knoll is loved and where the very soil has a quality of friendliness that we can never feel in any other fields. . . . We appreciate your trust in us and when

154

the calves are ready to sell we will refund the money." Whether the money was ever repaid isn't known but beef calves didn't sell for much deep in the Depression in 1933.

In 1927 Helen Keller, the famous blind-and-deaf woman, wrote Ingham: "It made me very happy when you came to listen to my story and for two successive contributions to the fund for the ever-lasting strength of the blind. It makes me humble to find myself so tenderly enshrined in the hearts of my friends."

A onetime Des Moines newspaper woman up against it in New York pleaded for sixty-four dollars (twenty-nine dollars for her insurance and thirty-five dollars on a dental bill). She got the money. Whether it ever was paid back isn't known.

The crippled girl wrote in 1929: "You used to give me a dollar every time you saw me and it always was a big help to me." Now she asked for twenty dollars to buy materials for making novelties to sell at fairs. "I think I can make real good. You are the only one I can think of who might loan me the money." He undoubtedly did. Maybe he got it back, maybe he didn't.

Ingham was glad to contribute an undisclosed but probably sizable amount toward the living expenses of former congressman Robert Cousins in his final poverty-stricken days at Tipton, Iowa. Cousins was one of America's and Iowa's all-time greats as an orator. His "Remember the Maine" speech in Congress, after the U. S. Battleship Maine was blown up in Havana Harbor in 1898, is a national legend.

A Mesquakie Indian living in the Des Moines area needed $377 to meet the debt on his car in 1937, "Plus a little extra for buying coal and other things this winter." He probably got the money.

Harvey Ingham, a jovial, paunchy man with a booming voice, never mentioned his generosity. But a lot of written evidence of his compassion survives because he was a cluttered man.

He had no secretary and he didn't file much. He didn't throw away much either. When he died, armfuls of correspondence and other papers were gathered in boxes. That is where details of his generosity have come to light. Perhaps other boxes were destroyed. Ingham became editor of *The Register* in 1902 and died in retirement at ninety years of age in 1949.

Charity is not the basis of his fame. He was known for his leadership in human affairs and the part he played in the spectacular growth and acceptance of *The Des Moines Register* and *Tribune* in Iowa. The newspapers were among the first in his early years to move away from politically oriented news to providing the reader with unbiased reports on what was going on around the world. Equally important, his was a clear eye in interpreting the great flow of events in his editorials.

He was far ahead of most Iowans and Americans in saying that only through an effective world organization could bloody wars be prevented. Though a Republican in politics, he strongly supported Democratic President Woodrow Wilson in his advocacy of The League of Nations after World War I. Ingham was one person Wilson especially wanted to see when he came to Des Moines in 1919 promoting the League.

Harvey fought early and hard for world disarmament, for woman suffrage, for full rights for blacks and Indians, for expansion of education, increased world trade, and responsible capitalism.

Quiet philanthropy was an unplanned and unscheduled sideline. Nevertheless, there was a sweeping grandeur about it all. The disordered collection of letters provides a look into the heart of an individual deeply concerned with the problems of his fellowman.

Some of the financial help went to unusual high up places. In May of 1933, for example, President D. W. Morehouse of Drake University sent a thank-you note to Ingham for a check "applicable to my personal expenses." Drake was having a tough time of it in that Depression period and evidently couldn't pay Morehouse's incidental expenses. Morehouse explained: "It [the check] is most timely since I always defray my own expense accounts."

In 1934 Morehouse acknowledged a one thousand dollar gift to Drake by writing: "Mr. Ingham, you have been an inspiration to me," and that same year an unnamed sum of his money went to Palestine. Hadassah, a women's Zionist organization, expressed thanks for "your generous contribution to carry on health work in Palestine. All the health work is non-sectarian and all the people who live in Palestine are the beneficiaries."

Similarly, a 1935 letter of appreciation from Anatolia College in Salonika, Greece, said: "I trust you are happy in feeling that what you have done all along the years has been well placed."

President R. M. Hughes of Iowa State College (now Iowa State University) displayed emotion in this 1930 acknowledgment: "I want you to know that your support is very deeply appreciated and that, in my judgment, your benevolence is placed in a very active cause for God." And President H. M. Gage of Coe College in Cedar Rapids, Iowa, wrote in 1937: "Your $100 looks big and means much to me."

That same year Ingham got from B. Shimek, noted University of Iowa botanist, a thank-you "for your generous help toward completion of the work for the extension of Lakeside Laboratory grounds."

On a more modest level, a preacher at Steamboat Rock, Iowa, couldn't afford to renew his subscription to *The Register* during the Depression. Ingham paid that bill. The preacher wrote: "Your quick action was more like the handclasp of a brother."

Another pastor in financial trouble wrote: "Your check came almost as a special providence for we have been desperately hard up of late, especially with unlooked-for doctor bills to pay."

A 1932 letter from Plymouth Congregational Church in Des Moines said: "We think that the Inghams have a genius for doing kind and thoughtful things and certainly this is one of them."

Father E. J. Flanagan of Boys Town in Omaha wrote in 1935: "Our divine savior knows just what is in your heart when you sent me this donation to feed the hungry and homeless boys."

Ingham was a life member of and generous contributor to the Mooseheart School in Illinois where fourteen hundred children and mothers were being taken care of in 1927. A Mooseheart note said Ingham gifts "will reflect in better manhood and womanhood for the future and will live on long after we have passed on to other shores."

A 1937 Des Moines letter said: "I doubt if any of your services have called forth or deserved greater appreciation than your gift to the Junior League Convalescent Home."

A deeply moved writer in an unnamed town said: "I kept the check about a week thinking I could get along without it and I meant to return it to you because, Mr. Ingham, I can not expect you to help us like that. Mr. Ingham, I sat down and cried when I got your letter."

And a Des Moines mother wrote in 1936: "If you can help us out a little so I can buy my daughter a little something for Christmas, she needs and wants a dress and a pair of shoes so bad. . . . Please forgive me, Mr. Ingham, I am heartbroken that I have to do this." The chances are the child got what she wanted.

He also had his own unadvertised student aid program. A girl in College View, Nebraska, told how Harvey helped her and her brother through Union College there. She added: "I am sure you will never realize how much good the wonderful gift you gave us did do."

Another student wrote: "I shall return the amount you advanced me within a year. Whatever progress I make at the end of my university career, I shall owe to your kindness."

Nor were his gifts just onetime propositions, especially in the education field. He sent Tuskegee Institute for blacks a $50 check in 1930 and that was his fourteenth consecutive annual gift to that institution. In another year Tuskegee commended Ingham for having contributed to the "improved life of the masses of our people—and to fit these young people for larger usefulness to their fellowmen."

He mistakenly sent two checks for $100 each to the Fargo Agricultural School in Arkansas in 1935. The school pleaded to keep both because it "was having the hardest time with high water and planting our crops." The school asked that the second check be considered the 1936 contribution. Harvey agreed.

Not surprisingly, he was a regular contributor to such organizations as the World Court Fund and the League of Nations Association, evidently $50 a year to each. A 1929 letter from the association said: "It is heartening to have you at the strategic point you occupy in the middle west to hold up the banner of the league." But the League of Nations failed and was followed by the United Nations which came into being in the 1940s.

Ingham long was an angel of the National Association for the Advancement of Colored People (NAACP) in Iowa, both in money and in editorial support in *The Register*. He was praised in an NAACP testimonial dinner in 1927 "for the services he has rendered our colored citizens in the last quarter century."

But Harvey ultimately came up against one problem that his generosity couldn't handle. Word got around Des Moines' down-and-outers that it paid to be near the front door of *The Register* when he came to work each morning. The result was the size of the group began growing rapidly. He found it was getting beyond him and he had to call a halt.

But he didn't do it all without notice. On the last day he "settled" with everyone on hand, giving each an amount that was somewhat more than the daily stipends of the past.

Monkey Business

*R*egister reporter Ben Stong usually was in hot water with the editors. Maybe he was unlucky but more likely it was his fault, a missed assignment or whatever. He was a brother of Phil Stong, famed Iowa author and a onetime *Register* reporter himself. Both Ben and Phil were pretty good drinkers and that could have been the source of Ben's difficulties with the paper.

The editors decided on one occasion during State Fair in the 1920s that a story of the Fair as seen through the eyes of a ten-year-old boy would be a good feature for the paper. They sent Ben with a youngster to the Fair. Ben was to write the boy's reactions to the highlights.

Stong soon became bored. He gave the boy a couple of dollars, told him to see the sights by himself and then report back to Ben relaxing in the administration building.

Ben was taking it easy when there was an outcry. The kid had stuck a finger in a monkey cage. A monkey promptly bit said finger off. Ben was in big trouble and so was *The Register*. The paper's insurance company was said to have paid the lad's parents a sizable sum in settlement.

The insurance agent in the case was reported to have commented mournfully: "Why is it when a kid's finger is bitten off, he has to be a violinist headed for a great concert career?"

Ben was deep in the doghouse with the editors for something or other when a juicy triangle story broke. Involved were two guys in a struggle over a mysterious beautiful woman. One of the men suffered injuries. Those were the days when editors were hot for pictures of good-looking women in such situations. Unpopular Ben was told to go out and get a picture of the woman and don't come back if you can't find one.

Stong had no idea where to go. There was no identification and no address available. But he was resourceful. He was a Drake University alumnus and had worked on university publications when he was a student.

He went out to the files of the *Quax,* the university yearbook. He looked at photos of long years ago, picked out a picture of an attractive young woman and brought it into the office as that of the triangle girl. She wasn't, of course, but Stong didn't tell the editors that. They printed the picture as that of the woman involved.

That sounds like a recipe for major trouble, big-money lawsuits and all that. But nothing happened. No complaints were received. Some power sometimes takes care of individuals such as Ben. He survived the crisis without a blemish. Ultimately he moved to Denver where he became a major public relations specialist. His brother Phil was the author of the classic Iowa novel *State Fair*. The Stongs were natives of Keosauqua, Iowa.

Death of a University

A student riot was the beginning of the end for Des Moines University.

The university, which had a peak enrollment of two thousand students, never recovered from the causes and effects of a violent disturbance May 11,1929. The religiously oriented institution was located on a handsome campus at Second and Euclid avenues, since occupied by the Park Fair Shopping Center.

The blowup began the morning of that May 11 when all thirty-four members of the faculty were fired. They lost their jobs mainly because of differences in religious beliefs, or lack of them.

Hundreds of students marched on the administration building the same afternoon. Police warded them off but peace was short-lived. That night the students attacked the same building where the board of trustees was in session. The rioters smashed windows with rocks and splattered the place with rotten eggs. They ran through the building looking for the trustees who had locked themselves in a restroom under a staircase.

The students turned their anger on photographer John Robinson and reporter Roy Porter who were in the building covering the story for *The Register*. The newsmen found themselves fighting for their lives. Robinson suffered a broken and bloody nose.

"Porter and I hid under a desk in the office," Robinson said afterwards. "The students broke into the building. I got a picture of them coming in. Somebody hollered: 'Get that damned photographer!' and they really got me. Two guys held me from the back and the guys in front took potshots at me. The football coach came in and pulled the guys off my back. That stopped the whole thing. The students didn't want to be identified by the pictures. We both were splattered with eggs."

Porter took some punching too and an egg in the ear. He grabbed a phone during the melee and fed a dramatic account of what was going on to *The Register* city desk. One of the headlines the next morning said: "Reporter, Beaten in Riot, Tells Own Story of Fight."

Porter told how he stuck his head out from under the desk when "Sock! A decidedly putrid egg landed on my left ear. Somebody socked me. I hit somebody else. What happened from then on is a puzzle except that I saw Johnny with his back against a filing cabinet taking them as they came. A young fellow aimed one at my ear. I ducked and let him have it. Three more moved in. We all went down together between the desks."

The police came and the students fled the building. But those outside didn't let up. They continued chanting: "Get Shields! Get Rebman!" Dr. Thomas Shields was board chairman and Edith Rebman was his secretary. They and the other five trustees had to have a police escort to get out of the building.

Classes reopened the next week but only because of a court order. The school limped along for the final weeks of the semester. The trustees terminated the university forever in September.

Religion appears to have been one major cause of the dissolution. The school had been founded by Presbyterians in 1889 as Highland Park College. The Baptist Church bought it in 1918, combined it with their Des Moines College that had been located at Ninth and College streets and changed the name to Des Moines University. In 1927 a fundamentalist group called the Baptist Bible Union of North America

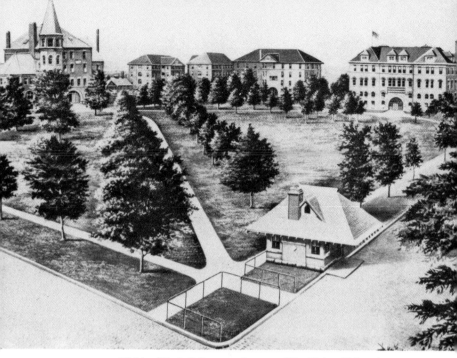

Highland Park College, predecessor of Des Moines University

took control. Shields was president of the Bible Union and became the strong man of the university.

In the succeeding months Shields let it be known that all faculty members would be required to agree to eighteen articles of religious faith. That angered a lot of professors and instructors. They said they'd quit first.

Dean Elbert Kagy of the pharmacy department was a Unitarian. He knew his attitude wouldn't pass with the Bible Union. He resigned along with J. Earle Galloway. Kagy and Galloway started the Des Moines College of Pharmacy downtown. They dealt a crippling blow to the university by taking all but two of its seventy-five pharmacy students.

The Bible Union saw to it that students got some moralistic heat too. The discipline committee summoned three women students who had taken part in a vaudeville skit in which one of them had turned a cartwheel. That was a most unladylike thing to do for the times.

The major issue centered around a charge of "moral turpitude" leveled against Shields and Rebman. They had occupied adjoining hotel rooms while in Waterloo. The trustees indignantly denied the charges. But the tension grew.

The last straw was Shields' action May 11 dismissing the whole faculty. Following the closing in September 1929 the university buildings stood idle and decaying for the next fourteen years.

In 1943 one Alfred Lawson of Detroit, Michigan, gave the campus a strange new lease on life. He bought the property for eighty thousand dollars and started "Des Moines University of Lawsonomy." He operated the institution under the name "Humanity Benefactor Foundation."

Lawson's place was weird and anything but a university. He had a fence built around it and welcomed no visitors and inquirers. He declared Lawsonomy was a substitute for all forms of education, was the "base of knowledge," and was concerned with "the knowledge of life and everything pertaining thereto." He kept himself virtually inaccessible.

The Internal Revenue Service made a big mistake on Lawson. Even though his institution was anything but a university, the IRS granted the place tax exemption as an educational institution. Not only that, Lawson was able to buy at less than five cents on the dollar a lot of World War II surplus equipment. He sold much of it to private buyers at a profit of more than $150,000.

Lawson admitted to federal authorities that all the living expenses of himself and family, including vacation costs, were paid by the institution. The IRS later canceled the tax exemption and forced payment of income taxes on the surplus sales.

Lawson's students apparently never numbered more than a few dozen at a time. They were not allowed to read any books except those written by Lawson. He once confiscated a basketball rulebook because he wasn't the author. He favored breeding a super-race of human beings by selecting superior partners for marriages. He changed the names of followers at his will.

Before coming to Des Moines, Lawson had attracted thousands of followers in Detroit during the Depression by demanding that all loans be made by the government at no interest. Another of his ideas that became popular with some people called for removal of "alien financiers who control the nation's wealth."

Some of Lawson's views were simple to understand. He opposed smoking, drinking, dancing, cosmetics, and eating meat. Another Lawson recommendation is guaranteed to make you shiver: "To keep the head, nose, ears, eyes, and throat free of decaying disorders," he said, "one should dip the head and neck into a tub of ice cold water upon rising in the morning and before going to bed at night. The ears should be allowed to fill up with water and the eyes should be kept moving about in the water."

He said the process of thinking involves the working of billions of mental organisms he called "menorgs." He claimed to have discovered the "law of maneuverability" which he said strengthened those who do right but punished wrongdoers.

He also claimed to have discovered a natural law that eliminated smoke from a coal-burning heating plant. He called the discovery a "smoke evaporator." Observers saw no smoke coming out of the university smokestack for two years. Workmen who removed the stack after he was gone found a 300-foot tunnel lined with concrete. The smoke purportedly had been released into the tunnel. Where it went from there nobody knows. Or maybe the place was heated in other ways.

Perhaps most important, Lawson was adept at talking people out of their money. One Ford factory worker in Detroit said his family had foolishly given Lawson some eight thousand dollars "and that's why we don't have a home of our own." Another woman told how she had given a good amount of insurance money to Alfred.

At the same time he always insisted he was penniless. He was fond of getting up at a local meeting and pulling his pants pockets inside out to demonstrate that he had nothing.

Lawson died November 29, 1954, in San Antonio, Texas. He was eighty-five years old. A month before he sold the campus to developer Frank A. DePuydt for $250,000. DePuydt and druggist Tom Couchman tore down the buildings and constructed a shopping center at a cost of $3.5 million.

Graduates of Highland Park College and Des Moines University included some big-name individuals, such as Conrad Nagel of Keokuk and Des Moines, one-time great Hollywood movie star; Ralph Budd of Waterloo, later president of the Burlington railroad; Carl Weeks of Des Moines, president of the once-famous Armand Cosmetics Company of Des Moines; E. T. Meredith, Sr., founder of *Better Homes and Gardens* and *Successful Farming* magazines and secretary of agriculture under President Woodrow Wilson, and Jack North, long-time sports editor of the old-time *Des Moines Tribune*.

A Fatal Step

Governor John Hammill was a witness to sudden death in downtown Des Moines.

The governor was one of four notables who agreed to review a parade sponsored by the Iowa Manufacturers Association October 7, 1929, on Locust Street.

Besides the governor, the reviewers were District Judge Herman Zeuck, former judge Hubert Utterback, and B. F. Williams, president of the Des Moines Chamber of Commerce.

The reviewing stand was the canopy over the entrance to *The Register* and *Tribune* building at 715 Locust Street. The four climbed out of a window on to the canopy top, the surface of which was partly metal and partly only glass.

A cameraman asked the reviewers to line up for a picture in their elevated location. Judge Zeuck happened to be in front of the other three. He moved toward the side. As he shifted his position, the governor said sharply: "Look out! Don't step on the glass, Judge!"

It was too late. Zeuck broke through the glass surface and plunged to the sidewalk below. He was dead on arrival at Broadlawns hospital of a broken neck and fractured skull. Judge Zeuck was forty and in his third year on the Polk County District bench.

The Register and *Tribune* quickly settled with his estate for a reported ten thousand dollars, a substantial sum of money in 1929.

Herman Zeuck (courtesy Judge Harold Ryan)

Night Baseball

Baseball people around the country looked upon Lee Keyser as some kind of a nut. He declared in 1929 that the game could be played well at night under lights. Moreover, he announced his Des Moines Demons in the old Western League would open their 1930 season at night.

"Most baseball men and virtually all the writers poked fun at him," wrote sports editor Sec Taylor of *The Des Moines Register.* "Some even insinuated he was a trifle crazy—that it was impossible to get enough artificial light on a ball park to enable the athletes to play the game expertly and to make the play clearly visible to spectators in the stands and bleachers."

Keyser, however, had assurances from General Electric engineers that the field could be sufficiently well lighted. Lee needed the attendance—the Great Depression was growing worse and many fans couldn't afford the price of admission. And what people did have jobs couldn't afford to leave them to go to a daytime game but often would be free to do so at night.

Meanwhile, the night baseball concept got all kinds of national publicity. Both Independence in the old Western Association and Lincoln in the old Nebraska State League liked the idea. They tried to beat Keyser to the punch. Both scheduled and played games before the May 2, 1930, Des Moines home opener. Sec Taylor, however, wrote their lights were inadequate.

"The contest here [May 2] was the first one played under adequate illumination," the sports editor wrote. "It was the game here that attracted nationwide interest."

Keyser spent eighteen thousand dollars installing lights, a lot of money at the time, at the old League Park across Sixth Avenue and west of the present North High School. An overflow crowd of more than ten thousand turned out to see Des Moines trounce Wichita.

"One hundred and forty-six projectors diffusing 53 million candlepower of mellow light, and the amazing batting of Des Moines' nocturnal-eyed players, made the opening night of the local baseball season a complete success Friday night," Taylor wrote.

"Baseball was played successfully after dark on an illuminated field, and the Demons won 13–6 in a contest that was normal in every respect so far as the playing was concerned."

The Demons scored eleven runs on eight hits and five bases on balls the first time they came to bat. The game was broadcast nationally over radio and overseas by short wave.

Taylor also reported that a picture taken of the game and crowd was put on display a few years later in the Baseball Hall of Fame in Cooperstown, New York.

Sec stood behind the plate with Keyser during the batting practice on May 1, the night before the game.

"The first pitch came in big as a pumpkin," Taylor wrote, "and big Jim Oglesby hit it on the nose. Keyser threw his arms around me and jumped up and down and shouted: 'It works! They can do it!' "

But the lights didn't work all the time, and they went out once at a moment of great suspense.

Ernest Canine, now retired in Scottsdale, Arizona, recalls a night

Baseball at night, 1930 (*Des Moines Register*)

game in those early years when Des Moines went into the ninth inning trailing an opponent 3–0. The Demons loaded the bases with two out and a good hitter at bat.

"Everybody was on edge," Ernie said. "A home run would give the game to Des Moines 4–3. There were two strikes on the batter. The pitcher wound up and sent the ball to the plate. "There was a crack of the bat and at that instant the lights went out, blew a fuse or something."

The ball couldn't be found either in the park or outside after the lights came back on. The fans and the team were dead sure it was a homer and Des Moines had won. But there was no proof and the opposing team wouldn't accept defeat. After a prolonged argument, the umpires decided the only fair thing would be for the batter to take his third strike over again. He did, and struck out, and Des Moines lost the game.

Some other minor clubs put in lights soon afterward but it wasn't until 1935 that the Reds installed the first Major League lights in the Cincinnati National League park.

The lights were not able to save baseball in Des Moines indefinitely. A number of years later, lack of attendance brought an end to the professional game for a period of years. The lights were taken to south of Ankeny to illuminate night construction at the old ammunition plant (now John Deere plant) during World War II.

Lights were common equipment just about everywhere in professional baseball when the game returned to Des Moines in the mid-1940s in the park built near the confluence of the Des Moines and Raccoon rivers.

Held for Ransom

Gangs kidnapped two top professional gamblers in Des Moines. After being held eleven days, Jimmy Sheridan was released in Galesburg, Illinois, in 1930 on payment of $10,000 ransom, a sizable sum of money in those days. Al Kiddie was freed in Des Moines after five days on payment of $8,700 in 1931. Both Sheridan and Kiddie operated wide-open gambling joints, even though every type of gambling was against the law.

There were no arrests in either case. True to the gangland code, Kiddie would provide no information to the authorities about his captors. This enraged Iowa Attorney General John Fletcher who responded by sending state agents into Des Moines to enforce the strict anti-gambling laws. Fletcher, a former district judge in Des Moines, declared gamblers had grown so powerful that they were able to prevent grand juries from returning justified indictments in gambling cases.

A third plot, to snatch major gambler Rich Kennelly, was foiled in 1931. Two would-be kidnappers swam across the icy Raccoon River in winter to escape pursuing officers. They were caught anyway, partly because of tracks they left in new-fallen snow.

A lot of kidnappings were committed all over the country in that period, the most notable being that of the infant son of Colonel Charles Lindbergh in 1932. The child was murdered. The wave of abductions led Congress to declare kidnapping a federal offense. The Sheridan kidnapping was the fifty-ninth in the nation in 1931.

Top professional gamblers probably numbered more than a dozen in Des Moines in those times. Illegality of gambling seemed perversely to guarantee its popularity with some people. They liked then, and like now, the adventure of doing things contrary to law.

The professionals, whether they broke the gambling and/or the anti-liquor laws of the time, didn't look upon themselves as necessarily evil. Said Nate Fidler, who was in that outer fringe: "Hey, we ain't criminal criminals." Meaning these violators were not shooting or beating up people, or engaging in such violent crimes as break-ins.

If you wanted to shoot craps against the "house," place bets on horses running at distant tracks, gamble on football or basketball, try your luck at card tables, play slot machines, or try your luck on punchboards or "barrels of fun" tickets, the chances were you could find the facilities somewhere in town or nearby most of the time.

Two racing wires for betting on horse races came into Des Moines at one time. You could also go to a place like Dave Fidler's on Seventh Street, give a few dollars to a bookie at the bar, he gave you a hand-written receipt with the name of the horse you selected, in the Kentucky Derby for example, and that was it. You went back and collected if your horse won, you didn't if it lost.

There was big money in gambling for the professionals. Kennelly testified the profits from the gambling operation at the old Mainliner Club on Fleur Drive across from the airport averaged ninety thousand dollars a year from 1941 to 1946, which was real dough. Thus, it was easy to see why kidnappers zeroed in on gamblers. They had the reputation of swimming in cash, and often they were.

Slot machines were plentiful in fraternal, veterans, and country clubs, taverns, drug stores. Many machines were the so-called "one-armed bandits," other varieties included payoff pinball machines.

As a rule, gambling operations were part and parcel of the then-unlawful business of selling liquor by the drink. Where there was gambling, there was likely to be illegal liquor. (Sale of liquor and beer were against the law everywhere in the early 1930s. Quite a contrast from the 1980s when even grocery stores began selling hard liquor.)

This is not to say gambling spots always had it free and easy. The law conducted frequent raids, made arrests that led to fines and sometimes jail sentences. As the chief of law enforcement for the state, the attorney general's office sometimes lowered the boom and closed up everything tight.

But it seemed that the professionals operated without much interference a good share of the time, perhaps as the result of payoffs to officers. Not much was said publicly about payoffs. But Al Rosenberg, operator of Mommie's Place (on Fourth Street south of the Kirkwood) once declared that a city council member demanded $100 a week protection money for the right to operate (liquor and crap tables) without hindrance from the law.

Other gambling spots included, at various times, 316 Locust; the Hubb Cigar Store at 221 Ninth; the Chesterfield, also known as the Mayfair, on Seventh Street (site of the Ruan building); the Kit Kat Club; the Argonne apartments; the Sports Arcade; the Viaduct Cigar Store on Seventh Street; and of course the Mainliner on Fleur Drive, the present location of the Crystal Tree dining spot.

Iowa's stringent laws against gambling have been wiped off the books in large part in recent years. Far more money has been bet since in lotteries, pari-mutuel betting on horses and dogs, bingo for money, and card games in taverns, than was wagered in the illegal gambling days.

Whatever professional gamblers are left are overshadowed by the state which itself is the biggest professional gambler in Iowa history. The state gets its cuts, exactly as the professionals do, by taking a percentage of the amounts bet.

A stranger entered the Fifth Avenue Cigar Store at 203 Fifth

Avenue in downtown Des Moines. The store was mainly a gambling operation that once had belonged to Jimmy Sheridan, a retired professional gambler. Sheridan happened to be there. The stranger talked with him and then they walked out together. They got into a car occupied by others and drove away. The incident was so quiet and quick that nobody noticed.

Yet it was perhaps the most spectacular Des Moines kidnapping ever. It took place at 6 P.M., September 2, 1930. Sheridan didn't cry out because he rightly feared he might be shot to death. The stranger kept him covered with a concealed gun.

The original demand for Sheridan's safe return was fifty thousand dollars, a huge sum for the times. His personal wealth was problematic. One estimate put his holdings at two hundred fifty thousand dollars to five hundred thousand dollars, an astronomical range. Others scoffed at those figures and said he was worth only twenty thousand dollars, including his home at 6001 Waterbury Circle, a classy address.

It was learned that the kidnappers immediately placed cotton over Jimmy's eyes and added glasses with tape over the lenses to make certain he couldn't see where they were going.

Eleven days of suspense followed. In that interim the newspapers splashed kidnap stories every day, stories of fact, rumor, conjecture, with headlines such as "Friends Fear Jim Sheridan Faces Death," "Omaha Seen as Key City in Kidnapping," and "Reports Drive Local Interest to Fever Pitch."

The shaken and anxious Mrs. Sheridan fell victim to an extortionist who called and said he would provide information on Jimmy in return for payment of one thousand dollars in cash. He told her to throw a package containing the money out a car window on Linden Street between Fifteenth and Sixteenth streets. She did so but never heard anything and the money was gone.

Although never proved, it appeared likely that at least some of the kidnappers were Des Moines characters. John (Go About Riley) Waters came to the Sheridan home the second day with the fifty thousand dollar ransom note. Waters, a Des Moines professional gambler and underworld individual, was picked up by sheriff's deputies and quizzed closely. He denied he was part of the kidnap plot and said he was forced to deliver the ransom note. The newspapers never learned whether he identified those who forced him.

The ransom note was in Sheridan's handwriting and was obviously dictated by the kidnappers. It soon became apparent Jimmy was being held somewhere in Illinois. Sheriff Park Findley went to that state to work on the case. On September 12, Mrs. Sheridan and two others, including Des Moines gambler Joe Swift, went to Aurora, Illinois. Exactly how it was done was never learned but the next day, September

13, a ransom of ten thousand dollars was paid secretly to somebody in Galesburg, Illinois.

Sheridan appeared free and unharmed twenty minutes later on a Galesburg street. He was brought home by automobile September 14. All he would say was: "I was kidnapped and I paid off. I paid all they asked. I am glad to be able to see my wife and family again. . . . All I want to do is forget about it. . . . It was a terrible experience and I hope I never have to go through it again."

The kidnap gang, reportedly of five men, never was caught and charged with the Sheridan crime.

Al Kiddie *(Des Moines Register)*

The kidnapping of Al Kiddie in November of 1931 touched off a bigger row than did the Sheridan abduction.

Details of how Kiddie was taken are sketchy except that it happened in Des Moines and he was held five days, originally also for fifty thousand dollars ransom. He was freed unharmed—pushed out of a slow moving car on Waterbury Circle after payment of eighty-seven hundred dollars. How that odd figure was arrived at was never explained. The release came not far from the Kiddie home at 538 Polk Boulevard.

The Kiddie negotiations, what was known of them, read like an old-time thriller. On instructions from the abductors, a go-between went to a certain acreage on the outskirts of the city and found two letters hidden in a shack near an oil tank.

The letters were both written by Kiddie at the command of the kidnappers. One to Mrs. Kiddie contained a demand for payment of fifty thousand dollars ransom. The other told the go-between to go to a certain place and wait for a phone call.

When the call came, the go-between asked for proof that the negotiations were genuine, that it was not another extortion scheme. The caller said to go to a certain spot in Woodland Cemetery. There the go-between found jewelry and identification belonging to Kiddie. The items were taken as a gesture that the proceedings were not just another phony extortion plot.

A couple of days later the go-between disclosed the kidnappers had agreed to accept eighty-seven hundred dollars. The currency was packaged and thrown out a car window at a designated spot on old Highway 32, which was the number of the road to Waukee. Release of Kiddie followed. Which in some people's minds should have been the end of the story.

But Attorney General Fletcher was burned up. He blasted Kiddie for saying that he didn't know who did it. "Such feigned ignorance on the part of the kidnapped and his friends," Fletcher said, "is an affront to the intelligence of every thinking person." He went on:

"The average person naturally makes this pertinent inquiry: How does anyone have the audacity to come into a city like Des Moines, that has 150 police officers in its employ and a substantial battery of other law enforcing officers, capture a fellow gangster, secrete him for five days, open negotiations for his release, arrange with other members of the gambling fraternity for a conference, meet the man carrying the ransom money, talk with him, obtain the money, return the person kidnapped to his home, without either the kidnapped or his friends having any conception of who the kidnappers are. . . . The brazen tactics of these gangsters are a challenge to the efficiency of the law enforcing bodies of the state, the city, and the county. The gangsters have challenged the law. The people should now challenge its officers to either rid the city of all persons of this kind or resign their jobs."

Fletcher declared that "the city of Des Moines is going to be cleaned of the gangster element, whether he be a gambling gangster, a booze gangster or just plain hanger-on gangster, spreading propaganda about the halls of justice and interfering with administration of the law."

The Kiddie case, he said, was "a demonstration of the audacity of the criminal operator. A man, who by general reputation, is allied with the gambling house fraternity of the city, was presumably kidnapped by another outfit of gangsters. The fact that one gangster has been mulcted by another outfit of gangsters is of little concern to this community, but the community is interested in the question of why either of these classes of gangsters should be permitted to operate within the limits of the city. . . . Kiddie, the kidnapped person, is commonly regarded to be a partner or co-worker with Jimmie Sheridan, who has operated a notorious gambling house in the city of Des Moines for many years past."

Fletcher expressed anger at what he called the power of gangsters to prevent indictments. He recalled the Sheridan gambling house in downtown Des Moines was raided October 3, 1929, by state agents. "A full and complete gambling operation was seized and a number of persons present were arrested," the attorney general said. He added that Sheridan admitted in the presence of officers that he owned the place, that he offered to pay the fines of those arrested, and he offered to plead guilty to operating a gambling house.

"The matter was taken before the grand jury of Polk County, fully presented, and Sheridan was not indicted," the attorney general said. "It was again ordered submitted to the grand jury and again no indictment was returned, although the officers of the Department of Justice testified to his admissions of guilt.

"The citizens of Des Moines should ask themselves why a grand jury of Polk County would not indict a man who admitted to the officers of the law that he was the owner of a full-fledged gambling house when the testimony of such admissions by reliable witnesses was before that body.

"The citizen of Des Moines should ask himself how much longer the Sheridans of this city are going to remain above the law, and why the gambling fraternity should be able to effectively enter the ramifications of the courts of justice and block their attempts to mete out justice."

Fletcher pointed out that the severe Depression had hit Des Moines and Iowa hard and costs of relief were skyrocketing. "In these times of financial stress, the men and women of Des Moines are giving every cent they can spare to feed the needy of our community," he asserted. "The gangster preys upon the very ones the citizens are sacrificing to help. He is a leech upon society, sapping not only its material substance but its morals. His presence is a challenge to the potency of our form of government. He must be hunted down, and in our efforts to hunt him down, we ask the cooperation of every good citizen of Des Moines."

Fletcher assigned eight of the fifteen agents on his staff to begin enforcing anti-gambling laws forthwith in Des Moines. Presumably that action spurred the police as well and wide-open gambling slowed down to a crawl. But such drives didn't seem to produce a lasting effect. Perhaps one reason for that was the desire of a number in the business community for a policy of allowing such things to go on. There was little question but that the city's wide-open reputation did bring Iowans from around the state to Des Moines seeking excitement and business people liked that extra activity.

An exciting chase after a gun battle highlighted the abortive attempt to abduct gambler Rich Kennelly in late 1931. It was a bungled operation all around.

Sheriff Charles Keeling had gotten a tip somewhere that kidnappers would seize Kennelly when he drove into his garage at 600 Fourth Street, in Valley Junction (now West Des Moines). Kennelly's extensive operations included the Hubb Cigar Store at 221 Ninth Street, a notorious gambling spot.

As the Kennelly car rolled into the garage, two men wearing handkerchiefs over their faces stood up. One was armed with a pistol, the other with a shotgun. They forced Kennelly from the car and took $255 from his pocket.

Before they could get anything else done, Keeling and Deputy Mickey O'Brien came into the driveway. They had followed Kennelly from downtown. Keeling fired a shotgun once and pistol twice at the suspects and O'Brien fired his pistol five times.

The balked kidnappers fired six shots at the officers before escaping out the garage back door. (It was a poor day for marksmanship. Fourteen shots and nobody hit on either side.)

The fugitives fled with the officers after them to the Raccoon River and jumped in even though it was December and the water was bone-chilling cold. They swam across and disappeared on the other side.

The officers raced around over the bridge to the south side and luckily picked up the tracks of one fugitive that led in the snow all the way to Forty-second and Welker where the trail was lost, briefly. Deputies picked it up again and followed it to a barbecue stand on Southwest Twenty-first Street. The suspect was inside trying to call a cab when the officers walked in. He ran out the back door.

This time the deputies traced him to a house at Fifteenth and Center streets. He had taken a cab there and the cab company reported he had been dropped off at 1431 Maryland Avenue. Officers surrounded that house and ordered him to come out. First he climbed out on the roof but climbed back in when he saw the law. When the deputies entered the house, he came down the stairs with his hands up. He was J. C. Smith, forty, a black man recently arrived in Des Moines from St. Louis. J. D. Charles, thirty, another black and a second fugitive, was arrested at his home at 1000 Tenth Street.

Again picked up in this case was Go About Riley Waters, along with Clarence (Doc) Eaton, another Des Moines underworld character. The authorities believed the plot was local and that others besides the black men were involved. Waters and Eaton were jailed for a time and questioned but released without charges being filed.

Both the black men were convicted. Smith drew a thirty-year sentence in Fort Madison penitentiary, and Charles one year in the county jail.

Kennelly emerged unscathed and was an often arrested but highly successful operator for decades afterwards. He and Kiddie were partners in a high-class roulette-and-blackjack place called the Club Belvedere on High Street between Sixth and Seventh, immediately west of St. Ambrose Cathedral.

The Belvedere featured chorus-girl acts, excellent food and

liquor, and gambling galore. Sportscaster Ronald Reagan liked to go there in the mid-1930s, not to gamble or drink but to date the chorus girls.

Lew Farrell (*Des Moines Register*)

It was a close touch-and-go in this period for another widely known character about town, Lew Farrell, who had changed his name from Luigi Fratto. He came out of gangland Chicago in 1939 to take over as the Mafia's man in Des Moines.

Known as "Cockeyed Louie," Farrell bribed public officials in Des Moines to let him violate gambling and liquor laws. He also sold at wholesale "Canadian Ace" beer, produced in a Chicago brewery with a Capone background. (Later he wholesaled Blatz beer.) Lew's share of the profits from the Sports Arcade gambling operation alone was $13,000 in 1947, a big sum of money for the times. But he was foiled when he tried to strong-arm his way with a gun into another big Des Moines gambling operation. And he was mixed up in the Teamsters Union rackets. A U. S. senator called him a "hood gangster" operating in the labor field. Farrell took the Fifth Amendment numerous times in Washington to avoid answering incriminating questions.

Yet more than anything else Lew wanted to be recognized as a person of respectability in Des Moines. To convince this author, he put a small son—who was perhaps maybe five years old—up on a chair. The little fellow was impeccably dressed in brand new clothes. At his father's command, the lad recited flawlessly the Pledge of Allegiance, down to the last words, "with liberty and justice for all." The jubilant father exclaimed: "See! That proves I am a patriotic American!"

It was one of the few times in his twenty-eight years in Des Moines that Farrell had a peaceful encounter with the press. More frequent were phone calls to reporters early Sunday, after he had seen the morning *Register*.

"Why are you doing this to me? I am a good citizen," Lew would cry, complaining maybe about a story involving him in gambling, his aluminum siding-business practices perhaps, or some labor union caper or other.

There is little doubt that Farrell bought off one Polk County sheriff. That meant Lew was protected against sudden county raids while that sheriff was in office. A Farrell son many years afterwards said his father paid a city public safety commissioner as much as $700 a week. That helped keep the police off his back. And a district judge did all he could to keep Lew out of trouble.

Making and receiving payoffs are plain unadorned crimes. But neither Farrell nor any corrupted public official ever was caught. In fact, Lew apparently never was convicted of anything in Iowa. The closest he came to taking a rap in Des Moines was when he and gambler Hymie Wiseman applied for a state sales tax permit for the Sports Arcade, their prosperous gambling joint at 612 Grand Avenue.

Wiseman was arrested for operating the Arcade. Their protection against the law had broken down for once. Ten customers were arrested also. Horse racing, football, and gambling forms were seized. Charges of conspiracy to violate the gambling statutes were filed against both Wiseman and Farrell. These were especially serious charges because the penalty on conviction was a mandatory three-year prison sentence. The case was based on the partnership application for the tax permit.

District Judge C. Edwin Moore came to the rescue. He dismissed the charges on the ground sales tax records were confidential and could not be admitted into evidence against the defendants. Wiseman thereupon pleaded guilty only to operating a gambling house and was fined $300. Wiseman didn't have to go to prison, nor did Farrell.

The interstate nature of the Mafia was demonstrated when two Kansas City mobster-brothers were jailed in Harlan, Iowa. Charles and Gus Gargotta were charged with robbing a night club. Farrell and his brother-in-law drove to Harlan to post $30,000 bond for the gangsters. Shelby County authorities demanded cash. Another Kansas City mobster brought the money (in bills) to Lew and the Gargottas were released. They never were tried. The county attorney dismissed the charges for "lack of evidence."

Lew appears to have been able to wield considerable power in the late 1940s within the Truman administration in Washington. A Farrell son, John, told Chicago and Des Moines newspapers in the late 1980s that family records indicated his father had "gotten to" federal officials and had arranged early paroles for four underworld characters. Freed from federal prison were Charles (Cherry Nose) Gioe, Paul (The Waiter) Ricca, Louis (Little New York) Campagna, and Phil D'Andrea.

Gioe, a close friend of Farrell and a former Des Moines resident, and Ricca had been given ten-year sentences in 1944 in connection with a $2 million motion picture shakedown racket. They were paroled in 1947 after serving only three years, and Campagna and D'Andrea were released as well. The *Chicago Sun Times* said the paroles "caused outrage among law enforcement officers and Chicago newspapers at the time" and that such notorious gangsters were expected "to spend a longer stretch behind bars." The *Sun Times* quoted the Farrell son as saying: "Somebody got to [a high federal official] to get these quickie paroles and I would say it was someone from my father's organization if not himself."

Lew was subpoenaed to appear before congressional investigating committees in Washington three times in the 1950s. He repeatedly took the Fifth Amendment when faced with such questions as: Had he participated as an advisor in midwest labor disputes involving the teamsters union? What was his relationship with then-teamster boss Jimmy Hoffa? Had he been in on plans to try to take over the wholesale supplying of liquor to the Iowa state stores? Had he pulled a gun on Pete and Gladys Rand in an unsuccessful effort to force them to give him 25 percent of the profits of the Mainliner gambling casino?

But no major federal action against Lew ever materialized from the hearings.

Farrell tried to build his image in Des Moines by spreading money around for various causes. He helped pay off a church mortgage and he organized and helped pay for dances sponsored by the Des Moines Junior Chamber of Commerce. He even was voted a life membership in the Junior Chamber.

On the other hand, Lew was indicted in the final months of his life on a charge of participating in a check scheme of more than $50,000. He declared his innocence.

The short (5 feet 2 inches) and stocky Farrell developed cancer in 1967 or possibly before. He hurried around the country, desperately trying to find a doctor or clinic that could make him well. He thought he had been successful. Mary Mills, first wife of this author, was diagnosed in August 1967 as having inoperable cancer. Lew called up. "Take Mary to the University of Wisconsin cancer clinic at Madison; they cured me," Farrell said joyfully. "I'm in good shape."

That may have been Farrell's last optimistic statement about his condition. Mary Mills died October 24, 1967. Death came to Lew Farrell exactly one month later, on November 24, 1967.

Cherry Nose Gioe had been chased out of Des Moines twice in early years, by the police and by his "friends." Jack Brophy, chief of detectives, ordered him to get out in 1936 and he left in a hurry. Brophy declared Gioe was "muscling in on the gambling racket." The detective chief told the police: "Every time you see him, throw him in jail. If he makes the break [runs], shoot him like a dog."

Gioe did return to Des Moines in 1942 and he was reported to have obtained a 25 percent share of the Mainliner operation. He left

Charles (Cherry Nose) Gioe (*Des Moines Register*)

quickly again, on the advice of others of his ilk, after the reported incident of Farrell pulling a gun on the Mainliner owners. Gioe's federal sentence on the movie shakedown charge followed a couple of years later.

As happens to many mobsters, the life of Cherry Nose came to a bloody end. He was killed in a gangland slaying in Chicago in 1954. Farrell was in Chicago at the federal building at the time. He was picked up for questioning but soon released. Asked years afterwards if he had ever killed anyone, he said no but he once was present at a killing. He didn't say who the victim was.

Wiseman was with Cherry Nose in Chicago when he was slain. They were getting into a car when Gioe was mowed down. Wiseman said they were partners in a plastics business. Wiseman was not wounded. He said he didn't know the assassins.

Cream of tartar, a substance used in baking cakes, played a role in a cat-and-mouse drama centering on Pete Rand at the Mainliner. Pete was sentenced to one year in the county jail on a gambling charge. He was supposed to stay there for a year—seven days and seven nights a week—no unexcused absences.

Eagle-eyed reformers discovered that Pete was being smuggled out of the jail every Saturday evening, picked up by his wife and taken home for a few hours, then returned.

Pete was arrested one Saturday night away from the jail. He gave this explanation for his absence: He was serving as jail cook. He was baking a marble cake and he needed cream of tartar as an ingredient. There was none in jail and he had gone home to get it. That turned out to be a poor alibi. There was plenty of cream of tartar on the jail kitchen shelf. Pete didn't get to go home on any more furloughs. The jailer was fired.

This Is Money?

Hard-up Polk County had its own "dollars" printed in the Great Depression. But nobody was arrested for counterfeiting. In fact, the 1933 Iowa legislature authorized such "money" which was called scrip.

The $125,000 Polk scrip went in large part to families on relief, mainly in Des Moines. Teachers and some other public employees also had to take 4 percent of their pay in the certificates.

The imposing-looking certificate carried a statement saying it was good for one dollar "in service or merchandise." Moreover, the scrip was supposed to pay for itself. Here's how: Every time the dollar was spent, the spender had to paste a special two-cent stamp in one of the fifty squares on the back.

County Treasurer Allen Munn sold the stamps. When all fifty squares were filled, the plan provided, the treasurer would redeem the certificates for a real dollar.

Unhappily, the scheme didn't work out at all. Some grocers and other merchants did accept the certificates and tried to keep them in circulation. But fifty large and small downtown stores balked. Public utilities and jobbers wouldn't take them either.

In addition, teachers disliked the scrip intensely. They didn't want the certificates in the first place and they detested the 2 percent salary cut that the stamps represented when something was purchased with the "money."

As it happened, none of the certificates was turned in with all the stamp squares filled. In many cases fewer than half the spaces were occupied.

The county was stuck with calling in the certificates and paying them off. Polk had to issue $102,000 in bonds to cover the losses. That was a real hardship in Depression times.

Two northwest Iowa lawmakers, Representative Charles Zylstra of Hawarden and Senator Garritt Roelofs of Sioux Center, pushed the stamp idea through the 1933 legislature.

Zylstra had attracted national attention in 1932 when he prevailed upon the Hawarden town council to pay people on relief jobs with scrip. The council issued $300 and then another $300 and it worked like a charm. A total of 482 of the 600 certificates were turned in with all the spaces filled. The other $118 is still in the hands of collectors and is said to be of high value in rare money circles.

Speaking of money, there came a time in the Depression when you couldn't even cash your paycheck, or a personal check. You couldn't draw money out of a savings account either because all the

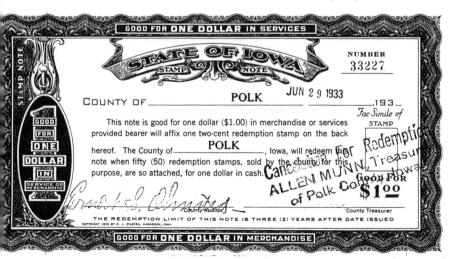

At each transaction user will buy a two cent redemption stamp, and sign his initials across the word "Holder", and the receiver will sign his initials across the word "Receiver", in each other's presence.

	POLK-CO. Polk County	POLK-CO. Polk County	POLK-CO. Polk County	POLK Polk County	POLK-CO. Polk County
HOLDER Polk County	POLK-CO. Polk County	9	10	11	12
13	14	15	16	17	18
19	20	21	22	23	24
25	26	27	28	29	30
31	32	33	34	35	36
37	38	39	40	41	42
43	44	45	46	47	48
49	The forty-ninth (49) stamp attached to this note must be dated in addition to placing initials thereon; and this note must be presented for payment within thirty (30) days thereafter or become null and void.				50

(FOLD HERE)

Polk County scrip

GOOD FOR ONE DOLLAR IN SERVICES

STATE OF IOWA
STAMP NOTE

NUMBER
33227

COUNTY OF POLK

JUN 2 9 1933 ..193_

Fac Simile of STAMP

This note is good for one dollar ($1.00) in merchandise or services provided bearer will affix one two-cent redemption stamp on the back hereof. The County of POLK , Iowa, will redeem this note when fifty (50) redemption stamps, sold by the county for this purpose, are so attached, for one dollar in cash.

GOOD FOR ONE DOLLAR IN SERVICE OR MERCHANDISE

County Auditor

County Treasurer

Cancelled for Redemption ALLEN MUNN Treasurer of Polk County Iowa Good For $1.00

THE REDEMPTION LIMIT OF THIS NOTE IS THREE (3) YEARS AFTER DATE ISSUED

COPYRIGHT 1933 BY C. J. ZYLSTRA, HAWARDEN, IOWA

GOOD FOR ONE DOLLAR IN MERCHANDISE

banks in the nation were ordered shut down by President Franklin Roosevelt for a so-called "bank holiday."

The president took action immediately on taking office March 4, 1933. He did so because people were drawing money out of banks so fast that even good ones were in danger of going under.

The money crunch left just about everybody stuck with only the cash he had in his pocket. Fred W. Hubbell, wealthy Equitable Life of Iowa official, found himself with only a five dollar bill.

"I'm going to have to break that to buy cigarettes," he laughed. Des Moines Chamber of Commerce secretary John Adams also had exactly five dollars. Gardner (Mike) Cowles, a top executive of *The Register* and *Tribune,* saw the "holiday" coming and procured a one thousand dollars bill at the bank. Then he realized it was not useful because nobody could make change for it.

The use of barter in business became widespread. *The Register* and *Tribune* started a "swap column" in the want ads. Some strange deals were made. A horse was traded for a flock of chickens, a typewriter for some rabbits, six pairs of curtains for a portable phonograph, a cream separator for a Ford roadster, some firewood for a cow, and a police dog for an automobile.

Businessmen extended credit generously. If you dropped in for a morning cup of coffee at a usual hangout and didn't have the necessary nickel, the waitress put it on the cuff. One guy paid for lunch for himself and friends with postage stamps. Families emptied their cellars of old returnable bottles to pay for groceries.

Paychecks were a major problem. *Register* and *Tribune* checks carried a printed guarantee they would be cashed when the holiday was over (which it was in a week).

Merchants accepted checks as IOUs, only they were called CABHs (Cash After Bank Holiday). The trouble was, you couldn't split up a twenty-five dollar or thirty dollar weekly paycheck (not bad money) to buy things at various stores. Thus, some companies paid wages in several smaller checks instead of one big one.

The people by and large took the crisis well. *The Register* said Des Moines "continued to rough it cheerfully" through the crunch. People had the feeling the worst of the Depression was over.

The pinch caught members of the Iowa legislature off balance the same as anybody else. Where they were going to get their next meal was a question for many. But not Senator Ora Husted. He had less than five dollars cash when he returned to Des Moines from his home in Truro. But he brought with him twelve dozen eggs and part of a hog that he used to pay some of his bills.

Car owners sometimes didn't have much for gas. One Des Moines driver barely reached a filling station when his motor went dead. "Well, I made it!" he shouted gleefully. "Now give me a dime's worth of gasoline." Which was more than half a gallon. Gasoline was as cheap as six gallons for a dollar.

Bad Boys

Iowa Governor Clyde Herring engaged in a spirited exchange with famed lawyer Clarence Darrow in 1935. Darrow came to Des Moines from Chicago to plead for release of a lifer in Fort Madison penitentiary. The prisoner had been convicted at fourteen years of age of slaying a little girl. Darrow said the lifer, Lyle Messner of Cedar Rapids, was basically a good boy. "I have hundreds of appeals made for good boys," Herring said, "But never for the bad boys. I wonder what becomes of the bad boys." With a twinkle in his eyes Darrow replied: "I think they all grow up and get elected to office." Herring took no action and Messner wasn't paroled until 1959 when he was forty-five years old.

Darrow, one of the world's great defense attorneys, enlivened the Des Moines scene several times over the years. He was an atheist and he said in 1938: "I went to [Unitarian] church this morning for the first time in twenty-five years. I liked the sermon. There was hardly any religion in it.

During a 1928 visit he commented: "This is a hell of a world we are living in and I am glad I am past seventy and do not have to go to Heaven."

Darrow was no abstainer. On a 1926 occasion when prohibition was in effect and there was all kinds of bootlegging in Des Moines and elsewhere, he said: "The prohibition question is being solved by—drinking."

A Governor Arrested

Anent the perils of politics, an Iowa governor was "arrested" for betting a pig on a football game.

The governor was Clyde L. Herring, a Des Moines Democrat. He was neither jailed nor fined. The hilarious incident took place in 1935. Here was the setting:

Ozzie Simmons was a star black fullback on the University of Iowa Hawkeye football team. The Minnesota Gophers were scheduled to play the Hawks November 9 at Iowa City. The Gophers were big and tough. They were poised to give Simmons a rough time.

Herring was asked at a press conference at the statehouse what he thought of Simmons' safety prospects. "If the referee doesn't take care of Ozzie, the crowd will," the governor declared. A storm of anger erupted in the Twin Cities when that comment arrived on the news wires. Minnesotans envisioned a howling mob roaring out of the stands in Iowa City.

Herring realized something had to be done before the game to defuse the situation. He arranged with his friend Governor Floyd Olson of Minnesota to bet an Iowa pig against a Minnesota pig on the contest. That drew a lot of laughs in both states and eased the tension.

Simmons wasn't mistreated and did fairly well. He carried the ball nineteen times and gained sixty-eight yards. Minnesota had to come from behind to defeat the fighting Hawks 13–6.

True to his word, Herring paid up with a quality hog named Floyd of Rosedale from the Rosedale farms near Fort Dodge. The Iowa governor went to St. Paul, Minnesota, and personally herded the creature, all marcelled and manicured, up the Minnesota capitol steps and into Olson's thick-carpeted office. The hog committed no social errors on the carpet and everybody was happy. Which should have been the end of the story but wasn't.

Back in Des Moines that same afternoon, one Virgil Case got a warrant for Herring's arrest on a charge of gambling for the hog wager. Iowa law at the time provided a penalty of up to a $100 fine or thirty days in jail for simple gambling. Municipal Judge J. E. Mershon signed the warrant.

Case was a gadfly and a natural-born hell raiser. He had been a secretary to a Des Moines mayor and publisher of a weekly newspaper.

Word of the warrant reached Herring while he was still with Governor Olson in St. Paul. Herring immediately engaged Olson as his attorney. Olson squelched a suggestion that the pig be auctioned off to pay a possible Herring fine.

"That pig stays in Minnesota regardless of what happens," Olson declared. He added that the bet wasn't a gamble anyway, that Minnesota had been a lead-pipe cinch to win.

Olson suggested that Herring stay in St. Paul where he could not be extradited because the Minnesota governor had to consent to extradition and he already was Herring's attorney. Herring observed that only the governor of Iowa could extradite anyone back to Iowa— and he was the governor.

Olson added a sly insult when he said it wasn't gambling because "nothing of value was involved." Herring shot back that Floyd of Rosedale was a "right good hog."

Govs. Floyd Olson and Clyde Herring, 1935 (*Des Moines Register*)

Case explained how he happened to file the charge. He said he had some spare time on his hands when it occurred to him a "good way to put in that time was to go over to Municipal Court and have the governor arrested. So that's what I did." He said his profession was "raising hell with public officials because they should be the first to set a good example."

Walter Brick, deputy municipal court bailiff, caused a stir of excitement at the statehouse a few days later. He showed up at Herring's office. Reporters thought maybe he was there to lead the governor away in handcuffs. Not so. Brick just wanted to talk over a planned court hearing on the charge.

The only action the deputy took that day was to join the reporters in eating apples out of Herring's fruit basket. (Besides apples, Herring was known at times to shut the door and provide the press with beer and Pella bologna, something no governor has done since.)

In the hearing, reporters and others testified that Herring hadn't committed the so-called offense in Des Moines, that the bet wasn't consummated until he and Olson met in Iowa City. Assistant County Attorney C. Edwin Moore, later chief justice of the Iowa supreme court, moved that the case be dismissed. Judge Mershon was glad to do so. The folderol was over.

For weeks afterwards, Herring enjoyed showing a clipping from an Iowa newspaper saying the governor should "pay no attention to those harassing him on the pig deal. Oinck! Oinck!"

Such trivialities aside, Herring was a key Iowa governor of the twentieth century. He rode into office with other Democratic state candidates in the President Franklin Roosevelt landslide of 1932, during the Great Depression. He was the first Democrat to win the governorship in more than forty years.

Herring was inaugurated in January of 1933 at a time of economic desperation for Iowans. Hogs dropped to as low as two dollars to three dollars per 100 pounds, corn to eight-and-a-half to ten cents a bushel. More than one thousand Iowa banks had closed since the agricultural depression started in the early 1920s. Tens of thousands of farmers lost their farms and homes through mortgage foreclosure. Unemployment in cities and towns reached record levels. Thousands of townspeople lost their homes in foreclosures, including Herring himself. He lost his beautiful home at 180 Thirty-seventh Street in Des Moines shortly after he became governor. He was unable to meet payments on a thirty-seven thousand dollar mortgage held by the Iowa-Des Moines (now Norwest) National Bank.

The Herring family stayed in the home and paid $125-a-month rent. He regained legal possession of the home within a couple of years.

It was said that he was unable to buy coal to heat the home late in the 1932 election year. Which was quite a comedown from the early 1920s when he was a millionaire Ford automobile dealer and real estate investor.

Herring's financial problems plagued him most of his four years as governor. His safety deposit box was sealed and his checking account of $301 was attached in 1936. The reason: Failure to pay a fifty seven hundred dollar judgment on a defaulted second mortgage on some property he owned. Herring paid that off and ultimately all his debts.

Despite his difficulties, the governor joined other elected state officials in voluntarily taking a $500 annual pay cut in 1933. That lowered his salary from seventy-five hundred dollars to seven thousand dollars a year. And at that time a governor had to provide his own living quarters. There was no state governor's mansion.

Herring's first two years as governor saw probably more far-reaching Iowa legislation passed than in any biennium before or since. It was in this period that the state sales tax, state income tax, and corporation tax were enacted to provide money for property tax relief. A sweeping bank rescue measure was passed, a moratorium delaying mortgage foreclosures, a state old-age pension system for penniless elders (since superseded by social security), a measure setting up a state liquor store system, a state relief system for needy families (financed by federal money), and a state planning board was created.

Herring and his lieutenants showed real leadership in moving quickly on the piled-up problems, not the least important of which was the insolvent condition of the state treasury because so much money was tied up in closed banks.

Herring worked hard, and he played hard as well. His exploits with women were a juicy topic of gossip, gossip that never got into print even though the press knew many of the details. Reporting was different in those days than in the 1980s. It was said Mrs. Herring put up with it all for reasons of her own. That situation became a political issue when Herring ran for re-election in 1934. Some Republicans circulated a printed sheet describing the governor's goings-on with women and the information was generally true.

The Democratic State Central Committee was alarmed. Committee members feared Clyde and the entire ticket were headed for defeat. Bill Millhaem, who handled the party publicity, wasn't concerned.

"If all the husbands who cheat on their wives and all the wives who cheat on their husbands vote for Clyde, it will be a landslide," Millhaem said. It wasn't a landslide but Herring did win by a comfortable seventy-four-thousand vote margin.

The governor was elated and combative the day after the victory. He told reporters that he would sue the Republicans for libelling him. He didn't. Reports later said Walter Maley, an assistant attorney general, advised Herring not to open that can of worms.

George Lloyd of Dallas Center was secretary of the Republican State Central Committee at the time. George was personally friendly with Clyde but a definite political opponent. Lloyd didn't join in sponsoring the juicy circular because he didn't think it was good politics.

Herring thought, erroneously, that George was involved. The governor got into his cups one night before the election and called Lloyd. "I've seen that dirty stuff you've put out about me," Clyde said. "Let me tell you, you just make me a good ladies' man and you'll elect me." Whether that was true or not, Herring did win.

Lloyd did fail in an attempt to embarrass the governor in an American Legion district meeting at Atlantic. Lloyd was present as a legion member in the Hotel Whitney when Herring arrived to address the organization's banquet. Lloyd told his Legion buddies, "I'll get the Governor and take him around to the rooms and introduce him to you.

Each of you get ready to extend your right hand and say 'hello Clyde' and then your left with 'have a drink.' "

The scheme appeared to work like a charm. Herring got loaded with liquor and Lloyd expected him to make a fool of himself at the banquet.

"Instead, Clyde came into the hall natty and stepping right along," George said. "He leaned over me and said: 'You son of a bitch, you thought you'd get me drunk, didn't you.' Then he made one of the best speeches of his life."

Herring was cheerfully careless about situations that would have been personally and politically embarrassing had they happened, say, in the 1980s. He was elected United States senator in 1936. He was feeling good at a Christmas party given that year by the Iowa Power and Light Company. He waved a one thousand dollar bill, an especially large sum in those days, for everybody to see, and said: "Look at what my friend Cy Leland gave me for a Christmas present." Leland was the top officer of the light company.

Herring returned home from Washington early in his senatorial career driving a custom-built Buick. Where did you get that, Clyde? "My friend Bill Knudsen gave it to me," he said casually. Knudsen was president of General Motors.

The propriety of accepting the thousand dollars and the car, and the wisdom of letting many others know about the gifts, didn't seem to trouble Clyde. The press knew about both gifts but didn't report them. The following incident did get into the papers:

Lucky Strike carried a series of full-page ads in the *Saturday Evening Post* quoting various senators as liking to smoke Lucky cigarettes. Herring was one of them. He received one thousand dollars for the testimonial.

"What will you do with the money?" reporters asked. "That goes to my favorite charity," Clyde replied. What is that? "Clyde Herring," was his answer.

Herring served one six-year senate term before being defeated in 1942. He subsequently was assistant director of the Office of Price Administration (OPA) in Washington before his death in 1945.

Meanwhile, the tradition of Floyd of Rosedale lives on, though not in the flesh. The original Floyd is long since gone, of course. But a statue-trophy of the animal became a traveling football prize between Iowa and Minnesota. Whichever wins the annual football game gets to keep Floyd for the ensuing year.

24 Prostitutes

A mysterious stranger approached a cab driver one night in front of a downtown hotel.

"This town has changed considerably since I was last here," the stranger said. "I used to know several good places, one in particular. . . . I went over there this evening but the party who ran it isn't there any more."

"What do you want, a woman?" asked the cabbie.

"I'd like to go to a place where they have more than one woman."

"I know of a good spot," said the driver. "Hop in and I'll take you there."

The stranger looked at his watch and said: "I'm afraid it's a little late now. Do you think I could visit this place tomorrow afternoon?" The cabbie said that could be arranged. He gave the address as 927 Fourth Street and to ask for Nellie. The cabbie, named Harry, presented the guy with his card.

The stranger didn't want a woman in that sense at all. He was an investigator sent in from New York in October of 1932 to search out the then-extensive Des Moines underworld of prostitution.

In three days and three nights he went to twenty-one brothels, met twenty-four prostitutes, talked to ten cab drivers and eight hotel bellboys, visited twelve hotels, and was accosted by eleven street-walkers.

His report, never before made public, is a rare document of a sleazy but real portion of Iowa social history. The report came to light many years ago in a gift of old books. The investigator listed names, addresses, telephone numbers, personal descriptions of the prostitutes and other individuals, reported conversations in detail, and gave prices which varied from three dollars to one dollar. (Iowa was deep in the Great Depression at the time and prices of everything were abnormally low.)

The infinite number of barefaced lies the investigator told in hiding his identity and purpose are a classic of dissembling.

The reason for the investigation was a sharp increase in Iowa syphilis and gonorrhea cases, serious venereal diseases often spread through prostitution. (Such diseases as herpes and the lethal AIDS were far in the future.) State Health Commissioner D. C. Steelsmith had become alarmed because reported cases of the venereal diseases had risen more than 50 percent in Iowa in one year, from a combined total of 3,202 cases in 1930 to 5,031 in 1931. The total rose a little more in 1932 to 5,122.

"If death records were to tell a complete story," an annual report

Dr. D. C. Steelsmith (*Iowa Official Register 1931–1932*)

of his department said, "syphilis would definitely be classed among the chief causes of mortality. Syphilis and gonorrhea present a health problem of enormous proportions."

Dr. Steelsmith knew the situation was even worse than the figures indicated. Some doctors over the state were lax about reporting diseases in those days.

Dr. Steelsmith appealed to the American Social Hygiene Association in New York for help in getting at the Iowa venereal facts so that action could be taken. The investigator was sent in on the promise of complete confidentiality. His name was never disclosed nor details of his report until now.

The investigator's task was four-fold: To find out where prostitution was principally being practiced; how easily accessible it was; the methods used by those in the business; and what the police were doing about it.

The report was plain spoken.

"An area exists on the [Des Moines] east side," the investigator wrote, "where prostitution is flagrantly practiced and the resorts are so closely grouped together that an atmosphere of a segregated district is created. This locality, which is not far from the [Des Moines] river and incidentally within a half a mile of the state capitol, is mainly that of a slum or deteriorated district, but no such area exists in the poorer sections on the west side of town."

He found much less prostitution on the west side. The investigator couldn't see why the differences should exist since the police vice squad charged with enforcing the law against prostitution had jurisdiction over both areas. But enforcement obviously wasn't uniform.

"On the west side the resorts are somewhat scattered," he said. "The operators, prostitutes, and third parties, such as go-betweens, continually and emphatically stated 'there isn't prostitution in Des Moines. The law is hot and they're watching' this place and that place. From the manner in which the business was carried on, it was evident that all in this part of the city were in constant fear of detection."

Such fears were at a minimum on the east side. Prostitutes "sat at the windows of brothels and openly and flagrantly accosted potential customers by window-tapping."

"When the prospective trade enters the resorts," the report continued, "they are immediately propositioned and immoral acts offered without hesitancy and without effort being made to determine the identity of the customer. When questioned regarding police authority, the prostitutes casually remarked 'oh they come around now and then.' It was evident that the vice squad visits the area mainly 'then,' otherwise the prostitutes would not indulge in such flagrant activities."

The investigator got into a brothel at least once by posing as a bill collector looking for a certain woman. And another time as a worker in a nearby plant. He found brothels especially thick on Des Moines streets in the East Second Street area.

He saw a woman seated at a window at 215 Des Moines Street. "She pulled the curtain aside, tapped on the glass and beckoned for me to come in," he wrote. He was admitted to a small sitting room adjoining which was a bedroom. "She promptly solicited me and offered to commit an act of sexual intercourse only for two dollars. I said I was just going across the street to the factory. On the way back I'll stop in and see you. Will you be here tonight in case I can't get back this afternoon? She said yes and there'll be another girl too. When you come back, be sure to ask for Mary. I said I would and departed."

As he did on all his calls, he wrote a personal description of this prostitute in his report. Apparently to aid police in identification later. In this case Mary was described as "thirty-five years old, five feet five inches tall, 150 pounds, dark brown bobbed hair parted on left side, round face, blue eyes, medium olive complexion, even and yellow teeth, wore a black satin dress."

Often the investigator posed as a businessman who had just come to town and had decided to "step out." He got into the brothels easily most of the time and used his various ingenious excuses to escape as soon as he had gotten the information he needed. He must have had a computer mind to remember the conversations and detail that he recorded from each visit.

At 213 Des Moines Street, where he also was window-tapped at, a prostitute wanted two dollars at first then cut the price to one dollar. She said she got to keep "only half what we make." The other half went to the brothel operator.

Cab drivers undoubtedly got a cut too by steering customers to certain places. The investigator probably never would have gotten in at the 927 Fourth Street place without Harry's card and repeating the phone number the driver had given him. Even so the operator named Nellie was suspicious of him. She said frankly that she didn't want to get hit by a big fine. Once he was in, however, she offered her own services for three dollars.

He got out of there by saying: "It so happens I was in the

neighborhood and thought I would come in and see if he [the cabbie] had given me a bum steer. I will be at leisure this evening and will return then." Which of course he had no intention of doing.

The situation at the Wellington Hotel at 417 Fifth Street, in downtown Des Moines, presented a different kind of a picture. A bellhop there was in the business.

"Now if you'll take a cheap room here," the bellhop said, "I'll steer you up against a very nice little broad. She's sweet and clean. All she wants is three bucks."

The investigator asked, "Why can't I go up to her room and see her?" The reply was: "No, the management wouldn't like that. You have to take a room. Take a room for a buck."

The investigator said he hated to invest one dollar and not be satisfied with the girl. Couldn't it be arranged any other way?

"No, you see they [the management] know she is working here, and of course if you go up to her room, the hotel wouldn't get anything out of it. They want the price of a room." That was the investigator's excuse to leave. He found the Franklin Hotel at Fifth and Locust had the same extra dollar-for-a-room charge.

His report indicated the larger downtown hotels were not in the prostitution business but sometimes were not too vigilant. Street prostitutes said the Hotel Fort Des Moines had a rule against prostitutes going to guest's rooms but that limitation could be avoided by walking up the stairs to the mezzanine floor and taking the elevator there.

The old Chamberlain Hotel at Seventh and Locust, site of the present Banker's Trust, apparently had the strictest policy of all.

"They don't allow any women to hustle here," said a bellhop. "If we [bellboys] suspect a girl is a hustler, we have to tell the house dick [detective] and he watches her. . . . The boys here don't deal in women. The house doesn't allow us to."

There were indications that some women had turned to prostitution in those difficult economic times because they couldn't make a living any other way. One street walker told the investigator: "I am not in this regularly but I lost my job and I had to give up my home so I'm living with my sister now. I've got to make money somehow. If I could get a job, I assure you I wouldn't be hustling."

The investigator spent another four days total checking into the prostitute situation in four other Iowa cities. He found some in Cedar Rapids and Mason City, a little in Marshalltown, and said Waterloo was "practically free of it."

Health Commissioner Steelsmith received the report of more than 100 pages in November 1932. He avoided all publicity on it as he had promised. Exactly what he did with the information is unknown but it is likely he forwarded it to the Des Moines police and to the departments of the other cities with a request for action. Undoubtedly they did act. But whether all the places were closed up for very long was unlikely. In Des Moines, for example, old-timers recall the window-tapping practice could be seen on Des Moines Street in the late 1930s and beyond.

But for whatever reason, the number of venereal disease cases reported in Iowa did go down in the two years after the report was received. The combined total of syphilis and gonorrhea cases reported in Iowa declined from 5,122 in 1932 to 4,376 in 1933 and all the way down to 3,420 in 1934. The 1934 total was 33 percent under the 1932 figure.

But the progress was short-lived. Reported cases of the two diseases soared to 6,834 in 1936, just about double 1934. That could have been due partly to greater emphasis on better reporting by Iowa doctors or to the fact that improvement in enforcement in such matters all too often is only temporary.

From Wheaties to the White House

The young sportscaster didn't know when he reported at the Fort Des Moines army post that he was in for a rough Sunday morning. He was a member of the U. S. Cavalry Reserve in the mid-1930s.

He mounted the horse he was assigned to in the riding mall. He galloped the steed toward the barriers. The animal didn't jump at all but went through the barriers and into the wall. The rider hit his head when he was thrown into the wall.

"I got dumped pretty good," recalled Ronald Reagan, president of the United States (1981–1989). He was sportscaster for radio station WHO Des Moines at the time. He was on the air from 1933 to 1937.

He suffered no permanent ill effects from the fall. He was told that the regular army cavalrymen at the fort had played a trick on him by giving him an obstreperous horse.

Reagan was the only U. S. president ever to have a Des Moines connection. Henry A. Wallace, who was a Des Moines resident much longer than Reagan, was vice president from 1941 to 1945.

Reagan lore from his radio days is substantial in Des Moines. He was personally popular in the city for his radio work. The breakfast cereal Wheaties was one of his principal radio sponsors. He was a Democrat at the time and the idea of becoming a Republican president in the White House was beyond his wildest dreams.

His nickname was "Dutch," given him by his father who thought he looked like a little Dutchman when he was born.

Reagan broadcast Chicago Cubs baseball games over WHO but he didn't do it from Chicago. Instead, he recreated the games at the Des Moines end of a Morse code telegraph ticker from Chicago, and he was excellent at it. He made his listeners feel that he was on the spot in Chicago actually seeing what was happening on the diamond.

He sat with a microphone next to a closed booth containing telegrapher Curly Waddell and a ticker. The ticker chattered. Curly typed maybe a single "B" on a sheet of paper and slipped it under the glass to Reagan, who then said into the mike: "The pitcher winds up and here it comes—a fast ball—just missed the outside corner, ball one." Or Curly might type "2BL" and Reagan would say: "He throws. It's a line drive over the shortstop's head, it goes all the way to the left field wall, and Jones is on second with a stand-up double."

He explained later: "I had to do it that way to compete with the guys who broadcast live from the ball parks." And compete he did.

Ensconced in American sports tradition is the way he handled the crisis one day when the wire went dead in the middle of a game. Then is when he used his resourcefulness and rich imagination to the utmost. He had a batter foul off half a dozen pitches in a row to use up the time. He also had the batter hit a long drive over the fence that would have been a homer but was just foul by inches. He had the pitcher stopping the action to tie his shoe laces. He had the batter stepping out of the box to put dirt on his hands. He described a fight among kids in the grandstand over a foul ball, and so on.

"And," he said with a laugh, "when the wire did come back on, it said,'Jurges popped to short on the first pitch.' " Nothing he talked about in the interim was true.

Reagan broadcast University of Iowa football games at Iowa City and numerous other sports events, including the Drake Relays. He was all set at one relays to describe a premier race when the Drake University president entered the booth to extend greetings to listeners around Iowa. The trouble was, he talked while the race was being run and Dutch had to remain helplessly silent.

The race was over when the president quit talking. Again, Reagan rose to the occasion. He returned to the air and recreated the race from start to finish, with so much excitement and tension in his voice that the radio audience didn't know but what the runners were performing right then and there. He was a delightful con man of the air waves.

Reagan believes he may have been one of the first, if not the first, Iowa announcer to broadcast a non-sports news event. He was serving as local announcer for an NBC band program one night in 1933 when he heard an engineer in Los Angeles say there had been a major earthquake centered in Long Beach, California.

Knowing that Long Beach was the home of many former Iowans, he relayed a brief report of what he had heard to WHO listeners. He added to that report as he got developments from Los Angeles. Calls from anxious relatives and friends of Long Beach residents swamped the station's switchboard. Reagan summoned help and by 3 A.M. the office was filled with WHO staffers handling calls and relaying whatever specific information was available.

On the social side, Dutch liked to go out to Cy Griffith's Moonlight Inn at Seventy-third and University west of town to have a beer or two. After he became famous, innumerable Des Moines people remembered, or said they remembered, drinking with him. If all who said they did really had done so, Reagan would have spent many a night passed out under the table. But he obviously wasn't a heavy drinker.

So far as the Chicago Cubs were concerned, Reagan felt in 1937 that it would help promote his regular season broadcasts if he carried some training camp accounts in early spring from California. He went to the Los Angeles area to do some recordings for broadcast on the team's prospects.

He had a hankering at the time to try out for the movies. He knew Joy Hodges, a Des Moines girl who had made good in Hollywood and also on the stage as an actress, singer, and dancer. He asked Joy if she would get him a screen test.

"I said: 'Why not?' " Joy recalled. "I said: 'Take off your glasses.' He took off his glasses and he had a very special something—an all-American boy look."

Reagan passed the test and signed a movie contract for $200 a week, an impressive salary in 1937. He was twenty-six years old.

He returned to Des Moines to get his things and to close out his job with WHO which said he could return to the station any time he wanted to. He hurried back to Hollywood, driving 650 miles the first day, 600 the second, and 660 the third, extra long drives in those days of no super-highways and slower cars.

His first picture was "Love Is On the Air," a fast-moving and light film about a radio announcer. He made four movies between May and October of 1937 and he was leading man in three.

His connection with Des Moines and Iowa didn't end immediately. Basil (Stuffy) Walters, managing editor of *The Des Moines Register,* thought Reagan breaking into the movies was a great story. He got Dutch to write a series of seventeen letters to the Sunday paper under the title: "The Making of a Movie Star."

The letters to *The Register* made delightful reading. He called himself a "Male Alice in Wonderland" and he admitted in his first report that he was scared of Hollywood.

"Ever since I signed the contract and committed myself to at least a brief whirl at the movies," he wrote, "I've had the same sort of feeling that a man must have in death row at Fort Madison penitentiary. He knows he has to walk up the scaffold and take it in the neck and is anxious to have it over with as soon as possible." (Iowa still had capital punishment.)

Reagan was put down good right away by movie people. He showed up in his "new white sport coat, tailored to measure and never before worn, which would show Hollywood I knew a thing or two and read *Esquire* regularly. Especially in combination with my new blue slacks."

A studio official exploded. "Where the hell did you get that coat?" he demanded. Reagan replied it was the latest in sportswear. "Sports my eye," the official grunted and sent him to the studio tailor for alterations.

"I hate to tell you what that tailor did to my beautiful coat," Dutch told the home folks. "All the tucks and pleats, all the looseness was ruthlessly whacked out while I stood and saw murder done."

A hairdresser made matters worse.

"Where the hell did you get that haircut?" she spit out, calling it "Bowl Number Seven." But that problem evidently was solved quickly. Reagan wrote nothing further about his hair.

Dutch next was turned over to the tender mercies of Perce Westmore, famed for making people "look like they ain't." Westmore walked around Reagan squinting, complaining partly under his breath that a certain studio official "must think I'm a Houdini. . . . Some of the mugs he signs up."

Dutch thought of the long drive from Des Moines to California. "I could see myself doing the same thing again," he wrote, "but pointed in the opposite direction. This time I decided, I'd take it easy—say thirty miles an hour."

But he wasn't sent home. His next great crisis was witnessing his first screen test. "I entered the projection room with all the eagerness of a hobo getting a free meal and came out like a whipped dog with its tail between its legs," he said. "It lasted only a few minutes but I was scrooched down so far in my chair that I was almost on the floor when it was finished."

He asked a studio official why he was hired. The guy "laughed so much I thought he was going to burst a blood vessel." His self-assurance didn't increase when rehearsals began for "Love Is On the Air." He kept wondering if WHO would live up to its promise and he could get his old job back.

Other actors sought to cheer him up. Edward Everett Horton said he hoped Reagan would "stick around—that the movies needed a new

Joy Hodges (left) and Arleen Whelan (top center) admire Jane Wyman's engagement ring, given to her by former Des Moines radio announcer Ronald (Dutch) Reagan, 1939.
(*Des Moines Tribune*)

face. I certainly hope they need mine." Ramon Navarro was similarly cordial.

The occasion Dutch dreaded most was the actual shooting of his first real movie scene. He said he was "as jittery as a June bride." If a studio associate hadn't calmed him down, "I believe I'd have fled screaming from the studio, jumped in my car, and started back to Des Moines."

He added: "No stage fright of college show days, of taking high hurdles on a spirited horse, making a sixty-foot dive, broadcasting the Notre Dame game—nothing I'd ever been through before approached my nervousness as I stepped on to stage eight, ready to be the leading man."

He "almost dropped dead" when the director approved the first scene without retakes: " A warm glow swept over me and I glanced rather proudly at the sidelines. I'd made my first movie scene. I was an actor."

Well, not quite. The director hadn't really given the scene the final OK. He stopped the shooting to give Reagan confidence. Dutch had to do the scene over again later "about a dozen times."

He learned to dislike the word "cut," especially when he heard that sharp command in the middle of a scene that was dissatisfying the director. "You get an all-gone feeling in the pit of your stomach that reminded me of the one and only time I got seasick when Lake Michigan got rough on an excursion I took from Chicago to Milwaukee."

The "Love Is On the Air" movie pictured Reagan as a rapid-fire newscaster waging a campaign against local gangsters. They succeeded in getting Dutch demoted to a children's hour program. Here he found the clue that led to a smash finish, a news broadcast from a truck in the midst of a gun fight.

"What radio announcer wouldn't get a thrill out of a scoop like that?" he asked. The picture took twenty-two days to complete.

Actress June Travis provided the love interest. She set Dutch back on his heels in one scene. The script called for her to whisper in his ear and for him to whisper in hers. To make the scene more realistic, the director instructed them to whisper something to each other.

Reagan "took the chance to ask her to have dinner with me." She whispered back: "No."

Later he did have a date with June. They went to an amusement park. He hit forty-five moving targets at the shooting stand, then showed her how to hold a rifle.

"She didn't say a word," he wrote, "but cut loose and pinged everything in the place, including the ping pong balls that bounced up and down on a water spout. Boy, she can shoot rings around me."

Reagan and June were called to the publicity department after the film was completed to make still photos to promote "Love Is On the Air." Dutch wrote: "June and I did some high class 'necking' portraits; that is, 'clinch' stuff that is supposed to make the hearts of the young beat a bit faster when they see them. That would have been fun if it hadn't been so terribly hot, and I was glad when noon came."

Besides "Love Is On the Air," he was the leading man in "Sergeant Murphy" and "Accidents Will Happen" and he had a minor role in a sea thriller titled "Submarine D-1" in his first five months in Hollywood.

He told how he got sick of ham and eggs: "The very first day of 'Accidents Will Happen,' we did a breakfast scene that lasted most of the day. Have you ever eaten ham and eggs from 9 A.M. to 2 P.M.? Well, don't, especially if you have to go on acting in front of a plate of half-eaten food. . . . After four hours, those once delicious eggs look a little pale around the gills, and so did I."

"Love Is On the Air" reached theaters in the fall of 1937. After the first showing, Reagan grabbed the film trade papers "to read the worst about myself." He was all set to "pack my trunk for the return trip home."

Instead, he wrote: "One paper went so far as to say 'Warner Brothers have a new find in Ronald Reagan, young leading man who promises to go places.'" Thus, instead of departing, he decided to "stick around and see what happens. If the studio and fans can stand it, I can."

Instead of hitting the highway back to Des Moines, he stayed on the road that led to a successful movie career, the governorship of California for eight years, and the presidency of the United States for eight more.

Girlie Show

C ome on in and see for yourself! Dancing girls all naked! Not a stitch on! Hurry hurry hurry!"

Grim-faced Gustave Alesch bought a ticket along with dozens of others. The time was August of 1935 and the place was a girlie show tent on the midway of the Iowa State Fair.

Alesch was no ordinary fair goer. The fifty-eight-year-old Luxembourger of Marcus, Iowa, was a state representative from Plymouth County in the legislature. He sounded off when he came out of the tent. "I figured the public was being defrauded and the girls would be hidden behind a string of pearls, a fan, or something," he said, "but the barker's promise was made good. Not so much as a court plaster interposed itself between the goggle-eyed public and the girls' epidermis." If the same thing happened the next year, he promised, he would get some "clean-minded men to go out there and clean it up with a club."

Fair officials denied the girls had danced nude. The officials said the dancers wore flesh-colored tights and only appeared nude in the dim tent light.

The management nevertheless loved Gus because his comments and threats generated a statewide storm of publicity for the fair. Whether the girls danced all the time in tights or only put them on after the Alesch blowup never was learned.

Girlie shows were long since gone from the fair by the late 1980s, probably because the sight of female skin had become so commonplace throughout society. Indeed, theater ads promoting nude dancers on stage regularly appeared in some newspapers.

Tony Gets Bopped

Hitting a *Des Moines Register* sportswriter over the head with a bat meant big trouble.

Gambler Clinton (Skeet) Petty found that out after a wild, early-morning altercation at the old Mayfair Club, 417 1/2 Seventh Street, in downtown Des Moines.

Petty called writer Tony Cordaro a "God damn stool pigeon" as he hit him twice, on the jaw and the head. Two Mayfair employees held Cordaro while Petty swung the bat. Tony suffered an extensive, bloody head wound that was dressed at a nearby drug store.

The attack took place in August of 1937, a robust period when seven gambling houses were operating in Des Moines. They offered slot machines and crap tables, and sometimes blackjack and poker, all thoroughly against the law. They also sold liquor by the drink, also thoroughly illegal at the time. Other places provided women as well.

In short, Des Moines was a wide-open town and there was no question but that business interests of the city wanted it that way.

Petty, who operated the Mayfair, had been angered by a story in the papers about gambling. He thought Tony was partly responsible, which wasn't the case. Cordaro wrote only sports.

In the turmoil, Tony hurled a chair at Petty. The chair missed Skeet and splintered against a post. There was a lot of pushing and shoving, punctuated by loud profanity.

Earlier in the evening, Tony had attended a gathering of sportswriters from around the Midwest to lay plans for covering a forthcoming major boxing bout in Des Moines. Charles Dunkley, a Chicago Associated Press writer, went partying afterwards with Cordaro. Dunkley had gotten drunk, as he usually did every time he came to Des Moines. He was known as the "night Mayor of Chicago." Cordaro evidently drank his share too. They arrived at the Mayfair shortly before three in the morning.

Dunkley probably had as much to do with starting the fracas as anybody.

"Charley had gotten obnoxious," a *Register* old-timer said. "He urinated at the bottom of the Mayfair steps. He said he had urinated in better places."

A Mayfair lookout saw through a peephole who had arrived and warned Petty. The explosion followed, with fights within fights. Club bouncer Louie Mays started to throw Dunkley out. Mays was a former professional boxer. Cordaro rushed to Dunkley's defense, with mixed results. Dunkley shouted: "Let's get a gang and clean out this place, just like we do in Chicago."

All this excitement was fully reported in long stories in both *The Register* and the old Des Moines *Tribune*.

A *Register* veteran said managing editor Basil (Stuffy) Walters "raised hell with Cordaro" but also declared: "They can't do this to the press." Walters sent reporters to all the night spots and the papers carried extensive reports about the goings-on.

"Stuffy closed up the town," said the veteran. Walters agreed he had done that very thing. "The stories did it," he said. "The town was shut up tighter than a drum."

But Mike and John Cowles, top executives of the newspapers, didn't want night life squelched and other civic leaders didn't either. "Mike and John were restive about it," Stuffy said. "The town soon opened up again."

Cordaro was a rotund individual (220 pounds) with black curly hair. He was strong and he could swing his fists with authority.

"Tony once knocked a guy through a plate glass window on Locust Street," said a *Register* reporter. "Another time a hotshot writer from Detroit thought he was a fighter. He and Tony got drinking. They made bets on who could lick the other. They went out to Riverview Park in the middle of the night and turned on the lights in Abe Frankel's boxing ring. They put on the gloves. Tony knocked the guy cold in no time at all."

Tony Cordaro on the witness stand, 1937
(*Des Moines Register*)

Cordaro had to be tough to stand up under the rap on the head he took from Petty.

There was considerable dispute in a court hearing over the size of the bat wielded by Petty and how hard he had swung it. Tony said it was an indoor baseball bat, about thirty inches long and two inches in diameter. A defense witness said, however, that it was " a little boy's bat that a kid had left up there." What a kid could have been doing in a gambling joint with a bat wasn't explained. And both blows, Tony said, "were struck with full force, like a batter uses when he winds up for a long distance hit."

Witnesses described in detail the lurid language hurled about during the combat, which prompted *The Register* to say: "There was much testimony not pleasing to the ear, and epithets normally heard only in livery stables were profuse."

Rough and crude though the times were, there still was a sensitivity toward women not to be found today. Municipal Judge Don Allen, who presided, warned the dozen women spectators that they could be shocked and might want to withdraw. None did.

Cordaro originally filed a charge of assault with intent to do great bodily injury against Petty and his two employees. In the end they pleaded guilty to a lesser charge of simple assault and paid fines of twenty-five dollars each.

The Mayfair battle was the only known time Dunkley got mixed up in a court case in Des Moines. But his exploits with liquor were legendary in the city. He came to Des Moines annually with dozens of other sportswriters to cover the Drake Relays. He was among the writers who always went to Aunt Jenny's place on the south side to get loaded up on spaghetti and Italian red wine, and to other places as well.

Dunkley frequently had to battle a bad hangover the next day while trying to cover the finals of the relays. On one occasion his condition was so bad that the story he sent by wire into the Associated Press office in downtown Des Moines was a disaster and almost unreadable.

An editor in the office rewrote the entire story and sent it out nationwide under the Dunkley byline. It was a case of one newsman saving another's skin, a rescue operation that used to take place quite often in the heavier-drinking days among the gentlemen of the press.

He Should Have Kept Still

Franz Jacobsen of Ottumwa was hanged by the neck until dead because he talked too much.

Jacobsen was sentenced to death in Fort Madison penitentiary in the late 1930s for the murder of his girl friend. Iowa still had capital punishment in those days.

The case came before Governor Nelson G. Kraschel in Des Moines. Governors had the power to reduce death sentences to life imprisonment. Kraschel chose to take that action. He so told his close friend, *Des Moines Register* reporter Gordon Gammack. The governor authorized Gammack to write the story but not to quote him.

Gammack wrote an exclusive story quoting "a reliable source" as saying Jacobsen would not be executed.

Jacobsen assumed an expansive mood when the Gammack story reached the penitentiary. Franz said he knew all along that he wouldn't hang because his uncle had a lot of pull with the Iowa Democratic party of which Kraschel was a leader.

Kraschel was incensed when word got back to him of Jacobsen's bragging. The governor decided to let the hanging proceed. Kraschel told Gammack of his new determination. That put Gammack in the embarrassing position of having to write another and contrary exclusive saying Franz would have to hang after all.

Jacobsen died on the gallows April 19, 1938. He went to his death calmly. One report said he sang "There's a Gold Mine in the Sky" before he was executed. He did no such thing. The story was a fabrication, not uncommon in the reporting of the times.

Nelson Kraschel, Iowa governor, 1937–1939
(*Des Moines Register*)

Slambang at the State Fair

A plane floated down out of the eastern sky aimed at the Iowa State Fairgrounds.

There is no airstrip on the grounds but the plane kept coming anyway. It cleared the midway going sixty miles an hour and no higher than the tops of the Ferris wheels.

To add to the tension, more than sixty-two thousand people crowded the grounds. Upwards of twenty-four thousand packed the nearby grandstand.

The plane touched ground in the infield of the racetrack some sixty feet short of a white frame house.

The plane hit the house with a crunch and a roar. The impact tore off the wings but the fuselage shot through the building and stopped upright fifty feet beyond. What was left of the house caught fire.

The pilot got out of the fuselage, staggered a bit and disappeared from sight of the spectators. An ambulance sped into the infield, picked up an individual prone near the wreckage, and darted away.

On getting outside the gate, however, the ambulance stopped and let the "patient" out. He wasn't injured. In fact, he wasn't the pilot. The ambulance call was only a ploy to enable the stunt pilot, Capt. F. F. (Bowser) Frakes, to escape arrest for deliberately crashing a plane. He had left the scene unhurt and unobserved.

It was all part of the fair's 1937 "thrill day" program. Frakes, a traveling performer, was paid $2,500 by the fair (quite a sum in 1937) for crashing the $500 World War I "jenny" biplane. The frame house had been flimsily built for the purpose of being crashed into.

Frakes violated federal law not only by crashing the plane but also by flying over a crowd and stunting at less than one thousand feet.

The fair staged a lot of spectacular "thrill" events in its 135-year

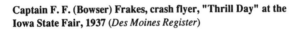

Captain F. F. (Bowser) Frakes, crash flyer, "Thrill Day" at the Iowa State Fair, 1937 (*Des Moines Register*)

history but the Frakes performance may have topped them all. Fair officials booked Frakes to build the crowd that day, and highly successful the strategy was, with the turnout exceeding sixty-two thousand, huge for the times.

The announcement that an intentional plane crash would take place on "thrill day" brought all kinds of publicity, and problems as well, which engendered still more publicity. The Iowa Aeronautics Commission filed an action in Polk County District Court to prevent the crash. Judge Frank Shankland refused to interfere. State and federal officials thereupon set up vigils at the Des Moines airport to keep Frakes from taking off. He foiled the law by flying out of a grain field east of the city.

In the crowd when Frakes landed were two aviation administration officials, one federal and one state. All they could do was watch helplessly when Frakes came down. He was not prosecuted, perhaps because he couldn't be located afterwards.

Fairgoers in 1914 saw another plane demonstration that would be as unthinkable now as the Frakes performance was in 1937. Pioneer flyer Lincoln Beachey flew in a plane-auto race around the fair track at a height of ten feet or less and hazardously close to the grandstand crowd. Beachey competed against famous driver Eddie Rickenbacker. The flyer dipped so low at one point that he barely missed the speeding car.

Lincoln Beachey (in plane) races Eddie Rickenbacker (in car) at the 1914 Iowa State Fair. (Iowa State Fair)

Rickenbacker was given a handicap of one-half mile in the five-mile race. Eddie won by five seconds. There were no mishaps. Beachey was killed the next year stunt flying at San Francisco.

An air race did come to a tragic end at the 1930 Iowa fair. Two planes of a barnstorming troupe known as the "Sons O Guns" collided over the northeast edge of the track. One plane piloted by a Leo Allen crashed into the crowd. Spectator Vernon De Vote of Mitchellville died of a fractured skull and seven others were injured. The pilot survived. The other plane got down safely.

The engine of the crashed plane tore loose and rolled at a fast clip into several planes parked in a nearby tent. A fair policeman tried to stop the catapulting engine with his foot. He didn't—and suffered a broken leg. That was devotion beyond the call of duty.

The fair staged the most thunderous of all of its purposeful crashes on the ground over the years. Great crowds for the times saw two deliberate "successful" head-on collisions of speeding steam locomotives in front of the grandstand.

In 1896 two forty-one-ton locomotives belching angry black clouds of smoke rammed into one another, each going an estimated thirty-five miles an hour, (thirty-five was fast in 1896). "It was a weird and awful sight," said *The Register,* "and yielding to the sense of the fearful from that fearful meeting, then only an instant away, the vast audience was stilled with breathless silence. Onward rushed the engines, and at a point a short distance west of the flag in the center, the awful crash occurred. The momentum they had attained hurled them upon each other with frightful violence. The collision was so awful that for an instant the solid earth trembled beneath the shock of the impact. Then there was the sound of escaping steam, crushing steel, splintered timbers, and the dull roar of water rushing from broken tanks, both of which were torn loose . . . and jammed forward with frightful violence into the gangways."

The smokestacks were rammed within two feet of each other. Both boilers were ruptured and the locomotive cylinders broken and shattered. "Altogether the wreck presented a frightful spectacle." A speed of thirty-five isn't fast now but the impact from a combined seventy miles understandably had a shattering effect.

The 1896 engines got their names from the politics of that era. The "Gold Bug" was named for William McKinley, the Republican presidential candidate who favored the gold standard for currency in the election that year. The "Silver Bug" was for William Jennings Bryan, the Democratic nominee who wanted silver as legal backing for American money. McKinley was elected.

The crash delighted fair officials by drawing a paid crowd of fifty-five thousand, the largest ever up to that time. Another five thousand free loaders watched from outside the fence.

The locomotives were old and pretty much worn out. The fair bought the engines from Frederick M. Hubbell for fifteen hundred dollars. Hubbell, an early Des Moines capitalist and railroad man, demanded his money upon delivery. New locomotives cost the paltry amount of forty-five hundred to five thousand dollars at the time.

The event attracted so much interest that the public for 100 miles around clamored for train tickets to travel to Des Moines to witness the collision. A total of 565 Iowans came by train from Winterset that day, 733 from Brooklyn, 371 from Grinnell, 542 from Atlantic, 223 from Newton. The Rock Island line brought 2,654 to the fair, the Des Moines Northern and Western 1,987, the Great Western 2,153, the North Western 1,794, the Burlington 761, the Wabash nearly 300. (How long has it been since rail passengers poured into Des Moines at that rate!)

In addition, not less than five thousand farmers streamed into town on their wagons. Charles Ashworth, a farmer three miles west of the city, said he was kept awake all night by the sound of teams of horses passing his home.

Fifteen thousand packed the old amphitheater to see the crash and an estimated forty thousand crowded around the fence of the half-mile track. Other thousands watched from the roofs of nearby machinery buildings and horse barns. The hillside to the east was black with people. The price of admission seems to have been a whole dollar, a goodly amount of cash then.

A second locomotive crash at the 1922 fair was a flop. The engines couldn't get going because the track was too short. One engine wasn't even damaged much.

But there was nothing dull about the resounding impact of two 112-ton metallic monsters at the 1932 fair. That fair was held in the depth of the Great Depression. Fair officials needed attendance badly. They resorted to another crash spectacular and it did the job. The day was rainy but the forty-five thousand attendance was ten thousand greater than the corresponding day in 1931. The turnout was unusually high seeing that striking farmers seeking higher prices were picketing roads around the state. That kept at least some away from the fair.

In accordance with tradition, the two engines went to their destruction bearing famous political names. The "Roosevelt" bore the name of the Democratic nominee for president in that national election year. The "Hoover" was named for the Republican president running for re-election.

The collision was a sight to behold. Each engine pulled a coach and tender on the three-thousand-foot track. The "Hoover" got a speedy start down the eastern slope. The "Roosevelt" came fast from the west off a mound built on the west edge of the fairgrounds.

A locomotive crash staged at the Iowa State Fair, 1932
(Iowa State Fair)

The engineers tied down the shrieking whistles, put both giants into high throttle, and jumped early on. The crowd leaped to its feet, those who weren't standing already, with dread anticipation as two huge machines roared toward collision.

They smashed into each other in a resounding crash. The boiler of the Hoover blew up, sending metal and wood debris in all directions. The cabs of both were crushed like eggshells. The Roosevelt coach blazed up and the flames spread to the Hoover coach. Both had previously been doused with gasoline. Dynamite placed in the couplings exploded in a mighty force that jarred the entire fairgrounds. Huge clouds of black smoke and steam enveloped the wrecks and in the center gleamed the burning coaches.

The spectacle was not without casualties. Mrs. Kenneth Meyers of Alexander, Iowa, at the fair on her honeymoon, suffered a severe scalp wound. She was 150 feet away. She was able to walk to the first aid station where her wound was dressed. She was hit by a wood fragment. Marvin Frincham of Des Moines suffered slight cuts on the

nose and arm from flying pieces of metal. He was 300 feet away.

    Critics assailed the fair board for spending forty thousand dollars to produce a dramatic show that was over in a few seconds. *The Register* said the cost of the crash was "nothing like forty thousand dollars," but the actual cost never was disclosed. An editorial in the newspaper said the crowd didn't come to see "one sum of money collide with another sum of money, both going up in a cloud of smoke."

    Rather, *The Register* continued, the people gathered "for a period of emotional suspense, heightened indescribably in the few seconds preceding the crash, and detonating the instant of the crash. There is, as the slang puts it, a 'kick' in that.

    "Essentially, that emotional appeal is probably no different from that which draws us by the millions to baseball contests, to stage and screen dramas, and to a hundred other places where we experience danger and uncertainty without risk."

    The Register congratulated the fair board for the collision "triumph."

Not So Long Ago

Far From Home

Two Japanese-American doctors were forced to seal shut their prosperous medical clinic in Los Angeles during World War II before they resettled in Des Moines.

They also had to seal three homes they owned before being rushed away.

"It was a sad state of affairs," said Dr. Tsutayo Ichioka. "I just left my car in the garage in Los Angeles. People sold their cars for as much as they could. We heard of some who sold their refrigerators for as little as ten or fifteen dollars."

Dr. Ichioka and her husband, also a physician, were among the 300 to 500 American citizens of Japanese blood uprooted from homes and careers on the West Coast and relocated in Des Moines in the war years.

The upheavals took place after the sneak Japanese bombing of Pearl Harbor December 7, 1941. That attack propelled the United States into World War II. The hundreds who came to Des Moines were among the one hundred ten thousand persons forced from the coastal states to inland areas. President Franklin Roosevelt ordered the massive dislocation to prevent spying and sabotage at naval and army installations and war industries on the coast.

The president acted after messages were intercepted in Japanese code from Tokyo saying spies had been recruited in San Diego and San Pedro, California, to provide military information. But no evidence ever was documented that any citizen born in the United States of Japanese blood was disloyal.

Memories of the tense national drama were revived in 1988 as Congress voted to pay twenty thousand dollars each to the estimated surviving sixty thousand evacuees. The bill, which was signed by President Reagan, also contained an apology to these Americans for the hardships they had suffered.

The removal action upset countless lives and families, left West Coast properties tied up and useless, and caused heavy losses in income and forced sales of personal possessions.

Other Japanese-American transplants in Des Moines told of a wide variety of losses. Ruth Fukuto said her father had to sell his Los Angeles poultry business at below its value. Ruth Wakida had to leave her barber shop and soft drink business in Fresno, California. Kiyoshi Minami had to depart from his wholesale and importing business in Seattle.

Bob Morishege was forced to sell at a loss the garage business he had operated for fifteen years in Selma, California. And Bob was unlucky enough to have his five-room bungalow back home destroyed by fire in 1945.

Kaz Arai was the victim of a strange twist. He had come from Honolulu eighteen months before to enroll in junior college at Sacramento, California. Kaz was forced into an internment camp and ultimately to Des Moines while his family back home in Honolulu wasn't disturbed at all. The relocation order didn't apply to those of Japanese descent in Hawaii.

Farm worker George Yoshida had to sell his pickup truck back home in Lindsay, California, for $115 even though he said it was worth at least twice that.

Today the sweeping relocation would be rightly regarded as a wholesale violation of the civil rights and the personal well-being of a lot of innocent people.

Nearly all the newcomers to Iowa were Nisei (pronounced Nee-say), which is the term for native American citizens born of Japanese parents. A few were "Issei," individuals living in America who were born in Japan.

Well over half the transplants who came to Iowa settled in Des Moines. An estimated 750 Japanese-Americans lived at one time or another in the American Friends hostel at 2150 Grand Avenue, Des Moines. They came from all walks of life, doctors, businessmen, students, mechanics, newsmen, mothers, children, office workers, farm workers, old, young. In addition to having to leave their homes, they suffered in many cases the indignity of confinement for months and often years in internment centers in California, Arizona, Colorado, Arkansas, and elsewhere.

The often-crowded centers were under twenty-four-hour guard and nobody was allowed to leave.

"Most people seem to think we were prisoners of war," said Frank Nakashima, a truck farmer from Whittier, California. "In a way we have been. . . . " But they were released after checking and allowed to go to interior destinations.

The newcomers arrived in Des Moines eager to work, and work well they did. They were not placed under any surveillance and they had plenty of job opportunities. The early 1940s were a time of serious labor shortages. More than 250,000 Iowans were away in the armed forces and all kinds of jobs were going begging.

At the same time, presence of the evacuees presented a test of tolerance for Iowans. On one hand, feelings ran high against Japan, not only for the treacherous Pearl Harbor attack but also for torture of American prisoners of war. And here came numbers of persons who were physically exactly like the enemy.

Even so, with only occasional exceptions, Iowans treated the evacuees well. Dr. Tom Abe, once of Los Angeles, served more than two years as resident physician and clinical director at Broadlawns General Hospital in Des Moines.

"I found only friendliness and courtesy here," he said. He and his wife and two children, both born in Des Moines, moved to Chicago in 1945. "I would like to have opened a practice in Des Moines," he said, "but my hay fever gets so bad I have to move on."

Abe Chambers, onetime mayor of Des Moines, hired two Nisei mechanics for his automobile business at 1201 Walnut Street. He heard rumblings. He called his employees together and gave them a chance to vote on whether to keep the men, Fred Kitigawa, thirty-one, and Chester Ishii, twenty-five. The vote was 13–2 in favor of the Nisei.

"The general attitude of our men was that Kitigawa and Ishii are American citizens who have become victims of circumstances," said Chambers. "After all, a person's standing as a man depends on how he thinks, not on who happens to have been his ancestors."

Chambers said both had been cleared by the FBI as loyal Americans. Another source said all the evacuees who came to Iowa were "proved loyal or they would not be here." (If that were so, why weren't they permitted to return to their homes?)

On another occasion, it appeared that, due to a mix-up, a large number of Nisei young people en route to Des Moines would have no place to stay when they arrived. "It would be a shame," declared Mrs. Frederick Weitz, a civic leader, "if Des Moines couldn't be hospitable enough to take care of these American boys and girls for a few weeks." Plans were hurriedly drawn for accommodations but were mostly not needed because many of the group were diverted elsewhere.

Another evacuee happy with his reception was Martin Marumoto, thirty, an employee of Midtown Motors in Des Moines. "We like it here because people are so kind to us," he said. Mrs. Marumoto told how she didn't like getting off a bus at first while going to work "because I was afraid the people would be staring at me. I was shrinking but they didn't." She was a pastry cook at Iowa Methodist Hospital.

On the other hand, a proposal to open a hostel in West Branch, Iowa, for Nisei farm workers had to be abandoned due to hostility in the community. And when stories of Japanese atrocities hit the papers in a big way, scattered anti-Nisei comments were heard. Iowa Relocation Director Frank Gibbs said he received critical anonymous calls. Some children shouted derogatory remarks on the street.

"No employer has shown any disposition to change his attitude because of the calls," Gibbs said. "We still have more job offers than people to fill them. Even though the phone calls and street remarks are rare, that type of procedure is to be deplored."

Willing and generally capable though they were, many Nisei needed specialized training. Twenty-four were placed in farm jobs in one batch and there were openings for at least that many more. "The difficulty," Gibbs said, "is to find individuals who know how to feed livestock and to milk cows." They learned fast, however. Another problem was tight-fisted employers. At one point, Gibbs said, about half the bosses were trying to hire the Nisei at "substandard wages." He advised the applicants to hold out for higher pay.

The professionals among the Nisei didn't make all that much either. Physicians worked for as little as $125 to $175 a month. The physicians were superbly qualified. Dr. Tsutayo Ichioka, thirty-seven, was interrupted by the war in her graduate studies at the University of Pennsylvania. She got her medical degree at the University of Southern California and spent an extra year there in heart research. Her husband, fifty-seven, was a medical graduate of Kyoto University in Japan. Her sister, Satsuki Nakao, twenty-five, was a pharmacist and she practiced her profession in Des Moines. Dr. Tsutayo said she and her husband saw "about 150 patients a day" in an internment camp where there were nine physicians taking care of 14,000 people.

"I don't think it was necessary to relocate us," she said. "It may have been for others, though. From the letters we've received from former patients out there [in Los Angeles] a lot of patients wish we were back."

She said she bought war bonds while in Los Angeles but couldn't do so in the camp because her pay was only $19 a month plus keep. She served as house physician at Mercy Hospital while in Des Moines.

Another physician to assume an important position in Des Moines was Captain Victor Nakashima who became a resident doctor at Mercy Hospital after four years in the army medical corps, including two years in combat areas overseas. At Karachi, then in India, Dr. Nakashima operated on "scores of American boys . . . all of whom were grateful for the care we could give and not one showed any indication they resented having a Nisei doctor."

Meanwhile, the Japanese-Americans moved into more and more diverse jobs in Des Moines. George Yoshida went to work as a maintenance man at Wakonda Golf Club for seventy-five cents an hour, then took a foundry job at the Wood Brothers Farm Equipment Factory at three dollars an hour. He became a watchmaker before retiring. Yoshida had spent twenty-two months and his family an additional ten months in an Arizona center before being released to come to Des Moines.

Bill Hosokawa was hired as an editor by *The Des Moines Register,* as was his brother. Kiyoshi Minami bought the old Rose Bowl Lounge at 2023 Grand Avenue, for eight thousand dollars and spent another five thousand dollars remodelling. Ruth Fukoto did well as a stenographer for a government agency. Masao Terai ultimately attained a position as supervisor at Firestone. Ted Hata was a refrigeration expert who started work at Moore Electric Company for twenty-five cents an hour before opening his own business.

Bob Morishege took a job at the Grand Central Service Station at Ninth and Grand Avenue. Henry Sakata was a florist shop employee. Sam Kurumoto and George Shimada went through Still College and became osteopathic physicians, Sam and his family settling afterwards at Webster City and the Shimadas at Marshalltown.

One young Nisei woman held a job as a welder. Quite a few others worked as housemaids for twelve dollars a week, the going wage at the time. Some, however, were lured away to Chicago where they could get fifteen dollars a week as maids.

By the end of 1944 there were 152 Japanese-American students in Iowa schools, mostly in Des Moines. Nearly 30 were at Drake University, others in the University of Iowa, Iowa State, and in various colleges, high schools, and grade schools. Minami had two daughters at Drake, a son and daughter at Roosevelt High School, and a son at Callanan Junior High. "This is a better town for education," Minami said.

It seems inconsistent, but the armed forces enlisted a lot of young Nisei men while government forced their brothers into resettlement. Fred Kitagawa, who had come to Des Moines to work for Chambers, had three brothers in the U. S. Army. Brent Yoshida saw service in the army all the way to Tokyo in 1945 while his brother George was interned and then relocated in Des Moines.

All Nisei automatically were ineligible for the draft during their first years in Iowa. That ban was lifted January 1, 1945, and 140 Nisei of military age in this state became subject to selective service. That improved their morale.

"They are anxious to go," said Gibbs. "They have regarded it as more or less a slam against them not to be considered for selective service on the same basis as anybody else."

The Nisei began arriving in Des Moines in mid-1942 and started leaving after the embargo was lifted on January 1, 1945, the year the war ended. "Almost to a man, those who returned went back to their former homes," said Dr. Nakashima, who had moved to the staff of the Des Moines veterans' hospital.

The Ichiokas reopened their clinic in Los Angeles. Fred Kitigawa started an auto repair shop back in California. Ruth Wakida returned to Fresno. "It doesn't sound inviting to go back now," she said, "but I was born and brought up there. Life begins and ends for me there."

Bill Hosokawa joined the staff of the *Denver Post*. The Reverend Lester Suzuki moved to Seattle where he became pastor-at-large for Japanese-Americans. Larry Kagawa took over as general manager for Occidental Insurance Company in Honolulu and he took with him Relocation Director Frank Gibbs as his assistant. By 1988, the wartime contingent of Japanese-Americans had dwindled to a handful in Des Moines.

"There are only six that we know of here," said George Yoshida. They were Yoshida, Ted Hata, and Masao Terai and their wives.

Asked to recall his state of mind when he was uprooted back in the 1940s, Yoshida said: "I didn't feel too good about it but what could you do? You can't fight the government. So we just followed each other out."

Asked about President Roosevelt's removal decision, Yoshida said: "I don't really suppose you could blame the man. He had his advice. He had national security to think of."

What about the $20,000 payment? Is it fair? "Oh my goodness, I can't express my feelings on that," Yoshida said. "I can't say I deserve it. I don't know about that."

Ted Hata, seventy-nine, who retired in 1987 after forty-five years in the refrigeration business, said he never was bitter over being shipped out of Los Angeles. "I was born in the United States and have always been a citizen in the United States," he observed. "When we got orders to go, we go." He had graduated from the University of Southern California before the war.

Asked about the $20,000 payment, Hata commented: "We lost more than $20,000 overnight. Congress is getting off cheap." He told of getting less than $100 for a fairly new Plymouth car when he left the west. He had to leave a house he owned. He felt lucky when he found a GI whose wife needed a place to live. He rented the house to them for $25 a month in return for her watching over the property.

Hata liked Des Moines: "The people here are very sincere. We were all well treated from the first. This is a nice place." And Yoshida in looking back was glad it all happened even though he disliked Iowa winters. "I wanted to get away from orchards and gardening in California," he said. "If I had it to do over, I would come to Des Moines again."

The Royal Prince

Royal Prince Rupert was a big flop. He had the ability to make love but couldn't become a father. He tried with many girl friends but no results.

So the Prince had to be turned into mostly sausage at the Iowa Packing Company plant in Des Moines. How he got to Des Moines is a story of high hopes and disappointment, of a lot of effort that came to naught.

Had Rupert been a human, he would have lived his life out peacefully and without penalty. But his royal highness was a handsome Hereford bull, the most valuable of his time.

He originally belonged to Governor Roy Turner of Oklahoma. The governor sold Rupert in 1943 to two Texas ranches for a then-record $38,000.

The Texans had every reason to believe the Prince would be worth the money. Their expectations seemed well-founded. Rupert's father was Hazford Rupert XV, a grand champion bull at the International Livestock Show in Chicago in the late 1930s. The Prince's full brother won another grand championship at the International a couple of years later.

The only reason anyone keeps a bull, however, is to breed cows to produce calves which grow into breeding stock or beef for the market. When calves don't materialize, goodbye bull.

Rupert undoubtedly enjoyed his life in Texas. He got plenty to eat and work was pleasant. But he accomplished nothing. In contrast, an Illinois bull later sired one hundred thousand calves in ten years. Rupert's lifetime output was zero. He was sterile.

The Prince had to go back home to Oklahoma. Governor Turner repaid the $38,000 plus expenses the Texans incurred in care and keep.

Iowa readers followed the Rupert story with zest in the *Des Moines Register,* which provided regular detailed reports. One intrigued reader was Wayne Fox of Des Moines. Only he wasn't at home. World War II was raging. Wayne was a captain in the air force stationed on far-off Saipan in the South Pacific.

Wayne Fox (courtesy Wayne Fox)

"My mother used to roll up the *Register*s every week or two and send them to me," he said. "I read about this bull. I decided I wanted to see what I could do with him if he still were around after the war."

Wayne had worked in his father's "Foxbilt" feed company before the war. They had had success with a similar problem. They had taken a $20,000 bull which had gone sterile after sickness and a high fever. The animal was given special feed mixtures and shots of testosterone, and was back impregnating cows in six months.

Rupert was still living in Oklahoma when Wayne got out of the service. "I called Turner who had Rupert around as a sort of pet," Fox said. "Roy told me that if I could get the animal going, he'd be half mine. I figured one calf from such a widely advertised bull would bring $100,000, so why not? I went and got Rupert in a double-horse trailer."

Wayne spent nearly two years trying to get Rupert on track in Iowa. Rupert was put on a reduction program that cut his weight from 2,300 to 1,425 pounds, a loss of nearly 900 pounds. Veterinary Dr. M. A. Emmerson of Iowa State University in Ames got into the act. Rupert absorbed lots of hormones, vitamins, and advice.

In addition, Fox bought a proved bull in 1948 for $1,000. The animal, Silver Letston, was slaughtered. Dr. Emmerson quickly transplanted the Letston pituitary gland into the Prince's neck to beef up his sexual powers.

That didn't do the job either. All hope gone, Fox regretfully sold seven-year-old Rupert to the packinghouse in February 1949 for $230 or about 16 cents a pound. The Prince had brought $18 a pound when first sold by the Oklahoma governor.

Not all of Rupert went into bologna. Quantities of tenderloin steaks went to Governor Roy Turner and Governor William S. Beardsley of Iowa and packages of Rupert hamburger to Lieutenant Governor Ken Evans of Iowa and the lieutenant governor of Oklahoma.

Fox said the Oklahoma legislature approved a resolution under which the flag was flown at half-staff over the state capitol in Oklahoma City at the time of Rupert's demise. The resolution said the entire nation was "stunned and bowed its head in sincere bereavement" at the passing of "one of Oklahoma's greatest non-producing sons."

Ruthie

Barmaid Ruthie gained world fame by carrying two full glasses of beer at a time on her big-breasted bosom without spilling a drop.

Ruthie (Mayita Photo)

Originally Ruth Williams, she operated Ruthie's Lounge at 1311 Locust Street, and other locations in Des Moines in the 1950s. Pictures of Ruthie doing her thing appeared in newspapers coast to coast, in foreign countries and seventeen magazines as well as the military newspaper *Stars and Stripes.*

Visitors from around the nation wanted more than anything else to "go see Ruthie." One enthusiast invited her to take a vacation at his expense in Clearwater, Florida. (She didn't accept.) Cecil B. DeMille, the noted Hollywood film director, stopped in twice. At his suggestion, she raised the price of beer from the going rate of seventeen cents a glass to fifty cents.

"He told me people came in to see me, not for the beer, and I should charge the higher amount," Ruthie said. Business didn't fall off at all.

She enjoyed profits of $250 a night, equal to well over $1,000 in 1990 inflated dollars. "I cried when I got only $200," she recalled.

She loved Monday nights to Thursday nights because that was when traveling salesmen poured in. She took in additional cash by selling pictures of herself for one dollar, plus one dollar for an autograph, and an additional one dollar if she added a sassy comment.

She was twenty-two years old in 1950. Her measurements were 48-inch double "D" bust; waist 19 inches; hips 33 inches; weight 118 pounds. One writer said she gave new meaning to the phrase "beer bust."

Ruthie denied she ever had wax, paraffin, or any other substance injected into her breasts to strengthen their carrying capacity. "Everything there was just me," she said.

Des Moines police brought charges of obscenity and indecency against her. Captain Louis Volz testified he saw her "balance a glass on her bosom and then pour beer into the glass from a bottle." Municipal Judge Harry Grund dismissed the charges. He said the act wasn't indecent and "no worse than performances seen on TV."

She presented a spectacular picture one time when she came to court wearing a purple suit, large purple hat and mink stole. She was married sixteen times to nine men, including three men at one time. One marriage lasted just twelve hours. "I woke up and he was looking for my safe deposit key," she said. "That was it."

Ruthie denied that she ever did the strip tease in Chicago. "I was an exotic dancer, not a stripper," she said. "I didn't take my clothes off. But then, I didn't have much on."

She said one of her biggest thrills was having her picture taken with President Dwight Eisenhower at the Iowa State Fair in the 1950s. She said the president wanted the picture "to show American boys in Korea." Whereabouts of that picture are unknown.

By 1990 Ruthie had long since retired and had been the wife of Frank Bisignano for thirty uninterrupted years. They lived quietly on Des Moines' south side. At sixty-two years of age she weighed 162 pounds, suffered from arthritis, and was hard of hearing but still lively.

She liked to recall that she had been in Hawaii six times on honeymoons in her life and had been around the world twice. She and a husband were granted brief audiences with Pope Pius XII and John XXIII in Rome. She said that husband was wealthy and gave "thousands of dollars" to the Vatican on both occasions. She said she told Pope John that what she tried to do with her life was make people happy. She said the Pope replied: "That is good."

She didn't explain what she did back in Des Moines to make people happy other than to say she was in "entertainment."

Lucky for Ruthie, the federal government never learned of her statement to the Pope. The government tried to assess a huge cabaret tax on the theory that the act "constituted entertainment." Her attorney argued that the act was merely "a convenient way to dispense beer." The courts held for Ruthie and she didn't have to pay.

For all she knows, Ruthie may be on the map of the Far East. At the height of her fame anyway, a pair of mountains in Korea were named "the Ruthies."

Archie

The story of Archie Alexander appears at first glance to be that of an ordinarily successful individual. He graduated from the University of Iowa with an engineering degree and three football letters in 1912. With various partners and associates, he built such projects as a big Union Pacific railroad bridge over the Platte River in Nebraska, a heating plant at the University of Iowa, a large sewage system, the East Fourteenth Street viaduct, and the Fleur Drive bridge in Des Moines. Archie and a partner went broke in the Great Depression, and recovered. Archie served as governor of the Virgin Islands in 1954 and 1955 under appointment from President Eisenhower. Alexander was condemned in the 1956 Democratic national platform for his record in the Virgin Islands job. He resigned because of ill health, not the partisan heat. The president expressed regret at his leaving. Archie was a leading Des Moines Republican of his time.

All of which constituted an unusual lifetime record for his era for a simple reason: Archie Alexander was a black man. His father was a janitor in what became Norwest bank in downtown Des Moines.

Archie was a teenager in 1907 when old Highland Park College at Second and Euclid refused him admittance because he was black. The University of Iowa accepted him the next year.

Among those with whom Alexander associated in construction projects was Glenn Herrick, well-known and successful white contractor.

The color problem came to the fore in 1944 when Archie and his wife bought an excellent home at 2200 Chatauqua Parkway in Des Moines for the then high price of $20,000. Owners of fifty-eight other properties in the neighborhood brought suit to cancel the deal. The suit pointed out that the abstracts of all homes in the area contained a provision banning ownership by blacks until 1948 at least.

The suit was unsuccessful. Archie Alexander died at sixty-nine years of age in 1958 in his Chatauqua Parkway home. His will set up scholarships that grew to $200,000 for engineering students at the University of Iowa, Howard University, and Tuskegee Institute.

Alexander's philosophy of life was demonstrated by a comment he made while a student. A white professor at Iowa expressed doubt that a black person could make it in engineering in the climate of those times.

"None of us knows until we try," Archie is reported to have replied, "and even then we keep trying."

Archie Alexander (*Des Moines Register*)

Mural Bites Dust

L loyd Cunningham knew nothing about painting and art. A farmer by trade, Cunningham nevertheless had a spectacular effect on modern art in Des Moines.

It was at his direction that an historical mural 110 feet long and 10 feet high was destroyed in 1946 at the State Fair. He had workmen saw up the big painting in the agricultural building and use the lumber in patchwork around the fairgrounds. Cunningham said he didn't like the mural and he needed the lumber. He was secretary of the fair board and manager of the fair.

Unemployed artists working under a federal WPA (Works Progress Administration) jobs program painted the mural in the 1930s. It colorfully portrayed a century of life in Iowa, including scenes of workers on farms and in industry, of landscapes, Indians, and so on.

Cutting up the mural raised a brief storm of protest around the state. Cunningham was unrepentant. "The mural wasn't art, it was WPA," he said. "It was an insult to Iowa farmers because it depicted them as club-footed, coconut-headed, barrel-necked, and low browed— those guys didn't look like farmers to me." The fair board approved the destruction.

The mural cost thirteen thousand dollars, of which the federal government paid ten thousand dollars in wages to the artists. The state footed a $3,000 bill for materials.

Democratic State Chairman Jake More blasted Cunningham. "An investigator whom I sent to see the destruction says a portion of the painting of [Indian Chief] Black Hawk was lying face down on the floor," More declared. "Pictures of Keokuk, Appanoose, Wapello, and other famous Indian chiefs and of early white-man pioneers were cut and thrown about in confusion. Other pieces of the painting had been nailed along the walls to fill up niches in the new woodwork and used as covers or roofs of booths and stairway arches."

In a sharp reply, the secretary said: "It was a joke to have that thing in a fairgrounds that is devoted to glorifying the Iowa farmer and his accomplishments." There was a lot of good lumber in the mural, Cunningham said, and "besides, the fair board was tired of being kidded about that picture."

A *Register* reporter took Cunningham to the Des Moines Art Center to get his opinion on various paintings on display. At one abstract painting the reporter asked: "You wouldn't have that artist paint your barn, would you?"

Cunningham refused to answer at first. "You son of a bitch, you are just trying to get me into trouble," he said. But then he relaxed. Asked what he thought of an abstract painting titled "Guitar with Fruit," he said: "If that is fruit it is indigestible. That picture doesn't mean anything to me at all. Either my imagination isn't fully developed or my art education has been neglected."

Before a painting named "Blue Horses," he said: "Now that's a picture I like. Of course, I never saw a blue horse but the color is nice and the animals undoubtedly are blue horses." He liked Marvin Cone farm pictures: "Whoever painted them either lives on a farm or has lived on a farm."

Told that an Edouard Manet painting on display was worth $50,000, Cunningham commented that he wouldn't trade twenty thousand bushels of corn for it. (Corn was worth $2.50 a bushel at the time.) He called "terrible" a Modigliani painting called "Bride and Groom." If they are bride and groom, Lloyd said, "they are pretty unhappy." The two persons in that painting had vertical lines dividing their faces. They looked as if they had been eating persimmons, Cunningham said.

"I just don't understand this modernistic stuff," he commented. He thought it was time to get rid of the state fair mural because it had "served its purpose." What was its purpose? "To give jobs to WPA painters, wasn't it?"

Cunningham suffered no lasting effects from his drastic venture into the realm of art criticism. The fair board didn't fire him. Indeed, the board members couldn't because they were co-conspirators. And what protests there were had come from a small minority of Iowans. A majority probably agreed with Cunningham about modern art.

What happened to the mural recalled the earlier fate at the fair of a replica of the Herbert Hoover birthplace cottage. (Hoover was the only native Iowan ever elected president of the United States.) The replica was a fair attraction for some time. Years later it was discovered serving as a bathhouse in the fair camp grounds.

Opal

An attractive brunette armed only with a syringe filled with Listerine robbed a downtown Des Moines bank of $2,950. The January 1947 robbery was one of the more bizarre of Iowa's countless bank holdups over the years.

Opal Dixon, thirty-five, bought the syringe and mouthwash at a 5-and-10-cent store in the loop. Moments later she entered the old Des Moines Bank and Trust Company, then located on Sixth Avenue, south of the Equitable building. Brandishing the syringe, she declared: "This is a stickup. Don't anybody move. I have enough stuff to blow the place to pieces and I'll go with it."

She took the money from a frightened teller, walked out calmly and disappeared into the sidewalk throng. She was wearing a gray coat and was bareheaded. (Most women wore hats then.)

Soon after the police, armed with a personal description, grabbed her as she emerged from the Equitable building. She confessed a short time later. The syringe and nearly all the money was found in a restroom on the Equitable eleventh floor. She had paid $75 dollars to a dentist in the interval.

Opal and her fifth husband and two daughters were living in the Cargill, a seamy downtown hotel. They had been knocking around the country, working some of the time. Opal was a rank amateur when it came to robbing banks but she did succeed in filching $582 from a St. Louis bank some weeks before. That money was gone when she tried her hand at doing it again in Des Moines.

"If I had gotten by with that job, my family would be eating juicy steaks today," she said. "I'm a nursemaid with a headache now. I'm sorry it all happened. I wouldn't advise any woman to take up bank robbing."

She went to the woman's reformatory at Rockwell City on a life sentence, which was mandatory for bank robbing in Iowa in those days. She got out after ten years, was returned for excessive drinking and other reasons, and finally was freed for good in the late 1960s.

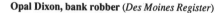

Opal Dixon, bank robber (*Des Moines Register*)

He Lost His Pants

*R*egister photographer John Neagle wobbled barefooted into his hotel in Chicago at two o'clock in the morning and was also minus his pants and money. Another time he showed up without his camera when he was supposed to take important pictures for *Look* magazine in a race for the presidency. Both times he was loaded with liquor, which was his condition all too often.

Nevertheless he was an excellent photographer, one of the best of his time in Iowa. He almost always got good pictures. He joined *The Register* staff in the late 1930s. *The Register* ultimately had to fire him after forgiving his drinking capers many times.

John was in the company of sportswriters Bert McGrane and Maury White on that fateful occasion in Chicago in 1946. It was the custom of the newspaper to send a team of writers and a photographer on an airplane tour of Big Ten universities each year prior to the opening of the football season. The team provided a words-and-pictures report for fans on the grid prospects of the various schools.

White was given an extra assignment on this trip. "It's your job," he was told, "to see to it that Neagle gets to the plane each morning." White said: "That meant I had to stay up a hell of a lot of nights and do a lot of drinking I didn't want to do, but I did it." Neagle and White roomed together on the road.

Maury White, left, and John Neagle (courtesy Maury White)

Chicago was the last stop on that tour. The *Register* trio looked over the Northwestern University team in suburban Evanston, then went to a north side Chicago hotel for the night. White had had notable success up to that point in keeping Neagle out of trouble. But Chicago was something else.

White arranged to have dinner with an old friend in Chicago and invited Neagle to come along. John said he had too much film work to do with shots taken from three of the schools they had visited. "John gave his word of honor he would not leave our hotel," White said. "I took his word of honor."

White got back to the hotel before midnight. "No Neagle," he said. "There is nothing I could do so I go to bed. I was sleeping away and, son of a bitch, all of a sudden the phone rings. It's a cab driver in the lobby. He says: 'I got your buddy downstairs in a cab. Come down and get him and bring some money and a pair of pants and a pair of shoes.' I look and it's two o'clock in the morning. I go downstairs with pants and money and no shoes and I pay off the cab driver. Neagle is potted and he puts on the pants. He walks barefooted up to the room."

White said Neagle gave this "fantastic" explanation: He had finished his picture work early in the evening and remembered a Chicago relative who lived eighty blocks across the city. He decided to visit that relative.

He reached the general neighborhood but wasn't certain of the address. He dropped into a bar (naturally) to get directions, and, of course, to have some drinks. The bartender said he didn't know where the Neagle relative lived but another patron said he did, and he offered to take John to the place. "So the guy takes Johnny and leads him through an alley," White related. "All of a sudden, John says, he is jumped by three or four men, ferocious men, and they stomp him to death almost. And they take his pants and shoes and a pretty good-sized diamond ring he is wearing, and all his money and his watch.

"He says he is lying there with his eyes closed, faking being dead while they are talking about whether they should kill him. Anyway they don't. So, this being John Neagle, this man without any pants or shoes or money, manages to stop a cab and talk the driver into taking him eighty blocks across Chicago. I am sitting there, listening in disbelief and admiring the great story. But then the son of a bitch talks himself into believing his own story and decides to call the cops. So he calls the cops. So, at three o'clock in the morning, two Chicago detectives come up to our room. They hear the story. They say: 'Where did this happen?' He tells them. They say: 'My God, that's eighty blocks away, that's silly.' That made Neagle, still potted, mad."

White went on: "There used to be a guy on the old Chicago *Herald-American,* picture editor I think, who was one of our old

Register and *Tribune* guys in Des Moines. So Neagle starts throwing his name around, the power of the press and all that, at these cops. They stand up there, Neagle and the cops, and argue with each other, and it's four in the morning when they finally clear out. And of course I have had a very poor night's sleep."

Both White and Neagle had problems when they got up. "We didn't want Bert McGrane, who was a crusty old gentleman, to find out about this," White said, "but John doesn't have any shoes and he can't go to the plane without shoes. To make matters worse, he wears some stupid-sized shoe. So I get up the next goddam morning and walk around trying to find shoes for Neagle. I finally get some that are too big for him but at least he has something on his feet." McGrane never caught on. Neagle told the editors back in Des Moines that he had been robbed in Chicago.

"Then Johnny tries to make up all that money, the shoes, the pants, the diamond ring, on his expense account," White said. "The office is so burned up at him that the editors do not send a photographer on the Big Ten football trip the next couple of years."

White had to go with Neagle on another occasion to either Oskaloosa or Ottumwa, Iowa, to see a black college team play a white college team. Such inter-racial contests were rare at the time.

Neagle took the necessary pictures. White spent considerable time after the game was over, asking both teams questions for the follow-up story. The crowd filed out. The place was soon deserted. "All of a sudden I can't find Neagle," White said. "I wait around and he doesn't show. So everybody's gone but the janitor and myself. I am standing down there on the floor not having any idea what to do because Neagle has the car. All of a sudden the janitor looks up in the balcony and says: 'Is that your friend?' There's this man weaving back and forth up there. Sure enough, it's Neagle.

"Well, Neagle had been born in this town, and the doctor who birthed him is still there, and John goes away from the game early and he goes to the doctor's and they are drinking and they go to a nightclub for drinks. And John tells me we are going back there for just one more drink.

"And we go although I don't want to. And everybody puts pressure on me to stay over and return to Des Moines in the morning. They are going to give me a bed and we're all going to stay and visit with his old friend."

White couldn't do that because he had to write a story the next morning for *The Des Moines Tribune,* an afternoon newspaper. "I know I've got to get down to the office in the morning and write the story, and it's winter," White continued. "And I keep saying no, we're going home now. Neagle gets mad and gets up and says: 'The only reason we're going home is because you can whip me.'"

Neagle drove seventy miles an hour on icy roads returning to Des Moines but luckily had no accident. White recalled: "Every time we pass a lighted bar, Neagle says: 'I usually stop for a drink in that place but we're not going to because of you, you sonafabitch.' "

Neagle deposited White at his home at 2:30 A.M.

"I stagger into the office at seven in the morning," White said. "Here comes Neagle, weaving out of the photography department. He'd been helling around the rest of the night. But he did develop the pictures."

Other *Register* newsmen went through hectic experiences with Neagle. This author had his hands full trying to keep John corralled at Jefferson, Iowa, in 1947. *Look* magazine hired me to cover a speech at Jefferson by Harold Stassen who was a leading contender for the 1948 Republican presidential nomination. Jefferson is sixty-one miles northwest of Des Moines.

Look editors told me to engage a photographer of my choice to take pictures of the event for the magazine. The afternoon before, I selected Neagle, believing that he would stay sober for the privilege of having his pictures appear in a national magazine.

I was wrong. John went right over to Dave Fidler's alcohol emporium on Seventh Street in downtown Des Moines that same afternoon and celebrated by getting gloriously drunk.

Stassen came by train to Des Moines early the next morning and motored the rest of the way to Jefferson. Newsmen gathered at the Rock Island to greet the candidate. Neagle was among them, suffering from a terrible hangover. Neagle took a couple of drinks at the station trying to recuperate but without success. Nevertheless, he kept nipping away at a bottle in the motor convoy to Jefferson, a county seat town of 4,400 population.

The situation at Jefferson presented excellent picture possibilities. Farm and small town people flocked in from the area as if it were a county fair or carnival day. Stassen spent hours before his evening speech talking with rural people to improve his rural image which was already good. He had served as governor of Minnesota and had delivered the keynote speech at the 1940 Republican national convention.

Stassen started speaking at 6 P.M. from the south canopy of the county courthouse. Five minutes before, Neagle came wandering down the street—without his camera. He had put it down somewhere while "relaxing" and had forgotten where. He was about to flop on his most prestigious assignment in years.

Suddenly he remembered he had been drinking in a certain home. He hurried there and found the place locked. The family had gone to hear Stassen. Fortunately, somebody located the family in the crowd.

A son rushed home and enabled John to retrieve his camera. Neagle did get back in time to take a few pictures before Stassen stopped speaking.

In this case liquor did interfere with John's usual good professional performance. The pictures he took for *Look* were not good at all. But he was rescued. Photographer John Robinson was there covering for the *Tribune* and his pictures went to *Look* in New York.

Neagle served in the Navy in World War II and spent a lot of his service time at a naval air base at Ottumwa, Iowa, ninety miles from Des Moines. John came to Des Moines frequently to party and to see such friends as Miles Sines, then picture editor of *The Register*.

Neagle got a ride to Des Moines one evening for the purpose of playing golf early the next morning with Sines. John relaxed all night and was in poor condition when he arrived at Sines' house at dawn for the golf date.

Unhappy Miles, seeing that Neagle was plastered, seated him on the front room sofa and ordered: "I'm going to make you some coffee. And don't you move till I come back. Understand?"

John obeyed but not for long. He decided he wanted to say hello to Mrs. Sines whose name was Natalie. John wandered upstairs and into a room where a woman was sleeping.

He gave her a whack on the fanny and shouted: "Hi Nat!" She screamed in fright. She was not Natalie at all but a teen-age business college student who stayed in the Sines home and took care of the children. Neagle probably scared her out of ten years of her life span. Mrs. Sines was in another room.

Miles was ready to assassinate John but didn't.

Another time Neagle and this reporter journeyed to Davenport, Iowa, on Thursday evening. The plan was to stay in Davenport overnight and to go to East Moline, Illinois, very early the next morning to cover an attempted smashing of a picket line in front of a strikebound farm machinery plant.

Neagle and I got a twin-bed room about 11 P.M. at the Black Hawk Hotel across the Mississippi River in Davenport and left a call for 5 A.M.

John, however, didn't want to go to bed right away. He said he was hungry and wanted a steak. He pointed out that he was Catholic and was forbidden at the time to eat meat on Friday which was only an hour away. He swore he would be right back, honest, so help me.

He left. I went to bed. The next thing I knew the phone was ringing for the five o'clock call and Neagle was just coming in the door, far far from sober. He had been carousing all night and hadn't had any sleep.

I poured a lot of coffee into him in an all-night restaurant but it did little good.

Covering picket line violence can be touchy and dangerous. Often pickets don't like newsmen. What would be the effect of injecting an intoxicated photographer into such a situation? It was plenty worrisome.

As it turned out, Neagle's condition proved to be an asset. The pickets had prepared grimly for the confrontation, and so had the police who were to battle on the other side. Into that tense arena strode Neagle, smiling and staggering, full of liquor and good fellowship. Swaying back and forth, he waved his arm and said with a thick tongue: "I wan . . . you guys to get out here . . . and do a ring-around-a-rosy and I'll . . . get your picture into the . . . *Des Moines Register.*"

Realizing that John had had too many, the pickets broke into laughter. They did the ring-around-a-rosy while John snapped pictures. The tension eased, for the moment at least. John was the most popular of the dozen or more newsmen on the scene.

The atmosphere changed quickly when a car appeared and the driver tried to jam his way through the picket line. A pitched battle took place, with the pickets trying to hold the car from going forward and the police struggling to push aside the pickets. The car got through but was dented and otherwise damaged. Both pickets and police suffered bumps and bruises.

Neagle had climbed up on a nearby railroad structure. He didn't fall off, as might have been expected, and he got a fine picture of the clash. He did the job he was sent to do, whatever his condition.

But time was running out for John. Liquor increasingly interfered with his work. The editors warned that one more liquor episode and he was done. He was found passed out on somebody else's front porch. That did it.

He went to California and his problems went with him. Miles Sines had been named to a top post on the *Long Beach Press Telegram* meanwhile. Miles gave John a job but he couldn't lay off the booze and again he was out. One of his last jobs was with the publicity department of the Queen Mary ocean liner docked permanently at Long Beach.

John was living in a desert city in California when he died in 1985. He is a hilarious but tragic character in the traditions of Des Moines journalism.

The Home Plate

An editorial writer may have saved the life of a downtown Des Moines bootleg tavern.

Beginning in the 1930s Louie Siegel ran the Home Plate Slide In Bar at 910 Locust Street. It was a popular place for relaxation. The patrons included many newspaper people, including Bob Blakely, editorial writer for *The Register*.

Louie served beer, which was legal, and hard liquor, which was not in bars at the time. Siegel could handle problems with the law. Paying a fine or paying off officers was part of the cost of doing business. But he could not stand difficulties with his landlord, the Hubbell estate, which owned the property.

Louie's lease expired. The Hubbells wanted him out. Louie panicked. He faced the loss of his livelihood. Whereupon Blakely sprang to the rescue.

Blakely, a blithe spirit, sent a hilarious letter July 22, 1948, to James Hubbell, Sr., a top official of the estate. "I have patronized taverns the length and breadth of the North American continent; also in Micronesia, Melanesia, and the Orient, and nowhere have I found so good a tavern as Louie's," wrote Blakely. "It is the closest approximation in this country to the English pub. As such it makes a vital contribution to our democratic society. There representatives of different social groups meet on a plane of convivial equality. Thus the chasms that are yawning between our classes are bridged. There the affairs of the day are discussed with information, energy, and wit. Thus, public education is improved."

The result, Blakely said, was that "busy persons from all walks of life relax and are refreshed and leave to do a better job. Thus our nation is strengthened," the letter continued. "There men and women meet in decent friendship. Thus the schooling of women to take a more responsible role in our society is promoted. There buddy knows where to meet buddy and wife knows where to find husband. Thus the bonds of home and companionship are reinforced."

Regarding Siegel himself, Blakely wrote: "He is a mature man who should have many years of life before him. This, however, is contingent upon his being active. If he is not able to have his tavern, he will waste and wither, and die, and his death will be on your hands. His host of friends will accuse you with their haunting eyes."

Blakely said the Home Plate was not just a local institution but was known "wherever newspapermen assemble. It is the locale referred to in 'The Whiffenpoof Song' in the line down where Louie dwells." The letter concluded: "Be assured, sire, of my continued esteem, provided you give Louie a lease."

It isn't known whether Blakely composed the letter after a considerable period of relaxation in the Home Plate. Whether the letter had anything to do with it, the lease evidently was renewed. The records show that police raids on the Home Plate for liquor law violations continued into the 1950s.

Visiting parents and friends at Raymond Blank Memorial Hospital in Des Moines, September 1948

Looking in Windows

A man on a tall ladder peered into a window on the second floor of the red brick building. He talked and laughed loudly. It was eerie because you couldn't see to whom he was talking.

Down on the ground two women stood on a bench and looked and talked into another window. Nearby another woman balanced herself on a cement block while concentrating on a window. On the other side two women and a man crouched on their elbows and knees as they looked into a cellar window just above the ground level. One woman was a blonde, the other brown haired. The blonde held a brightly colored book up to the window.

"Here, Mickey, here are your puppies running away from home," she shouted. "See! Here they go across the bridge." She turned a page. "Now four of them are on the hill. But the pokey puppy they can't find. He's lost again. Isn't that a shame?"

The red brick building is Raymond Blank Memorial Hospital in Des Moines. The adults acting so strangely were worried parents. Behind the closed windows were their small children, all ill of the dread poliomyelitis, also known as infantile paralysis. The youngsters had to be kept in isolation wards because the crippling and sometimes deadly disease is contagious. Thus the parents were barred from visiting them inside.

It was a heart-wrenching sight watching fathers and mothers trying to make contact with their little ones through glass and screens.

The hospital was caring for 70 polio patients in the September 1948 period. Medical science had not yet found a way to prevent the disease that was a dangerous threat to children every summer and fall.

Iowa reported 1,236 polio cases that year and about 60 percent were children nine years of age and younger. More than a dozen were under one year old. Eighty-one died, or nearly 7 percent. About two-thirds of the others experienced paralysis to a greater or lesser degree, although complications pretty much disappeared in most instances. But some suffered permanent handicaps, a few of which were severe.

But what was a little thing like a window pane or even a climb on a fifteen-foot ladder when Dad wanted to see his sick child? Each afternoon dozens of parents gathered on the south side of the hospital and on the north lawn to see their youngsters somehow.

The man on the tall ladder was Don Fisher, a thirty-six-year-old railway express agent from Chariton, Iowa. Inside was his three-year-old son Johnny who had been in the hospital isolation section for weeks.

Every day, or at least every other day, Fisher drove fifty-two miles from Chariton to Des Moines. Johnny waved delightedly as he watched his dad set the ladder against the building.

"Hi, Johnny. What are you doing? What? You have a car just like Billy's? That's fine." Johnny held up a toy automobile for his father to see. Billy was the little boy with whom Johnny played back home.

The Fisher tot was especially happy to see his father come because it always meant another present. On one occasion Dad brought two books, a set of educational cards, and two more toy autos. Johnny's mother was ill back home after having had another baby.

For the first ten days Fisher transported a ladder back and forth from Chariton, one end tied to the radiator with a piece of calico, the other to a door handle with rope. The ladder, however, hooked a car one night on the highway and was smashed to kindling. Neither car was damaged much. Don borrowed a ladder in Des Moines after that. He had to stand in the rain on the ladder once and luckily had his work clothes on on that occasion.

Johnny was very sick at first but showed improvement after three weeks. But he still couldn't stand up without holding on to something.

Mickey was the six-year-old son of Mr. and Mrs. Joe Blaha, a farm couple six miles southwest of Pocahontas, Iowa. Mickey also had been seriously ill but was starting to get better in September. His mother talked to him by the hour through one of the north windows.

Sometimes, when nobody wanted to share the window with her, Mrs. Blaha stretched out full length on the grill work by the cellar window and read in a loud voice such stories as the one about the "Pokey Puppy." Mickey got a lot of presents too. Mother had a jumping-jack clown which she showed him through the window before she sent it in to him. Holding up the clown she shouted:

"Can you see this, honey? Watch him jump this time. Do you suppose I could hang on a fence and jump over it like that? . . . You turned on your side? Why, Mickey, wasn't that swell?"

Then she said: "See him turn his head? He did that good, didn't he? When he turns his left side, he turns clear to the middle. She [the nurse] had him sitting up too. Mickey, I'm going to write Daddy and tell him about you sitting up. Maybe I had better even call him."

Mrs. Blaha observed to other parents: "If Mickey could just get the use of his hands, he could entertain himself so much. He could look at comic books." Turning back to the window, she shouted: "Mickey, I'll read to you again after a while. It's a long time before Mama goes."

Often at the same window with Mrs. Blaha were Mr. and Mrs. Sam Sloss, Jr., farmers near Guthrie Center, Iowa. Their two-and-a-half-year-old daughter Diana was in an iron lung much of the time. She had been in the hospital more than a month.

"For seventeen days Diana didn't breathe at all," said her mother. "Now she can get along out of the respirator three and four hours at a time. The doctors say she may have to stay in the hospital a year." But Mrs. Sloss was hoping four or five months would be enough.

"Did you know Gail is going to get his hair cut?" she shouted to Diana. "Are you going to get your hair cut? Can you wave goodbye now, honey? Isn't that nice? Can you hold a book by yourself? Isn't that good?"

To an onlooker, Mrs. Sloss said: "Diana can riffle the pages in a book now. Isn't it funny how you can get a thrill out of such a little thing?"

Similarly at another window, Mrs. Merlin Hutchinson of Des Moines happily reported that "Sandra walked across the floor for us a while ago." Mrs. Hutchinson balanced herself on a stool as she visited her daughter Sandra, six, through the window.

Polio was a feared scourge of families everywhere for three generations or more. Iowa's worst polio year was 1952 when 3,564 cases were reported, with 163 deaths and an unknown number of cases of permanent paralysis.

The turning point came in 1955 when Salk vaccine came into use. That immunizing agent has all but wiped out polio. No longer is it necessary for worried fathers and mothers to climb ladders outside a hospital to see and talk to their little ones afflicted with that dangerous disease.

Two Pilots

Paul Tibbets, Jr.
(Associated Press)

Oscar N. Tibbetts
(United States Air Force)

Two native Des Moines pilots with almost exactly the same last name made profoundly historic flights to Japan. One was a mission that resulted in an estimated eighty thousand deaths, plus injuries to untold thousands more. The other was a demonstration of help and compassion.

On August 6, 1945, Colonel Paul Tibbets, Jr., was at the controls of the plane that dropped the world's first atom bomb on Hiroshima, Japan.

On January 16, 1960, Major Oscar N. Tibbetts, with two "t's" at the end of his name, piloted a transport plane carrying thirty-six Iowa breeding hogs to Japan to help farmers devastated by a typhoon. Generous Iowans also sent sixty thousand bushels of corn by ship at the same time.

Colonel Paul Tibbets, Jr., now seventy-five and living in Columbus, Ohio, was born in Des Moines in 1915. He attended grade school in Des Moines until he was nine when the family moved to Miami, Florida. His father was a wholesale confectioner. His mother was the former Enola Gay Haggard of Glidden, Iowa. Colonel Tibbets had the "Enola Gay" name emblazoned on the nose of the atom bomb plane.

Major Tibbetts, now about seventy-three, was born in Des Moines in about 1917. The Tibbetts family lived at 2900 Cottage Grove Avenue. The major graduated from Roosevelt High School.

Colonel Tibbets said he never experienced guilt feelings over the atomic bombing that had been ordered by President Truman. "We were at war and the only way to fight a war is to win it," he said. "You use anything at your disposal. There are no Marquis of Queensbury rules in war."

The Enola Gay (Smithsonian Institution)

Hiroshima (Smithsonian Institution)

Major Tibbetts' agricultural flight grew out of a plea for help sent to Iowa from Japan by Sergeant Dick Thomas of Des Moines. He was on military duty in Japan's Yamanashi prefecture (state) when a harsh typhoon hit the farms there. Iowa responded with the hogs and corn.

The grateful Japanese expressed their appreciation by sending Iowa the prefabricated bellhouse now located on the statehouse grounds south of the capitol building in Des Moines. Included in the gift was a two-thousand-pound bell which Japanese tradition says will keep evil spirits away for a whole twelve months if you strike it 108 times at midnight on New Year's Eve.

Please Don't Prosecute

A weeping Des Moines police officer got down on his knees before Iowa Attorney General Robert L. Larson. The officer was suspected of taking bribes from big-time gambling operators. He tearfully begged not to be prosecuted but to be allowed to retire before long instead. Larson consented. He didn't say so but he didn't have enough hard evidence for a conviction. The officer retired.

That dramatic scene took place in the statehouse in about 1950 during an all-Iowa drive by Larson against statewide commercial gambling operations.

Strange as it may seem now, it was totally against Iowa law in 1950 to bet on horses and dogs, to hold lotteries, to play bingo for cash prizes, to play cards for money in taverns, and to gamble on riverboats. Now all such wagering is fully legal except for riverboat gambling and that is coming in 1991.

It must be said, however, that—law or not—plenty of large scale gambling was taking place around Iowa before Larson cracked down. He was attorney general from 1947 to 1953. What he went after in particular were the three thousand or more slot machines operating in the state, many thousands more payoff pinball machines and unlimited numbers of punchboards. Other less concentrated forms of major gambling existed in some big cities: crap tables, football handicap sheets, and horse race betting on distant tracks, but these setups were not widespread.

Also, alcohol violations were commonplace, especially of the law forbidding sale of liquor by the drink. But Larson decided he couldn't handle all those problems simultaneously and his best contribution would be to concentrate on ridding the state of the slots, pinballs, and punchboards. It was a rugged battle as it was.

Attorney General Robert Larson (*Des Moines Register*)

Slot machines, also known as "one-armed bandits," were the biggest problem. They were played in fraternal clubs such as the Eagles and Elks, veterans' posts such as the American Legion, in country clubs, night clubs, and taverns.

The slots made big money for owners and operators. Larson estimated the "take" in Iowa at $2 million a week, equal to more than $10 million in the inflated dollars of 1989. One machine could produce a profit of $700 a week or close to it, depending upon the location.

Slot machines are metal boxlike devices. The player puts a coin in the slot, pulls a lever on the side. Wheels whirl and stop with various combinations, usually of cherries, plums, lemons, and the like. Certain combinations cause the machines to return sums of coins to the player now and then. But tests run in Larson's time showed the machines returned only a little over 30 percent of the money risked and kept nearly 70 percent.

Punchboards, found on thousands of restaurant and cafe counters, on bars, cigar store counters, and in clubs, similarly kept most of the players' money.

The attorney general believed that most of the slots were locally owned up until about 1948. Then, out-of-state elements began taking over, said Earl Shostrom, one of Larson's assistants. "Strange stories began to be heard of gangsters from Minneapolis and Kansas City moving into Iowa," said the assistant. "These people reportedly demanded a share of the proceeds or, in some cases, demanded that the clubs use the syndicate's machines, of course for a sizable fee. These gangsters started with the less respectable clubs and threatened to complain to the police if their request was refused. The owners felt they had no choice but to accede to the wishes of the gangsters."

In early October 1949, Larson said in a public announcement: "We are going to rid the state of gambling." Larson immediately found himself traveling a hard road. He even had opposition from such topflight Iowans as Governor William S. Beardsley and State Auditor C. B. Akers.

Here was the problem: Slot machines were a major source of income for such respectable institutions as country clubs and veterans' and fraternal organizations. Some of the slot income went for charities as well as to pay expenses.

Members of those organizations were "good people" in their communities, substantial citizens. A lot of them objected to the Larson campaign. Furthermore, they always voted, and the 1950 elections loomed ahead. They might retaliate at the polls.

Beardsley convened a worried and tense group of officials in his statehouse office to discuss the situation with Larson. The officials wanted the attorney general to lay off the "good clubs." Shostrom was present and heard the discussion.

"The Governor and others declared they were shocked," Shostrom recalled. "They believed Larson was going down to defeat in 1950 and would take the entire Republican state ticket with him. They said he was alienating too many important Iowans."

Beardsley and Akers were among those up for re-election in 1950.

The attorney general also was told that doing away with slot machines would dry up a lot of campaign contributions. Larson replied that he didn't care what happened politically, he was going to enforce the law. In good conscience he couldn't do anything else.

The meeting broke up with the attorney general still adamant. Officials left convinced that political disaster was approaching and that Larson was a stubborn SOB.

The attorney general himself also felt certain he would be beaten. He had advised his assistants earlier to start looking for other jobs, and that the campaign would be political suicide. But he said he had become so disturbed by the expanding gambling situation that he had to do something no matter what the cost.

The primary election was to be held June 5 and the general election November 6, 1950. A lot happened that winter and spring, before the primary arrived. Delegations of important Iowa businessmen and other "good people" called on Larson. Typical was a group from a Marshalltown country club.

The Marshalltownians said they agreed with the attorney general in his moves against slot machines and other gambling paraphernalia in "bad" places such as sleazy taverns. But why not let the "good places" alone?

A puzzled look came over Larson's face. He leaned back, took an Iowa code book of laws off the shelf, leafed through it and said: "I can't find where the law differentiates. Maybe I am missing something. The way I read it, the law applies the same to everybody."

The attorney general also didn't flinch when a statehouse newsman asked: "Aren't you cutting your own throat politically? Won't you get killed off in the election?" Larson responded angrily: "I don't care if I do. It's the right thing."

Threats came. One source said Mrs. Larson received calls threatening harm to the two Larson children. Some attorney general staff members received threatening calls as well. Larson and the staff were not intimidated. The threats didn't materialize.

One of the attorney general's first moves was to notify local officials that they had to enforce the law. The attorney general directed his principal attention to county attorneys. This was a touchy business.

It appeared to most local officers that a majority of Iowans wanted gambling. The officers saw respected citizens enter law-breaking clubs. Conscientious lawmen found they had no backing when they did try to crack down. Thus, it was easy to "look the other way." They didn't like to do that but they felt they had no other choice. They couldn't beat the system.

Some county attorneys resigned from clubs rather than constantly be reminded that they were not enforcing the law as they were sworn to do. In some cases, Larson told county attorneys that he would institute proceedings to remove them from office if they didn't act. Without exception they did act. Things started to roll.

One of the most sweeping series of raids in Iowa history took place November 30, 1949, in Des Moines. Led by state agents, fifty-six raiders charged into forty-three spots and seized seventy-four one-ball pinball machines within the city and two immediately outside.

The Register said: "The raids were a convincing demonstration that Larson intends to go the limit in stamping out gambling in every part of the state, regardless of the attitude of local officials."

It took numerous moving vans to haul the machines to the courthouse. Sixty machines were valued at $750 each, a figure that probably would be nearly $4,000 each now.

Larson personally signed the search warrants which were issued by Justice of the Peace George Bidwell. The attorney general went along on the raids as did several of his staff.

Des Moines city police took part also but they didn't know where they were going or for what until they climbed into five cars driven by state agents. That was to make sure there were no tip-offs. There was little chance of that anyway because the raiders spread out and hit a lot of the places simultaneously.

One tavern operator did get word, however, and he hurriedly put a pinball machine out in the alley next to his place of business. He maintained the machine wasn't his. The raiders picked it up. The machines all were condemned and destroyed by court order.

Most if not all the raided spots are long since gone. Old-timers will remember some of the names, the Pied Piper, the Carnival Club, the Five Grand Tavern, and Diamond Horseshoe, Hotel Northwestern, the Silver Dollar, and the Q Club.

Other crackdowns took place elsewhere in the state. Raiders descended upon the swank Stork Club three miles south of Council Bluffs, and seized gambling equipment. Under pressure from Larson, Woodbury County Attorney Bernard Brown halted a $180,000 lottery just getting started at Sioux City under the auspices of the Veterans of Foreign Wars.

A local raid on the Eagles lodge in Boone resulted in the seizure of sixteen slot machines, a large dice table and half a bushel of poker chips, and the arrest of thirteen persons.

Boone County Attorney Paul Brown, a notable Des Moines attorney in later years, and Sheriff Steve Beaulieu got into the locked club through the coal opening into the furnace room. The slots, hidden away in a storeroom probably because of the enforcement heat, were taken away and destroyed.

I. T. Willis of Des Moines had brought the gambling equipment other than the slots to Boone. Willis was fined $800, as was the club manager, and Willis lost his car and the gambling equipment through condemnation.

In the midst of all the action, Larson said he received word that gambling forces would secretly provide him with $250,000 if he let his drive die out. He didn't.

"Suddenly," Shostrom said, "it became evident over the state that the campaign was having an effect. Letters started pouring in from families saying their husbands and sons had brought home a full paycheck for the first time in months and begging the Attorney General to continue his efforts."

Individual letters showed how widespread slots were, even in smaller towns. A Bernard, Iowa, mother wrote: "In our town, the machines were out for a while but they are all up again. Young boys put a lot of money in them. Every father and mother would appreciate it if they were seized."

A Tipton letter said: "Slot machines flourish in Tipton, Bennett, Cedar Valley, Durant, Rochester, and other Cedar County towns. Gambling for high stakes flourishes in clubs and some taverns."

Confiscated slot machines, Spencer (*Des Moines Register*)

A letter from Fort Madison, Iowa, reported: "This city has been running wild with gambling and liquor and the officials merely stand by. Card games are running wild twenty-four hours a day. Something should be done about it."

And then there were letters like this one from Dubuque: "If you would try and clean up your own city a bit on gambling instead of having your nose in everybody else's business, we would appreciate it very much in Dubuque. We will have gambling in Dubuque whether you are in or out."

Then, as always, gambling addiction had claimed some victims. An Iowa newspaper executive ruined his life and career by continuously playing slot machines. A farmer was reported to have lost a 160-acre place punching out numbers on the boards.

Ministers, seeing that the drive was not a flash in the pan, became Larson's best cheer leaders. They lauded the attorney general from pulpits all around Iowa. He in turn cautioned churches against using bingo games to raise money.

The next big tests came, not in enforcement but politics. Woodbury County Attorney Bernard Brown ran against Larson for the Republican nomination for attorney general in the June primary. It proved to be no contest. Despite Larson's own dire prediction and the worries of the other state officials, the attorney general won a smashing victory. He defeated Brown by a margin of more than two to one (Larson 167,619 and Brown 70,974). The other Republican candidates were not hurt at all.

The attorney general claimed afterwards that the Brown forces spent eighty thousand dollars in the unsuccessful effort to beat him, a huge expenditure for that office at the time. Larson also had no trouble whatsoever in the fall general election. He defeated a good Democratic opponent, 490,000 to 319,000. He did equally well in winning again in 1952.

"It became clear that Larson, who had forecast doom when he started the campaign, had badly miscalculated," Shostrom said. "Most Iowans did want gambling eliminated."

Not only that, slot machines were gone from Iowa, and so were payoff pinballs and punchboards, or nearly so. The drive had been a great victory. A check of state sales tax records in the summer of 1950 showed that not one slot machine was listed for registration in the state sales tax records in the seven months since late 1949.

Slot machines never have made a comeback in Iowa to this day, nor have punchboards. They both are still against the law, even in today's gambling-oriented Iowa.

Another interesting result of the anti-gambling battle was the change of minds about Larson in the Republican high command. Governor Beardsley and other state officials came around, becoming ardent Larson supporters. Few could argue with Shostrom's conclusion that the attorney general was the "primary political figure in the state."

Political observers believed that Larson probably could have beaten any candidate for any office from U. S. senator and governor on down in the 1954 election.

After three terms as governor, Beardsley had his heart set on running for the Senate in 1954. But he didn't want to take on Larson. The governor thereupon offered to appoint the attorney general to the Iowa Supreme Court to get him out of the way. Larson accepted. He never did want to serve in the Senate.

It so happened that Beardsley didn't run for the Senate. Reports said he couldn't get the necessary financial backing. He probably would not have gotten to serve if he had been elected. Unfortunately, he was killed in an auto accident on the north edge of Des Moines November 21, 1954, or fifty-three days before the end of his third term. He was the only Iowa governor ever to die in office.

Congressman Tom Martin of Iowa City wanted to run for the Senate that year. He didn't make the move, however, until he had checked with his fellow townsman Larson. (Larson was an Iowa City lawyer before joining the attorney general staff in Des Moines, first as an assistant.) Larson relayed back his lack of interest in the Senate to Martin who then ran for that office and was elected.

Larson served a number of years as chief justice of the supreme court. He died in retirement at eighty-eight years of age in 1986.

The Larson accomplishments in the mid-years of the century certainly are no indication of the way Iowans would act were they confronted with similar problems today. Far from it. In fact, the people of the state voted in favor of lotteries in a referendum in 1972, some twenty years after the great anti-gambling victory. The people did so by voting to knock out of the state constitution a provision banning lotteries. That provision had been in the constitution since it went into effect in 1857. And that ban had been interpreted as outlawing not just lotteries but all forms of gambling.

What it all adds up to is this: Bob Larson's Iowa disappeared in the twilight of the 1980s. Once "Bible Belt" Iowa has taken a 180-degree turn away from its longtime traditional anti-gambling principles.

Tax Trouble

A *Des Moines Register* reporter sat in a reception room at the statehouse waiting to see Governor William S. Beardsley. An internal revenue agent named Wilbur Lambert emerged from the governor's private office. The reporter knew Lambert. They had worked together before on income tax evasion cases.

"What are you over here for?" the reporter asked. "Is the governor in tax trouble?"

"He has a serious problem," the agent replied and walked out with no further comment.

"What was that IRS man over here for?" the newsman asked the governor a moment later. "What's the trouble?"

"Oh, just something technical," the uneasy Beardsley answered and would say nothing more on the subject.

The reporter knew he was on to something major. A governor in tax difficulty! But the reporter knew it was going to be difficult to get at, unless Beardsley were prosecuted in court. All income tax returns are super secret. Disclosure of confidential federal tax information was punishable by one year in prison and a one thousand dollar fine.

The story couldn't have been written on what Lambert had said. He would have been subject to prosecution and probably would have lost his job as well. The reporter didn't want that. The year was 1950. Beardsley had been in office a little over one year.

The reporter laid out the facts to *The Register* editors. They tried to break the story through *The Register*'s bureau in Washington. No luck.

Weeks passed, then months. The reporter worked on the story off and on, trying to pick up a usable peg that could not be traced to Lambert. Nothing proved available.

Those were the days when federal internal revenue collectors in each state were political appointees. The Democrats controlled the national government. Thus, it was no surprise when G. G. (Bert) Jeck, an old party warhorse from Atlantic, Iowa, was named collector in Iowa. He pretty much owed his appointment to Democratic State Chairman Jake More.

Having no other ideas, the reporter asked More if he would see what he could do about getting the facts of the governor's tax problem out into the open. Since the governor was a Republican, Democrat More was only happy to oblige. Contrary to law, Jake got Beardsley's thirteen thousand dollar IRS debt figure from Jeck and passed it on to the reporter.

Jeck and More were certainly vulnerable to prosecution for the illegal disclosure and maybe the reporter was also. *The Register* still couldn't carry the governor's tax story, however. Some lawful way to get the story into the open had to be procured. The governor himself provided it.

Rumors had been picking up steam around the state that the Internal Revenue Service was after the governor. The rumors reached a point that *Register* editors feared a rival publication or radio station would break the story before the newspaper could. To protect against that possibility, the editors sent two reporters to the statehouse late one afternoon to confront Beardsley with the rumors. The reporters argued the governor would be better off releasing the facts himself rather than be forced into it in response to publication somewhere. Beardsley

Governor William S. Beardsley, 1952

Jake More (Feiler Studios/courtesy Mary Jane More)

agreed. He disclosed that he had sent the check for thirteen thousand dollars to the IRS. The governor also issued a statement which said in part: "Federal income tax agents, after an audit of my income tax returns on farm and business transactions covering six years, requested payment of additional income tax. I have tendered my check for $13,000. This is purely a personal matter, which involved conforming to federal farm and business accounting requirements for tax purposes. Even though it is a matter of personal business, I recognize that it behooves the Governor to give the people of his state an honest statement of fact concerning it. My accountant advised me that he has settled numerous matters of this size without controversy."

The Register ran the copyrighted story the next morning, September 13, 1951, on page one under an eight-column banner headline.

Beardsley's private interests consisted of a drug store in New Virginia, Iowa, and a 900-acre southern Iowa farm. The federal audit covered the years 1944 through 1949. In one of those years, 1949, Beardsley drew a twelve thousand dollar salary as chief executive of the state. (A governor's salary was many times higher than that figure by the 1980s.)

Federal auditors were reported to have checked packing plants and sale barns for many miles around New Virginia in seeking out the

Bert Jeck, Iowa Internal Revenue collector, early 1950s
(*Des Moines Register*)

facts on Beardsley's tax returns. His farm was a heavy producer of hogs and he was known as a substantial cattle feeder at times. The federal probe apparently centered on whether he had reported all income from the sale of animals.

Beardsley never was prosecuted for tax evasion but he paid a heavy penalty in politics. He ran for re-election to a third term as governor in 1952. He was saved from defeat only by the coattails of Dwight Eisenhower, the Republican nominee for president. Eisenhower carried Iowa by a huge 357,000 majority. Beardsley survived by only 50,000.

That wasn't the end of the tax story. Federal officials suspected (rightly so) that both Jeck and More were responsible for the release of the Beardsley information. A federal investigator quizzed both Jeck and More. Jeck was especially alarmed. He kept saying: "They're going to get me! They're going to get me!" But the matter died down by 1954 without anybody being prosecuted.

More regretted his actions in the Beardsley case. Years later he said: "That was the worst thing I ever did in my life." Memories of the tax case pursued Beardsley into 1954 politics. As previously mentioned, he didn't get the pledges he needed to run for the U. S. Senate, and he died late that year in an auto crash.

Beardsley was a good speaker and excellent campaigner. He

might well have won a Senate seat had he not had the tax problem and had he lived.

Beardsley is a picturesque part of the statehouse lore because of an amusing incident. He went down to the cafeteria one afternoon for a Coke. Cafeteria manager Augusta Marsh charged him ten cents. A dime for a Coke is an outrage, he declared in a voice heard around the statehouse. I sell Cokes in my drug store and I know what you pay for that stuff, he said. Anything more than a nickel for a Coke is robbery. (Nickels and dimes bought a lot more during the 1949–1954 Beardsley administration than in the 1980s.) Whether Mrs. Marshall relented and charged him only a nickel is not known.

The Cargill Raid

It took six hours to find the women in the woodwork. Seven nude females were located packed behind a false wall in the Cargill Hotel on the northeast corner of Seventh and Grand in

downtown Des Moines. The hiding place was only two feet wide, eight feet long, and six feet high.

The discovery culminated the biggest vice raid ever in Iowa's capitol city. Eighty officers stormed the Cargill at 12:15 one Sunday morning in October 1951. The officers moved fast, but the prostitutes were quicker. They disappeared in a flash and were not unearthed until 6:15 a.m.

The law knew the women were somewhere in the building. Only by laboriously measuring spaces in various rooms of the three-story hotel were the officers able to calculate where they were and to make the arrests. "The women were stacked like cordwood," said Polk County Attorney Clyde E. Herring who led the raid. "It was stifling." He said they had to stand all the time because there wasn't room to sit or lie down.

Two other women and eight men were arrested as well. The nine women were fined one thousand dollars each in municipal court. The raiders found thirty-seven thousand dollars in cash in the room of

The Cargill Hotel in the 1930s
(Paul Ashby Collection, Iowa State Historical Department)

Lavonne Gillespie who owned the hotel. The Internal Revenue Service slapped a lien of more than half a million dollars on that money and other Gillespie possessions. The eight men were only charged with misdemeanors.

The Cargill raid has become a legend in Des Moines law enforcement annals.

Soviet Threatened

Riflemen stood on roofs of nearby buildings with weapons pointed down at the dense crowd around the entrance to Hotel Fort Des Moines.

Workers went around looking down manholes for explosives. Parking was banned on twenty miles of Des Moines streets. Hundreds of officers in uniform plus many more in plain clothes watched over the spectators. A horde of newsmen from around the country and around the world helped jam the streets. Signs appeared in the crowd saying: "The only good communist is a dead one" and "We butcher hogs, not people."

That was the "good morning" greeting which faced Soviet Premier Nikita Khrushchev when the communist leader emerged from the hotel September 23, 1959.

Khrushchev undoubtedly was the most important foreign head of state ever to visit Des Moines and Iowa. He stopped to inspect Iowa agriculture as part of his twelve-state tour of the United States. He gave no sign that the unfriendly signs bothered him.

What added greatly to the tension of the security forces that September morning was an unusual death threat. Before Khrushchev arrived, an Iowa physician had sent a letter to the State Department in Washington offering in effect to assassinate the Russian. The physician said the deed could be done by administering a substance to the visitor and the death would appear to occur from natural causes. Not only that, the physician said, the substance was slow-acting and death wouldn't have taken place until Khrushchev was back in Russia.

The alarmed State Department wanted no part in that. The department hurried one or more officers to Iowa. The Iowa Division of Criminal Investigation was asked to help. The division assigned State Agent Sam Kelly to stay with the physician all the time the Russian was in Iowa. Kelly even went with the doctor on his calls.

There was no known attempt. Khrushchev apparently never was in danger in his thirty-hour stay in Iowa, including overnight in the

Hotel Fort Des Moines. Authorities never released the name of the doctor who said he had acted out of patriotic motives. "I guess I asked for it," he commented. There was no way to get a lethal substance into Khrushchev's food anyway. He brought along his own chef to prepare the meals.

The Russian party went to Coon Rapids, Iowa, that morning to visit the farm of Roswell Garst, widely known seed corn official and agricultural activist. Extraordinary security precautions were taken en route. Officers with machine guns pointed out car windows preceded the Khrushchev auto. Armed national guardsmen were posted every half mile along the highway. A soldier stood guard on every bridge and one underneath.

There was a bit of violence at the farm where some 600 newsmen got in the way of Garst showing the fields to the Russian. But the force was not aimed at Khrushchev. Garst got so irritated that he began throwing pieces of silage at the news people and he kicked *New York Times* man Harrison Salisbury in the leg. Garst had nothing at all against mild-mannered Salisbury who just happened to be in the way of a wild kick.

There were no further angry incidents and Khrushchev returned to Des Moines where the Russian departed by plane and resumed his American tour. He said on leaving: "Let us be good neighbors."

Soviet Premier Nikita Khrushchev pats belly of Jack Christensen of Mason City, 1959. (*Des Moines Register*)

Khrushchev had a spirited clash with a Des Moines publisher in New York before going home. The Russian addressed the Economic Club in New York. Gardner (Mike) Cowles, a top official of *The Des Moines Register* and publisher of *Look* magazine, was at the meeting.

Khrushchev told the New York audience that he wanted Russians and Americans to become better acquainted. That brought Mike to his feet. "That being your feeling," Cowles said, "why is it, sir, that you will not allow your people if they wish, to listen to a broadcast from the United States, and why is it that you do not allow periodicals, magazines, and newspapers to be distributed freely throughout the Soviet Union, and why is it that the Soviet journalists resident in the U. S. are allowed to send any dispatches they want without any interference from the government or anybody else, why do you insist on censoring the dispatches of American correspondents in the Soviet Union?"

Khrushchev responded through an interpreter by saying he came to America under an agreement that banned discussions on the affairs of both countries. That brought demands of "Answer the question!" from the audience. "I am an old sparrow, so as to say," the angry Russian responded, "and you can not muddle me with your cries. . . . I come here as a representative of a great country, a great people who have made a great revolution, and no cries can deafen, can do away with the great achievements of our people."

Which brought more shouts of "Answer the question!"

"The question of what should be listened to or read should be decided," Khrushchev said, "not by an outside government or any outside influence but by our own people and by the government."

Which wasn't an answer at all, of course. One result of the confrontation was a statement by the Russian news agency Tass calling Cowles "provocative" and *Look* a "notorious" publication.

By 1989, or thirty years later, the Russian climate under Premier Gorbachev had changed considerably and a free press was functioning to a considerable extent in the Soviet Union.

Lincoln Picketed

An aura of peace and tranquility pervades the statue of Lincoln and his little son Tad on the statehouse grounds. No sign is there of the sharp controversy that broke out when the sculpture was created in 1961.

Pickets marched in protest at the scene. They didn't object to the Lincolns but to the fact that "no open competition" had been held among artists in choosing the design. They also said "neither the Iowa State Curator nor the Iowa State Capitol Planning Commission was consulted."

Perhaps more than anything else, the objectors didn't like the artistic qualities of the work. They said it was too much like the old-time classical monuments and out of date.

Iowa Secretary of Agriculture L. B. Liddy expressed another viewpoint as the statue was lowered into place. "The more my untrained eye looks at it, the more I like it," he said. "I think it is a decided asset to the statehouse grounds. I believe the Iowa farmer will like it also."

The statue was the work of Mr. and Mrs. Fred Torrey, elderly Des Moines sculptors. Mr. Torrey, seventy-seven, had done a number of Lincoln memorials around the country, including two small equestrian statues at the Lincoln tomb in Springfield, Illinois. The Torreys used a noted Mathew Brady photograph of Lincoln and Tad as a model in designing the Des Moines memorial.

An organization known as Iowa Friends of Lincoln asked Torrey to do the sculpture. The legislature approved the project. Donations from 5,167 contributors covered the twenty-five thousand dollar cost. The names of the donors were placed in a box in the base of the monument.

The controversy centered pretty much around three individuals: Torrey; The Reverend John D. Clinton, a retired Des Moines Methodist minister; and *Des Moines Register* reporter George Shane, who was a painter of distinction.

Mr. Torrey was a peaceable old gentleman who would not fight with anybody. He took no part in the conflict and was deeply distressed by it. The Torreys had moved to Des Moines from Chicago in 1957. He was an associate of famous sculptor Lorado Taft many years before.

The Reverend Mr. Clinton was executive secretary of the Friends group and its moving force. (Co-chairmen were District Judge Luther Glanton of Des Moines and State Representative A. L. Mensing of Lowden, Iowa.)

Shane was a leading figure in the Des Moines chapter of the Artists Equity Association which sponsored the protest. He maintained a running attack on the project in his newspaper stories.

The pickets, incidentally, had no impact either on the placing of the statue or the dedication a few days later. They were ignored.

The thirty-seven-hundred-pound sculpture is twelve feet high. It depicts a sitting father Lincoln with hand on standing Tad's shoulder as they look at a book. The Torreys reportedly got ten thousand dollars for their work.

The monument is on the esplanade down from the west statehouse entrance. The two Lincolns face south.

Both sides in the controversy fought the issue in letters to the editor in *The Register*.

Mrs. Kenneth Brown wrote: "The Brady photograph is a rare and sensitive one. But the Torrey statue . . . is a stiff petrified imitation. Lincoln's rugged ugliness, the towering greatness of his character and the brooding sense of tragedy which he could not banish, is all smoothed away in a prim, well-groomed empty face."

In contrast, Mrs. Mike Thomas of Des Moines wrote: "Having seen the statue, I can say it is magnificent. It evokes an emotional response of admiration for the man Lincoln. You sense the tenderness he felt for Tad. You sense the companionship between the two. It has two qualities. One is truth, the other is beauty."

The Register editorially agreed with the critics.

"It is unfortunate in our opinion," the newspaper said, "that the Lincoln society hasn't taken the approach of the kind the artists' group suggests. It is also unfortunate that the project was started by individuals before any approach was made to state officials."

The Equity association had said the model for the statue should have been selected by a qualified committee of experts in art and sculpture. *The Register* agreed, saying "that could give firm assurance as to the aesthetic value and appropriateness of the work."

A hilarious 1960s photo shows Old Abe getting a supply of snow on the head. *Register* photographers had been given an assignment to take a picture of the monument snowbound after a winter storm. But the snow had mostly melted before the cameramen could get there. A *Register* photographer thereupon got up on a ladder and adorned Lincoln and Tad with the white stuff for picture purposes. Cameraman John Houlette took this photo, which never before has appeared in print.

(*Des Moines Register*)

Wild Man in the Sky

An insane student pilot seized a plane at gunpoint from an instructor and took off on a low-altitude flight that paralyzed and terrorized downtown Des Moines for nearly four hours.

Roy Soderquist, a twenty-two year old with problems, swooped the plane perilously near buildings including the statehouse, the Polk County courthouse, and the Des Moines city hall. He dropped at times down close to busy streets and roads. He banked barely above ground on the east side. The plane was a single engine Cessna.

Tens of thousands of spectators, some uneasy and some downright frightened, watched as much as they dared from office building windows, roofs, sidewalks, and cars.

Soderquist had never soloed before. It was so tense a drama on the afternoon of January 29, 1957, that networks carried the TV pictures live nationwide.

Soderquist did get down safely in a crash landing in West Des Moines. He swallowed cyanide poison in a last minute suicide attempt but vomited up the pills before they could take effect.

"I just wanted to do this one thing before I died," he said. "I just felt the urge to fly low over the city. . . . The urge to do it was just too great to wait."

His distressed mother said Roy "was trying to show everyone the person he wanted to be rather than the person he is."

A jury found him mentally ill and he was committed for psychiatric treatment.

Hundreds of onlookers around metropolitan Des Moines will never forget those wild hours. "The first time I saw him it looked like he was coming right in the window," said Jack Bird, a registration clerk at the city hall. "I thought he was going to crash and I hollered 'look out,'" said district court bailiff Merle Clemens. "He came right up Court Avenue and just missed the courthouse."

District court clerk Michael Doyle reported: "One time he came swooping down next to the courthouse clock." Rose Kron, a courthouse employee, said: "I saw him right out there by the smoke stack over the county jail. He was below the top of the smoke stack. He just missed it."

It appeared a couple of times that Soderquist was going to crash deliberately into the west wall of the statehouse but he veered just in time, passing around the building at second-story level. The motor noise and the frightened nearness of the plane disrupted a public hearing before a legislative committee.

"It was quite an experience to look out and see that plane whizz by," said State Representative Fred Hall, a Humboldt, Iowa, Democrat.

Roy Soderquist pilots his stolen plane toward the statehouse, 1957. (*Des Moines Register*)

"The speakers would stop and a lot of people would rush to the windows."

C. R. Jeffries, who worked in the old Solar Aircraft plant, was standing at the intersection of Fleur and Valley drives when Soderquist came roaring north along Fleur which is the main artery to the airport.

"He came so low I'm telling you I ran," Jeffries said. "I honestly believed he would have landed the plane on Fleur if there hadn't been any traffic."

Polk County Attorney Ray Hanrahan said: "I was walking down Fifth Avenue (downtown) when he almost hit the Walnut Building at

Fifth and Walnut." Iowa Governor Herschel Loveless was downtown driving back to his office when he saw the plane. The governor said it appeared Soderquist "was going to hit the [old] KRNT - TV tower for sure."

An alarmed Des Moines housewife called and demanded that Loveless call out the National Guard "to do something about this flier." State authorities said they didn't know what the Guard could do.

A highway patrolman asked permission to shoot down the plane. The request was refused.

State Representative Howard Reppert, a Des Moines Democrat

and a celebrated World War II bomber pilot, watched Soderquist's performance with intense interest. "He was doing a pretty good job of flying," Reppert said. "There are up-drafts and down-drafts around tall buildings. He could have found himself in major trouble. Looking toward the Equitable building in downtown Des Moines, I didn't think he was going to make it a couple of times."

Officials ordered the top eight floors of the eighteen-floor Equitable building evacuated. Employees were told to take refuge in corridors away from the windows or in the basement. Several hundred did. Maintenance men with fire hoses were stationed at south corridor windows in case the plane should crash through. Four of the eight Equitable elevators were taken out of service and two of those remaining were placed on emergency standby.

Classes were interrupted in schools and the children taken to the cellars for safety in some instances.

Little work was done in downtown offices and the statehouse, or anywhere else in Des Moines for that matter. A chamber of commerce official estimated the loss in man-hours at between $150,000 and $200,000 or close to $750,000 at 1989 prices.

Another scary situation was the well-founded fear that the plane would run out of gas over the loop and crash, killing not only the pilot but a number of others as well. The gas should have been gone by 3:00 or 3:15 P.M. But Soderquist conserved fuel by throttling the plane speed down to eighty miles an hour and succeeded in staying in the air until nearly 4:00 P.M. There wasn't much in the tank when he landed.

Soderquist was a son of respected parents who lived in the little Wayne County town of Clio, Iowa, near the Missouri border. His father Rudolph was a carpenter.

Roy got himself in trouble in 1951 when he was a junior in Allerton, Iowa, high school. He ordered a camera and other merchandise from mail order houses and didn't pay for it. He sent at least one bad check. He also ended up with two draft registration cards, one under an assumed name. He pleaded guilty to both violations in federal court in Des Moines and was placed on probation for three years.

He moved to Des Moines after graduating from Allerton high in 1952. In 1956 he pleaded guilty in municipal court to a charge of contributing to the delinquency of a minor and drew a thirty-day suspended sentence.

Roy worked for the *Look* magazine subscription department in his early Des Moines years and later as a messenger and in the accounting division of Pittsburgh-Des Moines Steel Company. He quit the steel company four days before he took his spectacular plane ride.

He said he wanted at that stage to kill himself because "I had too many problems—I was in debt close to one thousand dollars and the job

I had had didn't seem to hold any future."

Roy got ready for the big adventure by buying a .25 caliber pistol and a .22 caliber revolver. He was carrying both weapons concealed on his person when he reported at the airport for a flying lesson before noon on the fateful day. In his heart he had a burning desire to solo.

"He had about fourteen hours and forty minutes dual time but we didn't think he was ready to solo yet," said instructor James Dolezal. "We taxied out to the end of the runway and checked the engine."

Soderquist handed Dolezal a note and told him to read it out loud. The instructor did so. It said: "In my hands is a certain device. I intend to take this plane up alone and return it here when it runs low on fuel [1/8 tank]. If you provoke me in any way you may get hurt—so please climb out of this plane and walk at least 100 feet in the direction the right wing points.

"Do not touch any controls. I certainly hope I do not have to put a bullet in your leg to prove I mean business. That might cripple you for a couple weeks.

"Yes, I do expect the police to be around when I land. Do I make myself clear? Now shut up out and away from this plane—or else.

"P. S. gun has hair trigger."

The note was printed in pencil in block type, and portions underlined in red ink.

"He had a gun in his hand so I got out," Dolezal said. "I couldn't get near enough to him to grab for it. I saw he really meant it. He was on the other side of the plane. I got out and ran. He gunned the engine and took off.

"I ran to the office and called the police. Then I went to the control tower and tried to contact him."

The tower didn't notice anything unusual as Soderquist asked for permission to take off. "He just called in 'This is 7170 delta. Am I cleared for take-off?'" the controller said. "I replied: 'You mean 7170 alpha, don't you?' He answered: 'Yeah, that's right.' I said: 'OK, clear for takeoff.' It was a normal takeoff to the northwest."

Soderquist took an immediate sharp turn to the right and headed low over the city. The controller said to himself: "I'll bet we get some phone calls over this." Little did he know.

Dolezal hurried into the tower and got on the air to talk to Soderquist: "Roy, I don't want to see you get hurt. Don't try any more of those low passes. This is Jim, your instructor."

After a brief interval, Dolezal spoke again: "Roy, everybody is worried about you. You have your mother all upset. She's coming out to talk to you. Your buzz jobs are 'way too low.' Very dangerous to everyone. If you read me, Roy, please acknowledge. You are in great danger of injuring yourself and others. Your buzz jobs are way too low.

I'm not giving you any guff. We know you are trying to show us how well you can fly. You've shown us. Your flying is fine so come on in. This will be all right if you can get her back in here OK."

All would not have been forgiven, of course, but Dolezal was willing to say anything to get Roy to come down.

The instructor repeated his plea perhaps twenty times, to no avail. Soderquist didn't hear him. He had the plane radio turned off.

At 1:45 P.M. Roy did come on the air to ask the tower for landing instructions. He got them immediately but went silent again and no further word was heard from him during the rest of the flight. It wasn't necessary as it turned out to halt other planes arriving and departing but all the pilots were warned of the situation.

The tower became crowded with other air controllers, police, and newsmen as the suspense grew.

Talk in the tower stopped abruptly when a fifty-one-year-old woman entered. She was May Soderquist, Roy's mother. She was brought to Des Moines in a Lineville, Iowa, ambulance, not because she was ill but because such a vehicle could move fast on the highway without fear of arrest. A controller went on the air and said: "Your mother is here. She wants to talk to you."

In a quavering voice she said: "Roy, do you hear me? If you hear me, I want you to know I'm so worried. Will you please answer, please." There was no response.

A few minutes later she took the microphone again: "If you hear me, Roy, please answer. Please come in and land. You've proved to everybody you can fly. Please land and take your punishment and don't endanger anyone any more." No reply.

Roy had wanted to come home to Clio on a visit several days before, but she wrote him a letter saying she was having other guests and there would be no room for him. "It might have hurt his feelings," she said. "He was supposed to come down Sunday anyway but he didn't show up at all."

She told how Roy had started taking flying lessons in 1953 but had to stop for the lack of money. "We made the remark he should quit flying, that he would never solo and that he was just wasting his money. Maybe that was the wrong thing to say."

Charles Coburn, another American aviation instructor, chimed in to say the company had had previous doubts about Soderquist. "We hadn't let him go alone because he acted rather odd," Coburn said. "I got suspicious when he told me he was cut out for flying, he was 'gifted to fly' and 'meant to fly.' He had a compulsion to fly."

Meanwhile, police, sheriff, and highway patrol cars ranged over the entire metropolitan area, keeping the plane constantly in sight.

Instructor Dolezal and Colonel Frank Berlin, the state aeronautics commissioner, took off in two planes to "fly chase" Soderquist and provide an unending flow of information on what he was doing. At 3:50 P.M. Dolezal or Berlin reported: "He's landed. The plane is up on its nose. Whew!" The crisis was over.

Here's how Roy described his last couple minutes of freedom: "I took two capsules filled with cyanide just before I brought the plane down. I picked out an open field to land in because I thought the capsules would kill me before anyone found me. I guess because I didn't swallow the capsules with water and because of the jostling I got in landing I threw up the cyanide and the police were right there too."

The West Des Moines police certainly were. The plane had hardly come to a halt (the damage was thirty-five hundred dollars) when two officers tore open the door, seized Roy and his guns, packed him in a squad car and sped him to Broadlawns hospital in Des Moines. There he was arraigned before Municipal Judge Ray Harrison on charges of robbery with aggravation and operating an aircraft without proper certification. The judge set bond at eleven thousand dollars and the police placed the prisoner under twenty-four-hour guard.

An examination showed Roy suffered no injuries of consequence. And he was eager to talk. He made it clear he hugely enjoyed the experience, that he savored the sense of power that was his during that zany flight.

"I got a big kick out of it," he said. "It isn't every day that somebody does something like that. The town had more excitement than it ever has had. I saw people on roofs and at office building windows all over town. I was watching them close and waved at them several times."

Flyer Soderquist *(Des Moines Register)*

He insisted that he was in no danger nor was anyone else: "I had the plane under control all the time. I had the flaps down and most of the time was flying at 80 to 100 miles an hour. I cut the throttle two or three times to give the people a little thrill but kept the plane above the stalling speed of 50 or 55 miles an hour. I had a lot of fun up there."

He said he never had any intention of hitting a downtown building or crashing into the statehouse. He took particular pleasure in buzzing the two plants of Pittsburgh-Des Moines Steel where he had most recently worked. He dropped to within a few feet of the ground at one plant. "I was just trying to give the employees a thrill," he said, "and I guess I did."

Soderquist was a brown-haired, brown-eyed man five feet nine inches tall, weight 162 pounds, no reason for anyone to notice him in a crowd.

He said the revolver he aimed at Dolezal wasn't loaded. "I wasn't going to kill him," he said. "The other gun [loaded] was in my pocket. I didn't intend to shoot. I didn't think it was likely he would put up any resistance. I hadn't thought of what I would do if he did resist."

The Polk County grand jury indicted him two days later for going armed with intent to do great bodily injury and in two weeks another Polk jury adjudged him "insane at this time." He was sent first to Anamosa reformatory then was tried and found innocent of criminal charges "by reason of insanity at this time." He was taken to the state psychopathic hospital at Iowa City and next to the state mental health institute at Independence where he underwent extensive psychiatric treatment.

Independence returned Soderquist to Polk County in September of 1958, saying he had improved and was sane. The held-over criminal charges were dismissed, the slate was wiped clean, and Roy Soderquist walked out of the courtroom a free man.

The wild flight illustrated a fundamental vulnerability of the modern, complex industrial civilization. An obscure person with one piece of equipment was able to create a feeling of total helplessness in a city of almost two hundred thousand population for nearly four hours. That would have been most difficult and perhaps impossible in the pre-machine age.

Not everybody on the ground was worried just about danger while Soderquist was on his hair-raising adventure. A merchant called police and demanded: "If that young man gets down safely, hold him because I have two bad checks he cashed at our store." The police learned that the daredevil of the sky had cashed five worthless checks for piddling amounts ranging from three dollars to ten dollars in recent days. Not exactly in the grand design Soderquist envisioned for himself when he temporarily seized the reins of power over an entire city.

Sources

In addition to the author's own recollections, this book is based in large part on material from the following sources:

Personal records of Harvey Ingham and Frederick M. Hubbell, and records in the Paul Ashby Collection, Des Moines;

Files of *The Des Moines Register* and *Tribune*, the old *Iowa State Register*, the *Des Moines Leader*, the *Des Moines Capital*, the *Des Moines News*, and the *Iowa Citizen*, all newspapers;

Annals of Iowa and *Iowa Journal of History*, both journals published by the State Historical Society of Iowa;

And the following books:

Andrews, L. F. *Pioneers of Polk County*. Des Moines: Baker, Trisler Co., 1908.

Brigham, Johnson. *History of Des Moines and Polk County*. Chicago: S. J. Clarke Publishing Co., 1911.

———. *Iowa, Its History and Its Foremost Citizens*. Chicago: S. J. Clarke Publishing Co., 1915.

Dixon, J. M. *The Valley and the Shadow*. New York: Russell Bros., 1868.

Gue, B. F. *History of Iowa*. New York: Century History Co., 1903.

Harlan, Edgar R. *The People of Iowa*. Chicago and New York: American Historical Society, 1931.

History of Polk County Iowa, 1880. Des Moines: Union Historical Co. and Birdsall Williams & Co., 1880.

Porter, Will. *Annals of Polk County and Des Moines*. Des Moines: George A. Miller Publishing Co., 1898.

Rule, Edith, and W. J. Petersen. *True Tales of Iowa*. Mason City: Yelland & Hanes, 1932.

The author also wishes to express thanks for assistance received on the various stories over the years from the following:

Register librarian Phyllis Wolfe and her staff, the staffs of the Iowa State Historical Library, The Iowa State Library, and the State Law Library; former President Ronald Reagan, Colonel Paul Tibbets, Jr., Merle Strasser, Earl Shostrom, Jake More, Mary Jane More, Wayne Fox, Ruth Bisignano, Dick Thomas, Agnes Wilbois, Maury White, Paul Brown, Kathy Swift, Nick Lamberto, Jim Muto, Harlan Miller, Gifford Strand, Carl Horstman, Jim Windsor, and Walter Shotwell.

Index

Dudley, 13, 21
Dunkley, Charles, 198–200
Dunlap, Flora, 103

Eaton, Clarence (Doc), 173
Eddyville, 22, 39
Eisenhower, Dwight, 220–21, 249
Elliott, Tommy, 34
Emmerson, Dr. M. A., 218
English, Dr. F. E., 60
Entwistle, Edward, 64–65
Equitable Life Insurance Company
  of Iowa, 50, 180

Farner, W. H., 24
Farrell, John, 175
Farrell, Lew, 174–77
Ferries, 16
Fidler, Dave, 167
Fidler, Nate, 167
Fifth Avenue Cigar Store, 168–69
Fisher, Don, 234
Fisher, Johnny, 234
Flanagan, Father E. J., 157
Flatboats, 85–86
Fletcher, John, 167
Floods, 20–23, 58, 81
Floyd of Rosedale, 182, 186
Fort Des Moines, 5, 7, 8, 10, 11, 12,
  21, 191
Fort Donelson, 34
Fort Madison penitentiary, 51, 173,
  194, 201
Fort Raccoon, 13
Foster, Mrs. Henry, 97
Four-Mile Creek, 8, 16, 58
Fox, Wayne, 217–18
Fox tribe, 3–6
Frakes, Capt. F. F., 202
Freemain, Nathan, 91
Fukuto, Ruth, 212, 215

Gambling, 167–77, 238–45
Gammack, Gordon, 201
Gargotta, Charles and Gus, 175
Garst, Roswell, 253
Gibbs, Frank, 214–15
Gilbertson, Gilbert, 105
Gillespie, Lavonne, 252
Gilliland, Shirley, 100

Gioe, Charles (Cherry Nose), 175–77
Godfrey, Col. George L., 63
Gold Rush, 15–18
Good, James, 100
Grand Opera House, 85, 87
Grant, Ulysses S., 54–55
Great Western Railroad, 84
Griffith, L. H., 153
Grimes, James, 25
Groves, Annie, 53

Haggard, Enola Gay, 236
Hammill, John, 150, 152, 163
Hammond, John, 122
Hanawalt, Dr. George P., 60
Hansen, Joe, 86
Hanson, Rowland, 126
Hardfish, Chief, 7
Harding, William L., 102, 103, 113
Harper, Ada, 84
Hata, Ted, 215–16
Hatton, Frank, 73
Havner, Horace, 122–26
Hawarden scrip, 178
Hawley, H. K., 125
Henry, John, 138
Herring, Clyde, 100, 181–86
Highland Park College, 160, 163,
  222
Hiroshima, 236
Hodges, Joy, 193
Home Plate Slide in Bar, 231–32
Hooker, E. F., 25
Hoover, Herbert, 84, 131, 134, 224
Hosokawa, Bill, 215–16
Hotel Fort Des Moines, 190
Houelette, John, 256
Houton, Anna, 84
Howard, Annie, 51–54
Howard, Charles, 51–54
Hoxie, Herbert M., 65–66
Hoyt Sherman Place, 57
Hubbell, Frederick C., 80
Hubbell, Frederick M., 77, 84, 100,
  205
Hubbell, Fred W., 180
Hughes, R. M., 156
Hughes, Thomas, 15
Hull, A. Y., 15
Humanity Benefactor Foundation,
  162